Marx and Anglo-Russian Relations and other writings

Brian Pearce is a translator from Russian and a historian of Soviet Russia.

D. B. Riazanov

Marx and Anglo-Russian Relations and other writings

Translated by Brian Pearce

Foreword by Al Richardson

Francis Boutle Publishers

Riazanov's work was originally published in 1918 by the Petrograd Soviet of Workers' and Red Army Men's Deputies.

English translation first published by Francis Boutle Publishers
272 Alexandra Park Road
London N22 7BG
020 8889 8087
Email: riazanov@francisboutle.demon.co.uk
www.francisboutle.demon.co.uk

ISBN 1 903427 13 4

Contents

Foreword

Al Richardson

The book the reader now has in his hands, the work of Russia's greatest Marxist scholar, appears for the first time in full in any Western European language, for those who are concerned to study the historical problems of Eastern Europe will only know it in its truncated German form. It comes at a most opportune time, for not only has the national question come bubbling to the surface there in ever more virulent forms since the collapse of ersatz socialism, but the appearance of several recent studies in Russia itself shows that the reputation of its author is finally enjoying a well-merited revival. It is little short of amazing that only two of the full-length books of this classic Marxist scholar have ever appeared in English. We are sure that our readers will join with us in thanking Brian Pearce, both for the translation and for the care with which he has introduced and explained it.

Nor is its relevance confined to the writer and his subject. The words of Marx and Engels have so often been quoted as the revealed truth of scripture that considerable doubt has arisen as to whether Marxist historical analysis can claim to be a method of thinking at all. Riazanov's admiration for their achievement is unparallelled, but any reading of what he has to say here shows that he is not afraid to correct their factual errors, to disagree most boldly with them in the light of further historical development, and to take them sharply to task when economic reductionism blinds them to the global strategies of the great powers. Recent remarks about the USA's intervention in Afghanistan being merely a matter of a projected oil pipeline remind us that this kind of thinking is not dead among the left.

And long before it became fashionable to do so Riazanov uses the correspondance of Marx and Engels to show where they differ. The evidence he collects proves that these are no trivial differences, particularly as regards Poland. And whilst their hostility to Russian imperialism never abated, Riazanov points out that, in spite of the efforts of the leaders of the German Social Democracy, it is unfair to harness either of them to Germany's war chariot.

By reminding us that Marx and Engels believed that the working class should have its own foreign policy separate from that of the bourgeoisie, he also shows why they never considered the national question on its own, but always linked it to class interests, and set it in its global context. At no time did they give the sort of automatic support accorded by much of the left today for any and every demand for national independence, but always held in mind broader strategic implications in all their international campaigns. For example, whilst Marx was not at all opposed in principle to the independence of the Balkan peoples from Turkish rule,[1] this took second place in his mind to any strengthening of Russia's position as the gendarme of European reaction that might be involved in it. In any case, in his eyes it was always subordinated to class considerations, from which the problem of national independence can never be separated in Eastern Europe – a lesson that has been confirmed time and again in the last 60 years, from the heroic Warsaw Uprising of 1944[2] to the more recent collapse of the USSR and Yugoslavia into their national components.

Many points Riazanov makes have wider implications for Marxist theory than appear on the surface. His analysis of the part played by the money economy in the rise of the Russian autocracy take us away from the traditional model of the Asiatic mode, and closer to that of the Tudor state in Britain and the European enlightened despots.[3]

But the most striking thing of all is surely the boldness with which Riazanov deals with all these questions. Marxism in his hands is creative, iconoclastic and vital. And what else can we expect from the man whom Stalin asked in 1929 why his picture was not in his office along with those of Marx, Engels and Lenin, only to receive the reply: 'Marx and Engels are my teachers. Lenin is my comrade. What are you to me?'[4]

Notes

1 See below, pp190–202, 'Marx and Engels and on BalkanQuestion'.

2 Cf Zygmunt Zaremba, ***The Warsaw Commune: Betrayed by Stalin, Massacred by Hitler***. Socialist Platform, London, 1997.

3 The best recent survey of the problem in Russian thought is Marian Sawer, 'The Politics

of Historiography: Russian Socialism and the Question of the Asiatic Mode of Production, 1906–1931, *Critique*, no 10–112, 1978, pp15–35.

4 'Le Meilleur connaisseur de Marx et d'Engels en URSS et dans le monde', *Cahiers du Mouvement Ouvrier*, no 3, September 1998, p64.

David King Collection

David Riazanov

D. B. Riazanov

Brian Pearce

To the generation of British and American Marxists who came to maturity in the late 1920s, Riazanov was well known as the author of *Karl Marx and Friedrich Engels* (1927), a translation of lectures given in 1922, the compiler of the symposium *Karl Marx: Man, Thinker and Revolutionist* (1927), and the editor of Plekhanov's *Fundamental Problems of Marxism* (1929) and of *The Communist Manifesto* (1930), to which he appended valuable notes. After being 'framed' in 1931, he became an 'un-person' in the official Communist movement, until the 1960s, when he re-emerged in Soviet reference books as a result of the so-called rehabilitations under Khrushchev. Apparently, his portrait then hung in the Institute of Marxism-Leninism in Moscow, which he founded, but where his very name was unmentionable for 30 years.

One British historian of Soviet Russia has described Riazanov as 'learned Marxist and *enfant terrible* of the party', and another as 'the wittiest man in the party, and far and away its best Marxist scholar.' It was doubtless both his knowledge of Marxism and his readiness to speak his independent mind that made inevitable his victimisation by Stalin.

Riazanov was born in Odessa in 1870 as David Borisovich Goldendakh (Riazanov was his 'party name': he also used the pseudonym Bukvoyed, that is, 'Bookworm'). He became a Marxist when still a teenager, after a brief spell as a Narodnik. He was soon well known among the revolutionary youngsters of Odessa for the reading list he compiled for them, consisting of works on world history, political economy, philosophy, sociology and the history of socialism and revolutionary movements. In 1890, he went abroad to work with Plekhanov's 'Emancipation of Labour' group on the publication of popular Marxist literature. Returning to Russia in connection with this work, he was arrested, and, after 18 months 'preliminary detention', was sentenced by administrative order to four years' imprisonment. After his release, he was exiled to Kishinev in Bessarabia, under police supervision. In 1900, he was allowed to go abroad again, and went first to Switzerland, then to Germany. Among the Russian Social-Democratic émigrés he belonged to a small group called *Borba* (The Struggle), which produced a critique of the draft party programme to which Lenin referred at the Second Congress (1903).

When the split came between Bolsheviks and Mensheviks, Riazanov sided with the latter. In 1905, he returned to Russia and worked for two years in the trade union movement and in the Social Democratic group in the State Duma. Briefly under arrest in 1907, he then went abroad again. The German Social Democratic Party asked him to write the history of the First International, and to edit the works of Marx and Engels. It was in this period that he published an abridged version of the first of our present works, as a supplement to *Die Neue Zeit*, the theoretical organ of the Social Democratic Party of Germany. At the same time he contributed to Trotsky's *Pravda*, and lectured at the party schools in Capri and Longjumeau.[1]

When the First World War came, Riazanov attended the historic conference at Zimmerwald,[2] and took up a position similar to Trotsky's, contributing frequently to *Nashe Slovo*. After the revolution of February 1917, he returned to Russia and resumed his work in the trade union movement. Politically, he adhered to Trotsky's *Mezhrayontsy* ('Inter-District Group') and joined the Bolshevik party along with the rest of them in July 1917. Riazanov remained, however, highly independent in his outlook: he was one of those who favoured the formation, after the October Revolution, of a coalition government of all the socialist parties; he was opposed to the dispersal of the Constituent Assembly, and he called for the repudiation of the peace treaty signed with Germany at Brest-Litovsk.

Riazanov was acutely aware of the problems that faced the Soviet government in a country where the peasantry constituted the majority of the population, and in a world where other countries had failed to follow Russia's revolutionary example. It was he who called the New Economic Policy 'a peasant Brest' – that is, a temporary settlement with the peasantry comparable to the peace treaty with Imperial Germany (Riazanov always had a talent for memorable formulations: it was he who defined Trotsky's role at the Second Congress as 'Lenin's cudgel'). His anxiety regarding the political dangers of the post-1920 situation led him to put down an amendment to the resolution on party unity at the Tenth Congress (1921) which would have gone further than the ban on factions by condemning any 'platforms', that is, any grouping around particular proposals when elections to party congresses were held. As is well known, Lenin successfully opposed this as impracticable.

Already in January 1918, Riazanov had said that if the proletarian revolution did not happen in the West there would be a danger of the restoration of capitalism in Russia, and from this he drew the conclusion that the Russian proletariat must retain, even after the October Revolution, a strong trade union movement for self-defence. At the Fourth All-Russia Trade Union Congress in 1921, thinking that the conditions of the NEP confirmed his fear, he argued for the independence of the trade unions from the party, so as to retain a safe stronghold for working-class interests in the event of the party falling under non-proletarian influence. His resolution was approved by the party's fraction at the congress, in preference to the one sponsored by the Central Committee. Stalin reacted vigorously to this hitch in the proceedings, and attacked Riazanov personally – ('Shut up, you clown!') Riazanov gave back as good as he got. However, Lenin intervened with a calm, reasoned speech, free from personalities, and the party fraction changed their minds. The Central Committee rebuked Riazanov for his 'anarcho-syndicalist' deviation, and decided to remove him from trade union work.

While exasperated by some aspects of Riazanov's political behaviour, Lenin appreciated his frank way of calling a spade a spade: for example, in the controversy in 1921 about the granting of concessions to foreign capitalists, he quoted with approval Riazanov's blunt remark that 'if we want to grant a concession, it is not meant to improve the position of the workers, but to raise the productive forces'. Nevertheless, the party leadership considered that the best outlet for 'Bookworm's' zeal would be the collection and publication of the writings of the movement's founders. To begin with, he was sent to Berlin. Lenin wrote to him on 23 September 1921: 'It is important to collect *all* the letters of Marx and Engels, and no one will do this better than you.'[3] Riazanov founded the Marx-Engels Institute and the Socialist (later Communist) Academy, and worked in the Commission on Party History.

Although research, editing, writing and lecturing were to be his chief occupations for the rest of his career, Riazanov continued to play some part in general political life. He was a member of the Central Executive Committee of the Congress of Soviets until 1928. At party gatherings, the old irrepressible Riazanov made himself heard from time to time. Thus, at the Eleventh Congress (1922), complaining of the arbitrary manner in which, it seemed to him, the Central Committee ruled the party, and pointing to the effect of this regime on members less spirited than himself, he said:

> The British Parliament, so they say, can do everything except change a man into a woman. Our Central Committee is far more powerful than that. It has already changed more than one not very revolutionary man into an old woman, and the number of these old women is increasing daily.

And at the Sixteenth Congress (1929) he interjected, sarcastically: 'They don't need any Marxists in the Political Bureau.'

Besides bringing out the first complete versions of such Marxist classics as ***The German Ideology*** in 1924 and the ***Dialectics of Nature*** in 1925, Riazanov worked steadily at the first comprehensive edition of all the works of Marx and Engels. In that connection, he was able to help Trotsky when the latter was exiled to Alma Ata in 1928–29. Riazanov provided him with paid work as a translator, editor and proof reader. The fees Trotsky received from this source supported himself and his family, and covered the cost of his extensive correspondence.

The year 1930 saw Riazanov's sixtieth birthday, and in his honour the Communist Academy published a collection of articles related to his special fields of research, entitled ***Na boyevom postu*** (At Battle Station): 'To the best Marxologist, a fighter for the emancipation of the working class, the founder of the Marx-Engels Institute, on his sixtieth birthday, this symposium is dedicated by his comrades, friends and colleagues.' The book opened with a resolution of the Central Executive Committee to award the Order of the Red Banner of Labour to Riazanov, followed by greetings from the Executive Committee of the Communist International, the Central Committee of the party and other leading organs.

Then, only a few months later, in February 1931, Stalin's axe fell. A group of former Mensheviks who had been working for years in Soviet institutions as economists, statisticians and the like were brought to trial on charges of counter-revolutionary conspiracy – and Riazanov was named as their accomplice. This affair, known to history as 'the Menshevik Trial', became a by-word internationally as a fraud, through a silly mistake in the scenario: the Menshevik émigré Abramovich[4] was alleged to have been in Russia, plotting with the accused, on a date when, as proved by photographs, he was actually attending a congress of the Labour and Socialist International in Brussels.

At the time of the trial, Trotsky was prepared to accept that the indictment of the ex-Mensheviks might be correct, especially as the principal accused 'confessed'; in 1936 he acknowledged his error. As regards Riazanov, however, he refused to believe that his old comrade could have involved himself in any anti-Soviet conspiracy:

> In the person of Riazanov, we have a man who for more than 40 years has participated in the revolutionary movement, and every stage in his activity has one way or another entered into the history of the proletarian party. Riazanov had serious differences with the party at various times, including the time of Lenin, or rather, *especially* in the time of Lenin, when Riazanov participated actively in the day-to-day formulation of party policy. In one of his speeches Lenin spoke directly of the *strong* side of Riazanov and of his *weak* side. Lenin did not see Riazanov as a politician. Speaking of his strong side, Lenin had in mind his idealism, his deep devotion to Marxist doctrine, his exceptional erudition, his honesty in principle, his intransigence in defence of the heritage of Marx and Engels. That is precisely why the party put Riazanov at the head of the Marx-Engels Institute, which he himself had created. The work of Riazanov had international importance, not only of a historico-scientific, but also a revolutionary and political character.

Speculating on how Riazanov had fallen foul of Stalin, Trotsky went on:

> For many years Riazanov was able to hold his tongue very prudently – too prudently – on a whole series of burning questions. But Riazanov was organically incapable of cowardice, of platitudes; any ostentatious display of loyalty was repugnant to him. One can imagine that in the meetings of the Institute he often flew into a passion against the corrupted youngsters of that innumerable order of young professors who usually understand very little of Marxism, but can excel in falsehood and informing... Riazanov fell victim to his personal honesty. The old revolutionist said to himself: 'to serve while holding one's tongue, with clenched teeth – good: to be an enthusiastic lackey – impossible.'[5]

A 'special' accusation was hurled at Riazanov in *Pravda* of 12 March 1931, aimed at destroying his reputation as a faithful editor of the writings of Marx and Engels. A letter from Marx to his daughter Jenny Longuet,[6] dated 11 April 1881, had been published in an abridged version in *Nachalo* in 1899. 'The original of this letter was given to Riazanov by the well-known Menshevik Lydia Tsederbaum-Dan[7] as long ago as 1895. This letter Riazanov carefully hid.' And *Pravda* reproduced the missing passage – some critical comments on Karl Kautsky, whom Marx had just met for the first time, describing him as 'a mediocrity' and 'a Philistine' who was 'too wise by half (he is only 26 years old), knowing better than anybody else'.[8] The fact that Riazanov had not given this passage to the public proved, it was claimed, that he was in league with the international social-fascists.

Trotsky guessed that what had happened was that the letter in question had been given to Riazanov by someone who attached the condition that it be not published while Kautsky was alive (he did not die until 1938):

> Comrade Riazanov had no alternative. In order to get possession of the letter he was obliged to accept the condition imposed. Anyone else in his place would have done the same. Having accepted this condition, he naturally carried it out. Thanks to his extreme prudence and loyalty in all matters of this kind, Riazanov was able to secure from our adversaries precious material from the heritage of our classics ... Whoever knows Riazanov knows that he, more than anyone else, must have ached to publish his valuable find. But he waited for the proper moment to do it.[9]

Trotsky's guess was confirmed by the letter from Lydia Tsederbaum-Dan to Riazanov, dated 4 July 1925, which was published in the Communist *Labour Monthly* of July 1931, along with the full text of Marx's letter. She refers to 'the conditions which I was compelled to impose', and asks Riazanov 'to remember that I am handing it over personally to you and not to the Institute, the personnel of which can be changed, and new persons, of course, will not feel themselves bound in any way'.[10]

Riazanov was expelled from the party, and also, of course, from all the other organisations to which he belonged, and which had considered themselves honoured by his membership. Exiled to Saratov, Riazanov found a job at the local university, and lived obscurely until the fatal year of 1937. He was then, on 23 July, arrested and subjected to intense interrogation. Among the charges against him was that he had maintained friendly relations with another exile, the Trotskyist Ivan Smirnov.[11] On this basis he was condemned, on 21 January 1938, by the Military Collegium of the Supreme Court of the USSR, to the supreme penalty, and executed at once. He had not confessed to any of the accusations against him, about belonging to 'a Trotskyist terrorist organisation' and so forth, which he boldly rejected as 'absurd.' The entire leadership of the party organisation in Saratov was 'liquidated' for having protected this comrade who, on his sixtieth birthday, less than a year before his exile, had been described in *Izvestia* as 'the most eminent Marxologist of our time', and in Pravda as 'a world-ranking scientific personality' who has given 'over 40 years to the cause of the working class'.[12]

Notes

1. The Bolshevik party school at Capri was held in 1910, and that at Longjumeau in 1911.
2. The Zimmerwald international conference of Socialists opposed to the First World War took place in September 1915. Its *Manifesto* was written by Trotsky.
3. VI Lenin, 'To DB Riazanov', 23 September 1921, *Collected Works*, Volume 45, Moscow, 1976, p309.
4. Rafael Rhein, called Abramovich (1880–1963), was one of the main spokesmen for Menshevism abroad.
5. LD Trotsky, 'The Case of Comrade Riazanov', 8 March 1931, *Writings of Leon Trotsky, 1930–31*, New York, 1973, pp194, 196–7.
6. Jenny Longuet (1844–1883) was Marx's eldest daughter.
7. Lydia Tsederbaum-Dan was Martov's younger sister, married to Theodore Dan.
8. 'Marx to His Daughter Jenny', 11 April 1881, in Dona Torr (ed), *Karl Marx and Friedrich Engels: Selected Correspondence, 1846–1895*, London, 1934, p389.
9. LD Trotsky, 'A New Slander against DB Riazanov', 1 May 1931, *Writings of Leon Trotsky, 1930–31*, New York, 1973, p237.
10. 'Marx on Kautsky', *Labour Monthly*, Volume 13, no 7, July 1931, pp447–52 (translated from *Bolshevik* [Moscow], 15 March 1931). In her letter to Riazanov dated 4 July 1925, Lydia Tsederbaum-Dan expressed 'complete faith' that he 'would accurately conform to the condition which I was compelled to impose'. Riazanov himself is described in the article as playing the role of 'a Menshevik savant and activist' (p447) and condemned for 'excising from the letter the deadly characterisation of Kautsky that it contains' (p448).
11. Ivan Nikitich Smirnov (1881–1936) had supported the Trotskyist Opposition, but had capitulated to Stalin in 1929. That did not prevent him from being accused of belonging to a 'Trotskyist-Zinovievist Terroristic Centre' and being a defendant in the first Moscow Trial.
12. Quoted by Boris Souvarine, 'DB Riazanov', translated from *La Critique Sociale*, 2 July 1931, in *What Became of the Revolution*, London, 2001, p130.

Introduction

Brian Pearce

Describing the mood in Germany in August 1914 which enabled the leaders of the Social Democratic Party to swing their organisation behind the Kaiser's government[1] in the First World War, Evelyn Anderson notes, in *Hammer or Anvil* (1945), that fear of Russia 'was undoubtedly felt by the vast majority of the German people. It was felt in particular by the working class, which for decades had been swamped with anti-Russian propaganda. True, German absolutism was bad ... But, compared with the barbarism of Russian Tsardom, it was decidedly the lesser evil ... Suitable quotations from Marx, Engels and others were sought and found' to justify Social Democratic support for a war by Germany against Russia, and one that was 'quoted again and again' was Marx's declaration in 1848 that 'only *a war against Russia* would be a war of *revolutionary* Germany'.[2] James Joll recalls, in *The Second International* (1955), that, already on 30 July, the editor-in-chief of the party paper *Vorwärts*, 'remembering what Engels and Bebel had said about the Russians, thought that this was the moment to say that, if attacked by Russia, "we will not have our women and children sacrificed to the brutality of the Cossacks".' And on the fatal fourth of August, Haase[3] spoke for the party in the Reichstag, to say: 'For our people and its peaceful development much, if not everything, is at stake in the event of the victory of Russian despotism, which has stained itself with the blood of the best of its own people.'[4]

To justify their alignment with German imperialism, the Social Democratic leaders harked back to the slogans of their movement's founders in the 1840s and 1850s. They omitted to examine the situation in which those slogans had been issued, to consider how that situation had changed, and had been recognised as changing by Marx and Engels themselves in later decades, and, above all, to confront the evidence that the situation had become fundamentally different since Engels' death in 1895. Yet there had been discussion in the international socialist movement since 1896 which pointed to the need to cease simply repeating old formulations regarding the proper 'foreign policy' for the Marxists of Western Europe. Riazanov's essay here presented in English translation was a contribution to that discussion: written in 1908, it was published in an abridged form in the German Social Democrats' theoretical journal, *Die Neue Zeit*, as a special supplement, in 1909 (the publication of the full text had to wait until after the October Revolution, in 1918).

Down to and including the time of the Crimean War,[5] Marx and Engels consistently and persistently advocated the promotion of war against Russia by the Western powers, because they saw Russia as a country where immense power was concentrated in the hands of a ruler who used this power to intervene against democratic revolutionary movements in Central Europe, and a country where there was no apparent possibility of this ruler being checked, let alone overthrown, by force from within. Russia's defeat in the Crimean War was followed by a number of reforms, notably the emancipation of the serfs in 1861.[6] At first, Marx and Engels (especially the former) were cautious in their estimation of the significance of these reforms. In his speech of 22 January 1867, Marx commented: 'However it may work in the future, for the present the serf-emancipation has increased the disposable forces of the Tsar', and he reiterated the old demand of the German revolutionary democrats: 'Europe must restore Poland' – that is, the Western powers must go to war against Russia in order to recreate the Poland of 1772, thereby setting a broad barrier between the 'realm of barbarism' and the countries of Central Europe where the revolution was brewing.[7]

In 1874 (in his article in the *Volksstaat* of 11 June), Engels wrote that 'even today official Russia is the stronghold and bulwark of all European reaction, her army the reserve of all other armies, ensuring the suppression of all the working-class in Europe'.[8] But it was in this article that, for the first time, influenced by news from the Tsar's empire, he admitted the possibility of a revolutionary upheaval in Russia. And when he wrote the article which appeared in the *Volksstaat* of 21 April 1875, he went further towards drawing practical conclusions from the changed situation. The overthrow of Tsardom was still a *sine qua non* for the revolution's success in Central Europe: 'it is by no means essential, however, for this overthrow to be brought about from outside, although a foreign war could accelerate it considerably'.[9] What *would* hold up the progress of the revolutionary movement in Russia would be 'a successful war'. Here was a hint of a change of policy from 'roll-back' to 'containment'.

Writing about the Russo-Turkish War of 1876–1878 in the New York *Labour Standard* of 31 March 1878, Engels noted that the Tsar had begun his war with Turkey for a reason which had never applied before, namely, to provide a solution to political difficulties at home. Russia would be forced to retreat by pressure from the other European powers, and this humiliation would intensify the domestic crisis, and so that revolution would be brought nearer which would change completely the prospects for successful revolution in the rest of Europe. The Tsar had lost his former liberty of action, and Russia's uniqueness in Europe as a country without an internal revolutionary movement had disappeared: nevertheless, the process that was beginning over there was not as yet very far advanced, Tsardom was still the 'main enemy', and no national movements must be encouraged anywhere that would play into the Tsar's hands, and help him strengthen his position.[10]

This was one consideration that led Engels to write to Kautsky on 7 February 1882, about the revolt against Turkish rule in Bosnia, that only after Tsardom had collapsed could Social Democrats let the South Slavs 'do as they please',[11] and to Bernstein on 9 October 1886, that the Bulgars ought not to attack Turkey in order to liberate their oppressed kindred: they must wait for the fall of Tsardom, just as the Alsace-Lorrainers must wait.[12] The mention of the Alsace-Lorraine question[13] points to another consideration that now increasingly began to weigh with Engels, namely, the danger of an all-European war begun through one or other of the powers adopting a policy of recovering 'lost' territories, whatever justification might be advanced. The Germany of the 1880s was very different from the Germany of the 1840s. The Social Democratic Party was great and growing. As Engels put it in the above mentioned letter to Kautsky: 'If it does [war breaks out], one thing of which we may be certain, namely that the splendid progress in the direction of revolution now being made in Germany, Austria, and Russia itself will be totally disrupted ...'[14]

In this last phase of his life, Engels stressed more and more emphatically the undesirability of war – of any war, war against Russia included. Nevertheless, he did not fail to insist that, if it should come, the defeat of Russia must be the first priority for revolutionaries everywhere. Writing to Wilhelm Liebknecht[15] on 23 February 1888, he expressed the view that, in a war between Germany and Russia, Bismarck[16] ought not to be overthrown by external agency *until* revolution was under way in Russia, and on 29 February he added that, in such a war, 'the Russians may get a fearful drubbing, and that would be the best of all'.

In his letter of 4 January 1888 to the Romanian Ioan Nadejde,[17] while reiterating that the overthrow of Tsardom was the first condition for the emancipation of the peoples of Central and Eastern Europe, he had gone on to insist that a European war was undesirable, and, in a phrase which interestingly foreboded a development in Marxist policy after his death, to add that, if such a war did come, 'one ought to wish that *every* participant should be defeated – if that were possible'.

In 1891, after the announcement of an alliance between Russia and France, Engels warned the French Socialists in an article entitled *Socialism in Germany*, that although the French Republic was certainly more advanced than the German Empire, nevertheless, as soon as that republic 'places itself under the orders of the Russian Tsar', things were no longer the same: 'Tsarism is the enemy of all the Western nations, even of the bourgeois of these nations.' In the event of war with Russia, the German Socialists would be obliged, 'in the interest of the European revolution, they are obliged to defend all the positions that have been won', and in doing this they would have to fight 'Russia and its allies, whoever they may be, to the bitter end'.[18]

The years of 1896 and 1897 saw massacres of Armenians in Turkey and a revolt by the Greek population of Crete, then under Turkish rule, aimed at union with Greece. The question of what the attitude of Socialists should be towards the Armenian and Cretan national movements met with a divided response among the leading spokesmen of European Social Democracy. In one of his last letters, to an Armenian named Atabekyants on 23 November 1894, Engels had opined that the liberation of Armenia from Turkish rule would be possible only when Russian Tsardom fell, and many Social Democrats now reacted negatively to the sympathy with the Armenians and the Cretans that was voiced in wide circles in Europe. The London *Justice* wrote on 26 September 1896: 'The bloodthirsty ravings of the Nonconformist press over the Armenian atrocities become more savage and hysterical every day ... There is no desire among the people here that any step should be taken that would have the effect of strengthening Russia in the East'; and on 1 May 1897, after referring to the 'Levantine lies' of the Greeks: 'The Russian government is the enemy of the human race, and the power to which the reactionists of every country look for support against the rising forces of democracy and Socialism.' To support the struggle for freedom of Turkey's Greek subjects would be to do just what the Tsar wanted, and that, above all, must not happen.

The opposite view was represented in *Justice* of 27 March 1897 by

'A French Socialist', who noted that, in the leading circles of the Second International, Wilhelm Liebknecht was alone in pronouncing himself against the Cretans. Against him stood Kautsky, Parvus and Rosa Luxemburg.[19] They considered that 'the only strong barrier in the Balkans against the great barbarous power of the East consists of those little nationalities who are far more annoying for the Russian Empire than the old, weak, decrepit Turkey'.

While Liebknecht opposed the slogan of a Balkan Federation, arguing that any 'independent' state in the Balkans would be in fact merely a client state of Russia, his opponents urged that the national movements of the South Slavs and the other oppressed minorities of the Ottoman Empire were facts that could not be wished away, and if Social Democracy turned its back on them, these movements would indeed turn to Russia as their only 'friend'. Rosa Luxemburg, though in general against the break-up of big states, saw the Ottoman Empire as an exception. There the Greeks and the other minorities had attained a degree of economic development higher than that of the decadent Turkish regime. She argued that 'Russia was no longer the hopeless bastion of reaction, to be weakened in every possible way', and also that 'one of the alleged bastions of defence against aggressive Russia – a viable Turkish state – was nothing but an illusion. Far from being artificially maintained, it and not Russia should be pressed to disintegration. The dead weight of Turkish rule was even incapable of *generating* capitalism – and thus, ultimately, Socialism: the sooner it was destroyed and split up into its constituent parts the better – and then this backward area might catch up with the normal processes of historical dialectic' (Peter Nettl, ***Rosa Luxemburg***, Volume I, 1966, p100).

Kautsky, writing in the ***Iskra*** of 10 March 1902 – 'How well Kautsky wrote 18 years ago!' was Lenin's comment in 1920[20] – pointed to a development of an even greater significance than the weakening of Tsardom. 'To Western Europe, Russia has long ceased to be a bulwark of reaction and absolutism. I think the reverse is true today. Western Europe is becoming Russia's bulwark of reaction and absolutism ... The Russian revolutionaries might perhaps have coped with the Tsar long ago had they not been compelled at the same time to fight his ally – European capital' – a reference to Tsardom's dependence on loans from the Western capitalists.[21]

In his article 'The Tsar Visits Europe ...', written in July 1909, Lenin said that the leaders of the international Socialist proletariat had from the 1840s onwards denounced Tsardom as the mainstay of reaction in the whole civilised world, but that, 'beginning with the last three decades or so of the nineteenth century, the revolutionary movement in Russia gradually altered this state of affairs. The more Tsardom was shaken by the blows of the growing revolutionary movement at home, the weaker it became as the enemy of freedom in Europe. But in the meantime, another international reactionary force had taken definite shape in Europe – the bourgeois governments ...'[22] A few years later, Lenin was to develop further that last point, defining the 'qualitative change' to monopoly capitalism, to imperialism, which had taken place in the most advanced capitalist countries. From then on, as he saw it, there could be no counterposing of Germany and Russia, either as a 'lesser' or a 'greater' evil from the Socialist standpoint. The old pattern had become wholly obsolete. After the First World War had begun, when Inessa Armand brought up in argument the line of Engels' *Socialism in Germany*, Lenin replied on 25 December 1916: 'For Germany in 1891 the war did not, and could not, have an imperialist character. You have forgotten the main thing – that in 1891 no imperialism existed at all (I have tried to show in my pamphlet that it was born in 1898–1900, not earlier), and there was no imperialist war, there could not be, on the part of Germany (by the way, there was no revolutionary Russia then, either: that is very important)'.[23]

In his critique of Engels' article 'The Foreign Policy of Russian Tsardom' (1890), written in July 1934 but not published until May 1941 ('On an Article by Engels', English translation in *Labour Monthly*, August 1952),[24] Stalin indicates that he sees imperialism as having begun earlier than Lenin allows. By concentrating on Tsarist Russia as the main source of danger of world war, 'Engels omits one important factor which later on played the most decisive part, namely, the factor of *imperialist* struggle for colonies, for sources of raw material. This had very serious importance already at that time. He omits the role of Great Britain as a factor in the coming world war, the factor of the contradictions between Germany and Great Britain ...'

This idea, of an earlier dating than Lenin's for the beginning of the imperialist epoch, does not appear to have been developed further by Stalin. It would certainly have drawn him into deep waters re-estimating political attitudes taken up in the 1880s and 1890s. Perhaps he does not distinguish sharply enough between 'imperialism' in the special sense given to the term by Lenin (monopoly capitalism, with its specific tendencies, both internally and externally) and the drive to colonial expansionism which antedates and prepares the way for it. That drive, of course, began long ago. One of the criticisms that Riazanov levels at Marx is that he failed to observe how Britain's intensified attention to India and the approaches thereto, from the 1780s onward, following the loss of the American colonies, brought under severer strain than ever before that Anglo-Russian solidarity to which Marx attributed such great importance in the history of Europe in the eighteenth century.

Riazanov's book is concerned mainly, though not exclusively, with Marx's 'Revelations of the Diplomatic History of the Eighteenth Century', originally published in a British newspaper in 1856–57, and reissued in book form in 1899 as *The Secret Diplomatic History of the Eighteenth Century*. Having become forcibly aware of the collusion between Britain and Russia in European affairs in the first half of the nineteenth century (with Russia zealous to put down all 'subversive' political movements, and Britain careful to discourage progressive developments in other countries which might threaten to impair her industrial monopoly), Marx sought to trace the prehistory of this collusion, and satisfied himself that it had begun at the beginning of the eighteenth century. Riazanov examines Marx's work with an appreciative but critical eye, and points to factual errors, to an inconsistent application of Marx's own historical materialism, and to signs of that tendency which lies in wait for every politician writing on historical subjects – to project contemporary politics into an essentially different setting in the past. His main concern, however, writing in 1908, is to show the context in which Marx formulated his views on Russia, and explain how times had changed, so that it would not be truly Marxist to go on repeating those formulations as though they still possessed whatever validity they had then.

Marx's 'Revelations' long remained unpublished in the Soviet Union. In the new edition of the *Collected Works* brought out in English by Lawrence and Wishart, in collaboration with the Institute of Marxism-Leninism in Moscow, after Volumes 1 to 14 had appeared, they were followed by Volume 16. It was obvious that Volume 15, which should contain the 'Revelations', was causing the editors a problem. Years passed and saw the publication of several more volumes in the series before, with Gorbachev and *glasnost*, Volume 15 was given the green light. Anyone could now discover that Marx had really made mistakes in his account of diplomatic history and had also made disparaging remarks about the Russian people.[25]

In 1969, Lawrence and Wishart brought out *The Secret Diplomatic History of the Eighteenth Century* in one volume with *The Story of the Life of Lord Palmerston*.[26] There were introductions to both works by Lester Hutchinson – interesting, but uncritical. The book is now out of print. When it appeared, the late EH Carr wrote a review which was published (without signature, as was the practice of the time) in the *Times Literary Supplement* for 28 August 1969, under the heading 'Marxist Hack-Work'. In this review, Carr sneered at both books as unimportant scribblings written to make money, and certainly not deserving to be reprinted. Actually, as Carr must have known, from Marx's *Correspondence* and from *Herr Vogt*,[27] Marx took very seriously the researches which resulted in these works. On Urquhart, in whose paper he published them, Marx wrote to Lassalle[28] on 2 June 1860 that though his views were 'subjectively reactionary', the activity they inspired was 'objectively revolutionary': he was not the mere 'fanatic' contemptuously dismissed by Carr. Engels, in his 1890 article entitled 'The Foreign Policy of Russian Tsardom', wrote of him: 'It is impossible, in England, to write about Russian foreign policy without at once recalling the name of David Urquhart. For 50 years he worked indefatigably to spread among his countrymen a knowledge of the aims and methods of Russian diplomacy, a subject he thoroughly understood; and yet, all he got for his pains was ridicule and the reputation of an unmitigated bore. Now the ordinary Philistine does indeed class under that head everyone who insists upon unpalatable subjects, be they never so important ...'[29]

Included in the 'Revelations' is a survey of Russian history, and Riazanov's critical discussion of this part of the book may profitably be compared with Trotsky's ideas on the subject as expounded in *Results and Prospects*, in the essay 'Concerning the Intelligentsia', the book *1905* and the reply to Pokrovsky's criticism of that work which appears as an appendix to the *History of the Russian Revolution*.[30] Riazanov holds the same view as Trotsky in rejecting the decisive role ascribed by some historians to the 'Tatar yoke' in the formation of the autocracy in Russia. He points, instead, to the role of internal social processes (though giving more weight to these than Trotsky does) and to the response to influences from the more advanced countries of the West (though stressing the economic more than the military factor). Pokrovsky accused Trotsky of endorsing the historical conceptions of Milyukov,[31] whose essential idea Riazanov quotes in this book. Trotsky did indeed agree with Milyukov in emphasising the unusually independent and dominant role of the state in Russia's development (and noted that Russian Marxists, in trying to counter excessive emphasis on the peculiarities of Russia's development, sometimes tended to 'throw the baby out with the bathwater'). 'Nevertheless', he insisted, 'it is a terrible exaggeration and a distortion of all perspective to say, as Milyukov says in his history of Russian culture, that while in the West the estates created the states, in Russia the state created the estates in its own interest.'[32] The efforts of the seventeenth-century Tsars would have been fruitless indeed if Russia's economy had not already been moving, even though too slowly for the country's security, in a progressive direction. (In that connection, incidentally, Trotsky made a prophetic comment on 'the immensely important role which state power can play in the purely economic sphere when, generally speaking, it is working in the same direction as historical development'.)[33]

*

* *

The principal documentary sources used by Riazanov are F de Martens' collection of Russia's treaties, published in Russian and French, with a commentary, the French title being ***Recueil des traités et conventions conclus par la Russie avec les puissances étrangères***; Volumes 9–10, 11 and 12, published in 1892, 1895 and 1898 respectively, cover the periods 1710–1801, 1801–31 and 1832–95 for treaties with Britain; the ***Sbornik*** (Miscellany) of the Imperial Russian Historical Society, of which 148 volumes were published between 1867 and 1916; and ***Arkhiv Knyazya Vorontsova***, the archives of the Vorontsov[34] family through the eighteenth and nineteenth centuries, published in 40 volumes between 1870 and 1895.

'Blackstock and Hoselitz' refers to ***Karl Marx and Friedrich Engels: The Russian Menace to Europe***, a compilation of the principal writings of Marx and Engels about Russia, edited by Paul S Blackstock and Bert E Hoselitz, published in 1953. Editorial insertions in the text and in the author's own notes occur in the footnotes. A number of obvious misprints and slips of the pen have been corrected, and a few initials, dates of publication and the like, added, without special indication.

Notes

I have adopted the now generally accepted form 'Tatar' rather than the long used but offensive'Tartar', except when it appears in a quotation (translator's note).

1. The German Kaiser (Emperor) during the First World War was Wilhelm II, who reigned from 1888 to 1918.
2. Evelyn Anderson, ***Hammer or Anvil***, London, 1945, pp19–20. The quotation from Marx is from 'German Foreign Policy and the Latest Events in Prague', ***Neue Rheinische Zeitung***, no 42, 12 July 1848, Marx and Engels, ***Collected Works***, Volume 7, London, 1977, p212.
3. Hugo Haase (1863–1919) was co-chairman of the German Social Democratic Party, and voted for the war credits in the Reichstag in 1914. He supported the USPD (Independent Social Democratic Party) from 1916, and was assassinated by a monarchist after the war.
4. James Joll, ***The Second International, 1889–1914***, London, 1955, pp170, 175.
5. The Crimean War (1853–56) was fought between Britain, France, Piedmont-Sardinia and Turkey on the one side, and Russia on the other.
6. Tsar Alexander II (1855–81) emancipated the serfs in 1861, but in such conditions that

many of them were loaded down with debt.

7. Karl Marx, 'Poland's European Mission', Speech at the Polish Meeting in London, 22 January 1867, Marx and Engels, *Collected Works*, Volume 20, London, 1985, pp200–1. At the end of the eighteenth century, Poland was gradually cut down in size, and finally disappeared from the map of Europe for more than a hundred years. The first partition of Poland, between Russia, Austria and Prussia, took place in 1772, the second, between Russia and Prussia, in 1793, and the third, between Russia, Austria and Prussia, in 1795. Poland was only recreated as a state at the Treaty of Versailles in 1919.
8. Frederick Engels, 'A Polish Proclamation', *Volksstaat*, 17 June 1874, Marx and Engels, *Collected Works*, Volume 24, London, 1989, p10.
9. Frederick Engels, 'Introduction to the Pamphlet *Social Relations in Russia*', Marx and Engels, *Collected Works*, Volume 24, London, 1989, p103.
10. Marx and Engels, *Collected Works*, Volume 24, London, 1989, pp226–9.
11. Frederick Engels, Letter to Kautsky, 7 February 1882, Marx and Engels, *Collected Works*, Volume 46, London, 1992, p194. Karl Kautsky (1854–1938) was the foremost theorist of the Second International, and Marx's literary executor. He followed the same political evolution as Haase during the First World War.
12. Frederick Engels, Letter to Bernstein, 22 and 25 February 1882, Marx and Engels, *Collected Works*, Volume 46, London, 1992, p104. Eduard Bernstein (1850–1932) was Engels' literary executor, and Kautsky's opponent during the 'revisionist' controversy of 1896, but also supported the USPD from 1917 onwards, after which he rejoined the Social Democrats.
13. Alsace-Lorraine had been part of the Holy Roman Empire until 1648, after which it was gradually absorbed by France. It was annexed by Germany after the Franco-Prussian War of 1870–71, but returned to France at the Treaty of Versailles in 1919. It was always a bone of contention between the two states.
14. Frederick Engels, Letter to Kautsky, 7 February 1882, Marx and Engels, *Collected Works*, Volume 46, London, 1992, pp193–4.
15. Wilhelm Liebknecht (1826–1900) was one of the founders and leaders of the German Social Democratic Party, and editor of *Volksstaat*.
16. Otto, Prince von Bismarck-Schönhausen (1815–1898), was the main architect of the unification of Germany, and its 'Iron Chancellor'.
17. Ioan Nadejde (1854–1928) was a Social Democratic journalist who translated Engels' works into Romanian.
18. Friedrich Engels, 'Socialism in Germany', October 1891, Marx and Engels, *Collected Works*, Volume 27, Moscow, 1990, pp242, 244.
19. Alexander Israel Helphand, called Parvus (1867–1924), was the first Marxist to apply the theory of Permanent Revolution to Russian conditions in the early twentieth century; Rosa Luxemburg (1871–1919) was one of the foremost thinkers of the Social Democratic left in Poland and Germany, murdered by Freikorps in 1919.
20. VI Lenin, 'Left-Wing Communism: An Infantile Disorder', June 1920, *Collected Works*, Volume 31, Moscow, 1966, p23.
21. Karl Kautsky, 'The Slavs and Revolution', *Iskra*, no 18, 10 March 1902, quoted by Lenin, 'Speech Delivered at a Meeting Organised by the Moscow Committee of the RCP(B) (Russian Communist Party [Bolshevick]) in Honour of Lenin's Fiftieth Birthday', 23 April 1920, *Collected Works*, Volume 30, Moscow, 1965, p527; 'Left-Wing Communism: An Infantile Disorder', June 1920, *Collected Works*, Volume 31, Moscow, 1966, pp22–3.
22. VI Lenin, 'The Tsar Visits Europe and Members of the Black-Hundred Duma Visit England', 11 July 1909, *Collected Works*, Volume 15, Moscow, 1963, p461.
23. VI Lenin, 'Letter to Inessa Armand', 25 December 1916, *Collected Works,* Volume 35, Moscow, 1966, p268. Inessa Fyodorovna Armand (1874–1920) was a close collaborator and confidant of Lenin. Cf Michel Pearson, *Inessa: Lenin's Mistress*, London, 2001.

24. Frederick Engels, 'The Foreign Policy of Russian Tsardom', Marx and Engels, *Collected Works*, Volume 27, Moscow, 1990, pp11–49; JV Stalin, 'On An Article by Engels', *Bolshevik*, no 9, May 1941, English translation in *Labour Monthly*, Volume 34, no 8, August 1952, pp364–9.
25. Volume 15 of the English edition of the Marx-Engels *Collected Works* was finally published in 1986. Some extracts, with an introduction by Maximilien Rubel, had previously been published under the title of 'Excerpts on Russia from Karl Marx', in *New International*, Volume 17, no 6 (whole number 151), November/December 1951, pp360–3.
26. Henry John Temple, Third Viscount Palmerston (1785–1865) was successively Foreign Secretary, Home Secretary and Prime Minister for most of the period from 1830 to his death, and largely directed British foreign policy during the first part of Victoria's reign.
27. Karl Vogt (1817–1895) had been a deputy to the Frankfurt Assembly, during his exile received subsidies from Louis Napoleon, and slandered Marx and Engels. Marx replied to him in *Herr Vogt* (English edition, New Park Publications, 1982).
28. Ferdinand Lassalle (1825–1864) was the founder of the General Association of German Workers, the first successful organisation of the working class in Germany, which united with the 'Eisenachers' to set up the German Social Democratic Party.
29. Frederick Engels, 'The Foreign Policy of Russian Tsardom', April and May 1890, Marx and Engels, *Collected Works*, Volume 27, Moscow, 1990, pp13–4. David Urquhart (1805–1877) was a Tory MP (1847–52), a supporter of Turkey, and the editor of the *Free Press* and the *Diplomatic Review*. Cf Gertrude Robinson, *David Urquhart*, Oxford, 1920; GA Hutt, 'David Urquhart: A Forgotten Friend of Marx', *The Plebs*, Volume 15, no 2, February 1923, pp68–71.
30. LD Trotsky, 'Results and Prospects', *The Permanent Revolution*, New York, 1972, pp28–122; 'On the Intelligentsia', *Revolutionary History*, Volume 7, no 2, pp83–98; *1905*, New York, 1972; 'Appendix 1' (to Volume 1), *History of the Russian Revolution*, London, 1965, pp471–7. Mikhail Nikolayevich Pokrovsky (1868–1932) was chairman of the Moscow Soviet during the Russian Revolution, and the author of *A Brief History of Russia* (London, 1933). For his controversy with Plekhanov and Trotsky on Russian history, cf Samuel Baron, *Plekhanov in Russian History and Historiography*, Pittsburg UP, 1995, pp33–62.
31. Pavel Nikolayevich Milyukov (1859–1943) was an historian and leader of the Russian Constitutional Democrats (Cadets) during the Russian Revolution. His *Ocherki po istorii russkoy kultury* was published in St Petersburg in 1898.
32. LD Trotsky, 'Results and Prospects', 1906, *The Permanent Revolution*, New York, 1969, p40 (translation emended).
33. 'But if the general course of the internal economy of this enormous country had not been moving in this same direction, if the development of economic conditions had not created the demand for general and applied science, all the efforts of the state would have been fruitless.' LD Trotsky, 'Results and Prospects', op cit, p42.
34. Prince Semen Romanovich Vorontsov (1744–1832) was the Russian ambassador in London, 1784–1806.

Karl Marx on Anglo-Russian Relations

D.B. Riazanov

Published by the Petrograd Soviet of Workers' and Red Army Men's Deputies in 1918 and translated into English by Brian Pearce.

Preface

The work now offered for the attention of Russian readers was undertaken by the author in the autumn of 1908. The revolution of 1905–07 had shown that the old foreign policy programme which the Social Democrats, in the wake of Marx and Engels, had inherited from the radical democrats was in need of critical revision. In order to perform that task it was necessary, first of all, to study how the views of Marx and Engels on questions of foreign policy had evolved. And it was precisely in this field that what may be called 'Marxology' showed big gaps. The *Collected Works* of Marx and Engels published by Mehring[1] had got no further than the revolution of 1848–49. Eleanor Marx's[2] attempt to publish some of her father's writings concerned with the events of the 1850s proved, on closer examination, to be very inadequate. Consequently, I had to do a great deal of preliminary work, and to start by getting to know the entire literary heritage left by Marx and Engels. Although this work was considerably facilitated by the fact that the late Lafargues and Bebel[3] put all the archives of Marx and Engels at my disposal, it called for careful examination of many journals and newspapers, and, as a result, produced some completely fresh material.

The coming of the world war suspended publication of the *Collected Works* of Marx and Engels beyond the period 1850–52, together with that of the documentary history of the First International. Only certain sections of this work had been published in the journals of the German and Austrian Social Democrats, *Neue*

Zeit and *Kampf*, and also in the *Archiv für die Geschichte des Sozialismus und der Arbeiterbewegung* published in Vienna under the editorship of Professor Karl Grünberg.[4]

The critical study which now appears in Russian acquainted Europe's Social Democrats for the first time with the views of Karl Marx (his subsequently published correspondence with Engels showed that, in this sphere too, much that appeared under Marx's name was actually by Engels) on the historical development of Russia's hegemony in Europe. It was also the first serious attempt at a 'revision' of the views of Marx and Engels on the Eastern Question and on the question of Russia's role in the field of international politics. The previous attempt, made by Rosa Luxemburg and Karl Kautsky, in their polemic with Wilhelm Liebknecht concerning the questions of Crete and Armenia, to show that one could not go on dogmatically repeating the old views of Marx and Engels, despite a number of correct critical observations, was inadequate because it proceeded from a quite incorrect notion of the way the relevant opinions of the founders of scientific socialism had developed.

This Russian edition is an almost literal reproduction of the German version which appeared as a supplement to *Die Neue Zeit*. I have merely restored, from the manuscript which I retained, some passages which Kautsky considered too specialised for the German reader, and also some critical remarks addressed to Mehring, who took up, on the dispute between Marx and Lassalle about problems of foreign policy, the same opportunist position as on the dispute between Liebknecht and Bebel, on the one hand, and Schweitzer[5] on the other, about problems of domestic politics – the cuts, in this case, too, being made at Kautsky's request.[6]

The demands of practical activity just now prevent me from reworking and supplementing certain chapters. Shortly after the appearance of my study, and even in some cases simultaneously with it, new materials and works were published, both in Russian and in other languages, which would have helped me to illustrate more effectively the arguments I develop (the works of DM Polievktov, I Lyubimenko, J.F. Chance, William Robert Scott and others).[7]

I hope that I may be able in a subsequent publication to deal, if only in the form of detached notes, with objections evoked by what I have written.

D Riazanov
September 1918

Notes

1. Franz Mehring (1846–1919) was one of the theoreticians of the German Social Democratic left, the first editor of the collected works of Marx and Engels, and the author of a well-known biography of Marx (English edition, *Karl Marx: The Story of his Life*, London, 1936) (translator's note).
2. Eleanor ('Tussy') Marx (1855–1898) was Marx's youngest daughter, who made an unfortunate marriage to Edward Aveling in 1884 (translator's note).
3. Laura Lafargue (1845–1911), Marx's second daughter, married Paul Lafargue (1842–1911), the founder of the French Workers Party, in 1868. August Bebel (1840–1913) was a founder and leader of the German Social Democratic Party and of the Second International (translator's note).
4. Carl Grünberg (1861–1940), a historian of Law who held a chair at Vienna University before the First World War, founded and edited this *Archiv*, which was the first major journal of labour history (translator's note).
5. Johann Baptist von Schweitzer (1833–1875), a supporter of Lassalle and President of the General Association of German Workers, opposed the unification with the Eisenachers to set up the Social Democratic Party. He was finally expelled for his contacts with the Prussian authorities (translator's note).
6. On the differences between Mehring and Riazanov on these matters, cf Franz Mehring, *Karl Marx: The Story of His Life*, and DB Riazanov, *Karl Marx and Friedrich Engels* (1927), especially pp112–7 (translator's note).
7. The references are evidently to MA Polievktov, *Baltiisky vopros v russkoy politike posle Nishtadskago mira*, 1721–1725 (1907), I Lyubimenko, *Istoriya torgovykh soobshchenii Rossii i Anglii*, (1912); JF Chance, *George I and the Northern War: A Study of British-Hanoverian Policy in the North of Europe, 1709–1721* (1909), and WR Scott, *The Constitution and Finance of English, Scottish and Irish Joint Stock Companies to 1720* (1910–1912) (translator's note).

Chapter One

The Counter-Revolutionary Role of Britain and Russia in 1848–49

The revolution of 1848, which swept like a whirlwind all across Western Europe, stirring not only Vienna but also Berlin, halted at the frontiers of Russia. The momentary alarm caused in St Petersburg soon subsided when reports were received from the Third Section that 'all was well'.[1] And Russian absolutism, lurking like a wild beast that awaits the best moment to leap upon its prey, watched attentively the ups and downs of the revolutionary struggle in Germany, while concentrating its forces on the Western frontier.

'The Tsar is standing at the gates of Thorn', wrote the *Neue Rheinische Zeitung*.[2] This was the circumstance that determined the entire foreign policy of the German democrats and their extreme left wing, grouped around the *Neue Rheinische Zeitung*. The paper's editors declared openly that 'only a war against Russia would be a war of *revolutionary* Germany, a war by which she could cleanse herself of her past sins, could take courage, defeat her own autocrats, spread civilisation by the sacrifice of her own sons as becomes a people that is shaking off the chains of long, indolent slavery, and make herself free within her borders by freeing herself from without'.[3]

On the other side, Nicholas and Nesselrode,[4] who were even then engaged in secret negotiations with the 'Grapeshot Prince' (the future Wilhelm I),[5] merely continued the traditions of Russian diplomacy when, in a circular dated 6 July, they complained bitterly about the unjust suspicion to which Russia had been subjected in Germany since the time of the March revolution. 'War against Russia', wrote

Nesselrode, 'was proclaimed as one of the most necessary tasks of the moment.' Russian absolutism called for respect for the treaties of 1815, the aim of which had been to perpetuate the fragmentation of Germany, and protested most vigorously against the unification 'dreamt of by democrats who are yearning to draw Germany, at any price, into war with her neighbours'.

The heavy paw of 'the Russian bear' had already been felt in the energy with which the attempted rising in Prussian Poland had been suppressed. And Russian absolutism had quite openly intervened in the Schleswig affair,[6] compelling Prussia to wage merely a 'sham war', in order to conclude it immediately with an armistice. Among the 'three most reactionary powers in Europe' which sided with Denmark, the *Neue Rheinische Zeitung* named Britain along with Russia and Prussia. 'Prussia, England and Russia are the three powers which have greater reason than anyone else to fear the German revolution and its first result – German unity: Prussia because she would thereby cease to exist, England because it would deprive her of the possibility of exploiting the German market, and Russia because it would spell the advance of democracy, not only to the Vistula, but even as far as the Dvina and the Dnieper'.[7]

We can see already in the London correspondence of the *Neue Rheinische Zeitung* this change in attitude towards England and the man who was then in charge of her foreign policy, Palmerston, whom not only the members of the Holy Alliance,[8] but European liberals as well, had regarded as a champion of constitutionalism and national unification after the events in Italy and Switzerland in 1847.[9] But this fierce enemy of the British labour movement and true servant of British capital, who had defended constitutional Belgium as a bulwark against France, supported the Swiss liberals with his 'moral' authority and with money, and protected the interests of British trade in the Apennine Peninsula against Austria, was 'shocked' by the revolution of 1848 to no less an extent than Nicholas. He realised all too well that any fresh successes by the revolutionary movement on the continent would strengthen Chartism in Britain, and he exerted every effort to keep the revolution within definite bounds. Hence also his stubborn opposition to German unity, insofar as this could be accomplished only by a victory of the people over the crowns. Every defeat suffered by the revolution in France and Germany meant at the same time a defeat for Chartism in Britain and a strengthening of Britain's counter-revolutionary role.

Summing up the results of the revolutionary movement of 1848, the *Neue Rheinische Zeitung* wrote in the New Year article published on 1 January 1849:

> But England, the country that turns whole nations into its proletarians, that takes the whole world within its immense embrace, that already once defrayed the cost of a European restoration, the country in which class contradictions have reached their most acute and shameless form – England seems to be the rock against which the revolutionary waves break, the country where the new society is stifled even in the womb ... A revolution of the economic relations in any country of the European continent, in the whole European continent, without England, is a storm in a teacup. Industrial and commercial relations within each nation are governed by its intercourse with other nations, and depend on its relations with the world market ... And only a *world war* can overthrow the old England, as only this can provide the Chartists, the party of the organised English workers, with the conditions for a successful rising against their gigantic oppressors. Only when the Chartists head the English government will the social revolution pass from the sphere of utopia to that of reality. But any *European war* in which England is involved is a world war, waged in Canada as in Italy, in the East Indies as in Prussia, in Africa as on the Danube. A European war will be the first result of a successful workers' revolution in France. England will head the counter-revolutionary armies, just as it did during the Napoleonic period,[10] but through the war itself it will be thrown to the head of the revolutionary movement, and it will repay the debt it owes in regard to the revolution of the eighteenth century. The table of contents for 1849 reads: *Revolutionary Rising of the French Working Class, World War*.'[11]

While the *Neue Rheinische Zeitung* had, on 2 July 1848, mercilessly set out the long list of all the crimes committed by Germany against the liberties of various peoples and in defence of absolute power, and had said that even in the very heart of Russia Germans were the mainstay 'of the one autocrat and of the smaller ones', and that 'the reaction in Britain had Hanoverian troops at its disposal',[12] on 15 February 1849 it wrote somewhat more gently:

> Up to now it has always been said that the Germans have been the Lanzknechte of despotism throughout Europe. We are far from denying the shameful part played by the

> Germans in the shameful wars against the French revolution from 1792 to 1815, and in the oppression of Italy since 1815, and of Poland since 1772; but who stood behind the Germans, who used them as their mercenaries or their vanguard? England and ***Russia***.[13]

In the preface to his article 'Wage Labour and Capital', in which Marx explained why the *Neue Rheinische Zeitung* had until then not engaged in a detailed analysis of the economic relations which constitute the material basis of class and national struggles, he said that the editors had considered it their principal task to follow, first and foremost, the manifestations of class struggle in current day-to-day practice. Then he again enumerated the chief stages of the February and March revolutions and showed how 'Europe, with the defeat of the revolutionary workers, had relapsed into its old double slavery, the ***Anglo-Russian*** slavery'. And, promising that he would now analyse economic conditions in greater detail, Marx sought not only to examine the relations between wage labour and capital and to prove 'the inevitable destruction of the middle bourgeois classes ... under the present system', but also to show 'the commercial subjugation and exploitation of the various European nations by the despot of the world market – England'.[14]

However, he was unable to fulfil his promises. On 19 May appeared the last issue of *Neue Rheinische Zeitung* printed in red, in which Marx repeated the conclusion of the leading article in the New Year issue: 'The table of contents for 1849 reads: ***Revolutionary Rising of the French Working Class, World War***. And in the East, a revolutionary army made up of fighters of all nationalities[15] already confronts the alliance of the old Europe represented by the Russian army, while from Paris comes the threat of a "red republic" '.[16]

Marx and Engels were mistaken. Hungary was crushed by the Russian army, and hopes of a social revolution in Britain, of a victory for Chartism, proved as unjustified as the hope that the French proletariat would recover after the June slaughter and give a fresh and even more powerful impetus to the revolutionary movement.

Reaction, growing stronger, trod closely behind Marx. The defeat of the petit-bourgeois democrats on 13 June 1849 compelled him to quit Paris for London,[17] where he soon applied himself to bringing out the *Neue Rheinische Zeitung* in the form of a periodical.

While Prussia and Austria were in tow to Russia, the French bourgeois republic was in tow to Britain, where foreign policy was still in Palmerston's charge:

> The role of mediator which Cavaignac[18] and the National Assembly played in Northern Italy, in order, together with England, to betray it to Austria – this one day of rule destroyed 18 years of opposition on the part of the *National*. No government was less national than that of the *National*, none more dependent on England ... none was more servile towards the Holy Alliance ...[19]

And who supplied Russia with the funds that enabled her to carry out her counter-revolutionary mission? Britain. At the beginning of 1850, Nesselrode wrote to Prince Vorontsov the following triumphant lines:

> We have recently had a striking proof of the sympathy with Russia which still exists in Britain. The evidence is the reception given to our loan, in spite of 'Cobden, Peace & Co',[20] as the *Morning Chronicle* amusingly calls the present leader of the free-traders. Just think, the loan has been subscribed to the extent of £16 million. After this, let people say, if it pleases them, that in Britain they don't love Russia any more.[21]

It would indeed be hard to say which was more zealous in supporting the leader of France's Black Hundreds[22] in his task of restoring order – Russia or Britain. In its issue for 29 November 1851, the British *Economist* wrote: 'The President is the guardian of order, and is now recognised as such on every stock exchange in Europe.'[23]

And Nesselrode wrote that Russia, in her representations to the President, always stressed the 'indisputable merit which he had acquired by checking the revolutionary spirit', approved of everything that he had done in the interests of order, and recommended that he keep unwaveringly along that same path.[24]

The *coup d'état* of 2 December 1851 meant the final triumph of the counter-revolution. The constitution was rescinded in Austria, and in Germany, after the Cologne trial of the Communists[25] and the destruction of the last vestiges of the workers' unions, the blackest and most cynical reaction prevailed. After the humiliation in Warsaw followed the ignominy at Olmütz, and the London Protocol of 8 July 1852. Schleswig-Holstein was again attached to Denmark.[26]

And who were the principal authors of the London Protocol? Britain and Russia. The old Anglo-Russian slavery extended once more over all Europe. Prussia fawned on Russia more slavishly than ever. As Tsar Alexander II[27] put it (that dearly beloved nephew of a still more dearly beloved uncle, the future Wilhelm I): 'The more they insult Prussia, the more closely she clings to us.' Relations between Russia and Britain were most friendly, so friendly that Nicholas I prepared to divide with Britain the inheritance of 'the sick man', since he was quite confident of Prussia and Austria. Russia's number-one slave-owner was poorly acquainted with the psychology of slaves.

For Marx, this triumphal march of reaction was not unexpected. He had already in the autumn of 1850 come to the conclusion that there could no longer be any question of a real revolution for the time being. He had been brought to this conclusion by a close study of the prevailing economic conditions and an analysis of the events of 1849 and 1850. He showed how the boom in industry and trade which had begun in 1848 and grown stronger in 1849 paralysed the revolutionary upsurge and made possible the victory of reaction. The Continent's economic dependence on Britain was revealed no less clearly in time of prosperity than in time of crisis. The Continent followed Britain slavishly. 'Just as the period of crisis occurs later on the Continent than in England, so does that of prosperity. The original process always takes place in England: it is the demiurge of the bourgeois cosmos.'

The *political* enslavement of continental Europe to Russia was complemented by its *economic* enslavement to Britain. The revolution of 1848 had been wrecked on the resistance of Russia, the despot of Europe, and equally on the resistance of Britain, the despot of the world market. While it was from London that stretched all those economic threads in which the world market was entangled, consolidating the dependence of continental Europe on the London Stock Exchange, it was in St Petersburg that those fetters were tirelessly forged in which the defeated revolution was struggling, and there that all the machinations and intrigues were woven with which the European courts, from Berlin to Madrid and Lisbon, ensnared their peoples.[28]

This was the political climate in which Marx resumed his economic studies which had been broken off by the revolution. What he saw as of primary importance was to study the 'demiurge of the bourgeois cosmos', and to endeavour to solve the riddle of bourgeois society. 'The enormous amount of material relating to the history of political economy assembled in the British Museum, the fact that London is a convenient vantage point for the observation of bourgeois society, and, finally, the new stage of development which this society seemed to have entered with the discovery of gold in California and Australia'[29] – all this led Marx to apply himself afresh to his researches, starting again from the very beginning and critically working through all the new material.

The first fruit of this work was the *Critique of Political Economy*, in which Marx began fulfilling the promise he had made 10 years previously to the readers of *Neue Rheinische Zeitung*.

But, during the 1850s, Marx did not confine himself to studying 'the bourgeois cosmos'. He studied no less diligently 'the mysteries of international statecraft'. London was not only the most convenient point for observing economic relations in the world market, it was also the place, as The Hague had been in the eighteenth century, where, more quickly than anywhere else, the stock exchange bulletins reflected, just as a sensitive barometer reflects the slightest variations in the atmosphere, every disturbance, however slight, in the sphere of international political relations.

Only in the Britain of that time was such a phenomenon possible as the formation, all over the country, of a whole series of 'Foreign Affairs Committees' – societies which devoted themselves exclusively to studying problems of foreign policy, following closely the activity of the Foreign Office and subjecting every move it made to the most exacting criticism.

But it was not merely Marx's personal inclinations that impelled him to 'investigate the mysteries of international statecraft and follow the diplomatic trickery of governments.' Peremptory need to obtain paid work obliged him to take on the duties of the European correspondent of the *New York Tribune*, the leading Anglo-American newspaper of that time. Because, as he put it, he spent very little time on work strictly connected with his job as a newspaper correspondent, this meant that he ranged extremely widely in his choice of subjects. And among the studies which distracted him from his most important economic research and which, obviously, had very little connection with it, a considerable place was occupied by study of the history of international diplomatic relations.

We have seen what the impressions were that influenced Marx, already before he came to London, in forming the conviction that Britain and Russia were actually allies in the struggle against the revolution. His stay in London strengthened him still further in his view of the counter-revolutionary nature of the policy pursued by Palmerston, whom the Prussian camarilla of that time saw as an agent of revolution, and the Prussian liberals saw as a champion of constitutionalism and no less a defender of the idea of nationality than Napoleon III.[30] It was quite understandable, therefore, that he should take an interest in the work of David Urquhart, who had for 20 years been tirelessly exposing the intrigues of Russian diplomacy, accusing Palmerston of subservience to Russia, and also enthusiastically lauding the charms of Turkish rule in the Balkan Peninsula. It was this antagonism towards Russia and constant opposition to Palmerston that provided the basis for a *rapprochement*, not only between Urquhart and the revolutionary émigrés from Poland and Hungary, but also between him and Marx.

It would be wrong to suppose, however, that Marx was, in this matter, influenced by Urquhart alone. This was out of the question, if only because the two men proceeded from quite different principles, and the tasks they set themselves were absolutely divergent. Not only did Marx not share Urquhart's Turcophil tendencies, he mocked them, as we see from the following humorous sketch of a stubborn eccentric who went into raptures over Turkish freedom no less than over Turkish baths:

> This gentleman, of Scotch birth, with medieval and patriarchal recollections of home, and with a modern British civilised education, after having fought for three years in Greece against the Turks, passed into their country and was the first thus to enamour himself of them. The romantic Highlander found himself at home again in the mountain ravines of the Pindus and Balkan, and his works on Turkey, although full of valuable information, may be summed up in the following three paradoxes, which are laid down almost literally thus: If Mr Urquhart were not a British subject, he would decidedly prefer being a Turk; if he were not a Presbyterian Calvinist, he would not belong to any other religion than Islamism; and thirdly, Britain and Turkey are the only two countries in the world which enjoy self-government and civil and religious liberty.[31]

This is how Marx writes, in his well-known pamphlet, *Herr Vogt*, about his relations with Urquhart and his party:

> Urquhart's writings on Russia and against Palmerston had interested, but not convinced me. In order to arrive at a firm view, I undertook the laborious analysis of Hansard's *Parliamentary Debates* and the diplomatic Blue Books from 1807 to 1850. The first fruits of these studies were a series of leading articles in the *New York Tribune* (end of 1853) in which I demonstrated Palmerston's involvement with the St Petersburg cabinet on the basis

> of his transactions with Poland, Turkey, Circassia, etc. Shortly afterwards I had these articles reprinted in the *People's Paper*, the organ of the Chartists edited by Ernest Jones,[32] together with additional passages about Palmerston's activities. In the meantime, the *Glasgow Sentinel* had also reprinted one of the articles, 'Palmerston and Poland' which attracted the attention of Mr D Urquhart. After a meeting with me he persuaded Mr Tucker in London to bring out some of the articles in pamphlet form. These Palmerston pamphlets were later sold in various editions in numbers ranging from 15,000 to 20, 000.

Marx's pamphlets really did have immense success, and contributed in no small extent to destroying the legend created around Palmerston's name, not only in Europe, but in Britain itself. Marx ruthlessly exposed all the contradictions in Palmerston's policy and showed how, *de facto*, he was an agent both of counter-revolution and of the diplomacy of St Petersburg:[33]

> Yielding to foreign influence in facts, he opposes it in words. Having inherited from Canning[34] England's mission to propagate constitutionalism on the Continent, he is never in need of a theme to pique the national prejudices, and to counteract revolution abroad, and, at the same time, to keep awake the suspicious jealousy of foreign powers. Having succeeded in this easy manner to become [*sic*] the *bête noire* of the continental courts, he could not fail in being set up as the truly English minister at home. Accused by the one party of being in the pay of Russia, he is suspected by the other of Carbonarism ...[35] Poles, Italians, Hungarians, Germans found him in office whenever they were crushed, and their despots always suspected him of secret conspiracy with the victims they had allowed him to make. Till now, in all instances, it was a probable chance of success to have him for one's adversary, and a sure chance of ruin to have him for one's friend.[36]

Marx might have added: except in the case of the heroes of order. *They* could always count on his sure friendship. How correctly Marx evaluated this counter-revolutionary role played by Palmerston, his actual alliance and collaboration with the other leaders of European counter-revolution was shown by the entire subsequent political activity of the noble lord. One needed to possess all the political sagacity of the German liberals of the 1850s to continue, even after the revolution of 1848, to see in Palmerston a defender of constitutionalism *quand même* and a protector of oppressed nationalities.

It was typical that Vogt should explain the attacks by Marx's 'clique' on Palmerston as being due to Marx's hatred of Vogt and his friends. Even Lassalle was under the spell of this continent-wide legend, and was disposed to explain and justify many of Palmerston's actions by his alleged anti-Russian policy – including those carried out under the influence of the cabinet of St Petersburg, or which met with full approval on the part of esoteric Russian diplomacy. How right Marx and Engels were in regarding the Crimean War, insofar as it was an act of *official* Britain, as merely a 'sham war', even though it cost a million lives and milliards of francs, has been shown by all subsequent literature on the Sebastopol campaign.

Closely connected with Marx's articles on Palmerston were his numerous articles on the Eastern Question and the Crimean War in the *New York Tribune* in 1853–56, which were assembled and published by Eleanor Aveling under the general title of *The Eastern Question*.[37]

To get out of analysing and explaining the relevant views of Marx by simply mentioning that, in private letters, he – *quelle horreur!* – called Palmerston a 'paid agent' of Russia is too easy a way of evading the real question of how correct was Marx's evaluation of Palmerston's policy. It is enough to point out that Palmerston was regarded as a Russian agent, and his honesty called in question, not only by Urquhart, but also by many others in Britain, including Porter, the author of the well-known work *Progress of the Nation*.

Mehring was able to arrive at his conclusion that Lassalle was essentially right only because he reduced the dispute between Lassalle and Marx, in the main, to the question of whether or not Palmerston was a Russian agent. This also accounts for the unexpected conclusion drawn by Mehring that Palmerston's policy is defended against the charge of deliberate treachery by the entire actual course of events!

Palmerston guided Britain's foreign policy from 1830 to 1851, with short intervals, and then again, also with short intervals, from 1852 to his death in 1865. It was quite natural that Marx should have formed more and more firmly the view that, behind the *de facto* collaboration between Britain and Russia in combating the revolution there was hidden a personal collaboration, a solidarity of ideas, between the cabinets of St James's and St Petersburg. However contrary to nature such an alliance between constitutional Britain and despotic Russia might seem from outside, a whole series of facts – not only after 1850, but also earlier – pointed to the existence of such a hidden collaboration, which was not interrupted in the period when the rule of the Whigs in Britain was replaced by that of the Tories.

> When, in March 1849, Lord Dudley Stuart[38] introduced in the House of Commons a motion condemning Russia's occupation of the Danubian Principalities, Lord Palmerston vigorously defended the action of the Imperial government, and proved its right to maintain order in the Principalities. But the most eloquent defender of Russia's policy in the East was Disraeli, the later Lord Beaconsfield:[39]... When the Russian ambassador, Brunnow,[40] informed Palmerston of the entry of Russian troops into Hungary, the noble Lord received the news with obvious indifference, merely murmuring in reply: 'Get it over quickly' ... Walking a few paces further on, Baron Brunnow encountered the Duke of Wellington,[41] and hastened to tell him the news. After a moment's reflection, the Duke said: 'Try to act *en masse*, with forces sufficient to crush the revolt at one blow. Wage war on the grand scale, with large means – you have them.'[42]

It was only after the Crimean War that the anti-Russian tendencies of the British Conservatives more or less crystallised. But until the 1860s, whether a Tory or a Whig ministry was at the helm of state, the British big bourgeoisie, in alliance with Russian absolutism, no less willingly trampled in the mud all the principles of liberalism, *once it was a question of restoring 'order'*, than did, in our time, the 'radical' ministry of Asquith and Grey,[43] in alliance with Russia's Lyakhovs,[44] when they helped the Shah of Persia bombard the Mejlis and strangle the Persian revolutionaries. And the naive European liberals of the 1850s, in the hopes they placed in constitutional Britain, showed themselves no less naive than the Russian Cadets, when they support the present Anglo-Russian alliance, and yet 'refuse' to see that behind the Lyakhovs stands Hartwig,[45] and 'cannot believe' that behind Hartwig Grey is hidden.

But Marx did not confine himself to studying the diplomatic records for the period between 1807 and 1850. The very persistent sympathy of the Whigs with Russia caused him to make an excursion into the history of the eighteenth century, when the Whig oligarchy ruled Britain almost without a break. And his supposition that the old Anglo-Russian slavery, into which Europe had fallen again after the February revolution, was the result of an alliance between Britain and Russia, that the *de facto* collaboration of which Marx had not the slightest doubt was based on a definite link between British and Russian diplomacy, became transformed into a firm conviction when, 'while looking through the diplomatic manuscripts in the possession of the British Museum I came across a series of English documents, going back from the end of the eighteenth century to the time of Peter the Great, which reveal the continuous secret collaboration between the cabinets of London and St Petersburg, and seem to indicate that this relationship arose at the time of Peter the Great'.[46] But it was not only the diplomatic correspondence he found that provided him with new material which had, he thought, not been used by anyone up to that time. Not less important was the new material he obtained from the pamphlet literature of the eighteenth century, of which he had an unrivalled knowledge. He applied himself with characteristic fervour to working scientifically through these publications. Unfortunately, out of all his great labours on this subject he managed to publish, as he mentions in *Herr Vogt*, only an introduction, entitled *Revelations of the Diplomatic History of the Eighteenth Century*. This work appeared first in the Sheffield and then in the London *Free Press*, newspapers which were organs of David Urquhart. This is the work, also prepared for publication by Eleanor Marx, but, like *The Story of the Life of Lord Palmerston*, published only after her tragic death, which appeared under the title of *The Secret Diplomatic History of the Eighteenth Century*.[47]

In the *Neue Rheinische Zeitung* Marx gave an incomparable example of publicistic activity, showing himself able, out of a confused mass of apparently quite accidental facts of contemporary history, having no connection with one another, to extract and bring to the forefront those that were of fundamental significance, so as to reveal the actual roots of the past, and discover in them the seeds of the future. In *The Eighteenth Brumaire of Louis Bonaparte*, hot on the heels of the events concerned, he depicted with a hand of genius the basic outlines of the history of the French revolution of 1848, and showed in a masterly way that the Napoleonic coup d'état was its inevitable consequence. In *Revolution and Counter-Revolution in Germany* there unfolds before us a concise description of the principal moments in the revolution in Germany and Austria. In their origins, however, these works, like *The Civil War in France*, were not historical but publicistic writings, and if they have been transformed for us into model histories of contemporary events, if their fundamental conclusions have been confirmed and reinforced by all subsequent historical literature, this merely shows once more how profoundly *historical* the publicist Marx was, how objective was his exposition, despite all his *subjectivism*.

In the *Revelations*, on the contrary, we have our only example of Marx studying the political history of Britain, and also, and especially, of Russia. In that distant past he sought the answer to the riddle of Russia's colossal might and, along with it, of the old Anglo-Russian slavery beneath which all Europe groaned.

Was this work as successful as his other works? Did Marx succeed in providing a materialist explanation of the history of the Russian colossus? Did he manage to throw light on the secret of Anglo-Russian diplomacy from the standpoint of the materialist conception of history? Does this work supply the key to understanding the mistakes he made in evaluating certain events of contemporary history, those mistakes which are now recited over and over again, with delight, by every 'Marx-shatterer'? And if there were undoubtedly such mistakes, are they to be explained by the unfitness of the method of investigation, or by an inconsistent use of this method?

Before answering these questions we will acquaint the reader with what this work of Marx's contains. This we will do in all the greater detail because it has remained quite unknown to the immense majority of readers.

Notes

1. The Third Section (of the Imperial Chancellery) was Russia's secret police between 1826 and 1880 (translator's note).
2. The passage reads: 'But from the East an apostle of revolution is approaching impetuously and irresistibly. He is already standing at the gates of Thorn. It is the Tsar. The Tsar will save the German revolution by centralising it' (Marx and Engels, *Collected Works*, Volume 7, London, 1977, pp89–90). Thorn (in Polish, Toruń) stands on the Vistula, close to the border which then separated Prussia from Russian Poland (translator's note). The following excerpt from an address to the Tsar by Nesselrode on 20 November 1850, in which, on the occasion of the twenty-fifth anniversary of Nicholas I's accession to the throne, he gave a review of his foreign policy, serves as an excellent commentary on the words of the *Neue Rheinische Zeitung*: 'The events of 1848 made even more important the role of preserver and guardian of order which Providence had assigned to You since 1830. This was achieved by the calm way in which Your Majesty caused to subside the first consequence of that storm which burst over Europe, showing neither excessive haste, nor timidity, nor fear, but waiting only for that moment to appear on the scene which You, in Your wisdom, considered the most suitable. Left alone among the ruins of the ancient states of continental Europe, You quietly assembled Your forces so as to be able, if the need arose, to defend the inviolability of Your territory and to employ these forces in defence of others' (*Sbornik Russkogo Istoricheskogo Obshchestva*, Volume 98, p294) (author's note).
3. Marx and Engels, *Collected Works*, Volume 7, London, 1977, p212 (translation corrected) (translator's note).

4. Nicholas I was Tsar from 1825 to 1855. Count Karl Vasilyevich Nesselrode (1780–1862) was his Foreign Minister (translator's note).
5. Prince Wilhelm of Prussia (who became King in 1861 and German Emperor during 1871–88) was held responsible for the bloodshed in Berlin on 18 March 1848 and, at his father's request, left Germany for England for several months. The nickname is sometimes translated as 'the cartridge prince' (translator's note).
6. The duchies of Schleswig and Holstein (occupying the isthmus which links southern Denmark to the continent of Europe, and separating the Baltic from the North Sea), though linked with Denmark through their ruling houses, had long enjoyed virtual independence. After her loss of Norway in 1815, Denmark attempted to annex the duchies. The German population resisted, and in 1848 the duchies broke away and appealed for support to the German states. Prussia declared war, but waged only a 'sham war'. Britain and Russia supported Denmark, and Prussia yielded victory to the Danes. This surrender aroused great indignation among revolutionary democrats in Germany (Marx-Engels, *Collected Works*, Volume 7, London, 1977, pp421–5; Volume 10, pp392–5; Volume 11, London, 1979, p49) (translator's note).
7. Marx-Engels, *Collected Works*, Volume 7, London, 1977, pp424–5 (translator's note).
8. The Holy Alliance was signed in Paris by Alexander I of Russia, Francis I of Austria and Frederick William III of Prussia on 26 September 1815. Its aim was to prevent the spread of revolutionary ideas in Europe (translator's note).
9. The election of Pius IX as Pope (Giovanni Maria Mastai-Ferretti, 1846–1878) led to tension in Italy in 1847, as he was thought to hold 'liberal' views. Austria and the petty Italian states dependent on her made threatening gestures against him. Palmerston prevented actual armed conflict. In Switzerland, seven predominantly Catholic cantons formed a league, the *Sonderbund*, to resist anti-clerical policies. In 1847, the Swiss diet decided to suppress this 'separatist' grouping, and a brief civil war followed. Austria and France backed the *Sonderbund*, but Palmerston refused to join them in intervening on its behalf, and the rebellious cantons had to surrender (translator's note).
10. England was at war with France for practically the whole of the time in which Napoleon I Bonaparte was Dictator and Emperor (1799–1815) (translator's note).
11. Marx-Engels, *Collected Works*, Volume 8, Moscow, 1977, pp214–5 (translator's note).
12. Marx-Engels, *Collected Works*, Volume 7, London, 1977, pp165–6 (translator's note).
13. Karl Marx, 'Democratic Pan-Slavism', in *Neue Rheinische Zeitung*, no 222, 15 February 1849 Marx and Engels, *Collected Works*, Volume 8, Moscow, 1977, p372. By *Lanzknechte* (or *Landsknechte*) he means mercenary soldiers (translator's note).
14. Marx-Engels, *Collected Works*, Volume 9, Moscow, 1977, pp197–8 (translator's note).
15. The Hungarian revolutionary army included many volunteers from other countries, especially Poland (translator's note).
16. Marx-Engels, *Collected Works*, Volume 9, Moscow, 1977, p454 (translator's note).
17. Cf Marx-Engels, *Collected Works*, Volume 10, Moscow, 1978, pp105–6 (translator's note).
18. Louis-Eugène Cavaignac (1802–1857) played a leading part in suppressing the June uprising of 1848 in Paris, and held power in France for the rest of the year (translator's note).
19. Marx-Engels, *Collected Works*, Volume 10, Moscow, 1978, p76. Cf also *Collected Works*, Volume 7, London, 1977, pp402–3, 480–1. In 1848, a rebellion broke out in Lombardy and Venetia, the North Italian provinces then under Austrian rule. The Italian kingdom of Piedmont-Sardinia declared war in support of the rebels. The government of France's 'Second Republic' created by the Paris revolution of February 1848, instead of supporting the Italians, attempted to 'mediate'. Cavaignac was the head of the French government, and the *National* was the organ of the ruling party of 'moderate republicans' (translator's note).
20. Richard Cobden (1804–1865) was a radical MP and leader of the Free Traders and the Anti-Corn Law League (translator's note).

21. From the letter of Nesselrode to Prince Vorontsov dated 7 (19) February 1815 (*Arkhiv Knyazya Vorontsova*, Volume 40, p361) (author's note).
22. The Black Hundreds was an organisation of extreme Russian chauvinists founded in 1905 with links with the Tsarist police, and which carried out massacres of Jews (translator's note).
23. Quoted by Marx in *The Eighteenth Brumaire of Louis Bonaparte*, *Collected Works*, Volume 11, London, 1979, p170. 'The President', soon to be the Emperor, was Louis Napoleon Bonaparte (translator's note).
24. From Nesselrode's letter to Prince Vorontsov of 7 (19) March 1852 (*Arkhiv Knyazya Vorontsova*, Volume 40, p421) (author's note).
25. The Cologne Communist Trial of 1852 found seven German workers guilty of high treason on trumped-up charges (translator's note).
26. Referring to the Warsaw Conference of October 1850, Engels wrote: 'The Russian Tsar went to Warsaw, where he sat in judgement as the arbiter of Europe. He appointed his creature Christian of Glücksburg heir to the Danish throne. He humiliated Prussia as it had never been humiliated before, prohibiting it even the slightest craving to exploit the German aspirations for unity, and forcing it to re-establish the Federal Diet and submit to Austria.' ('The Role of Force in History', March 1888, Marx and Engels, *Collected Works*, Volume 26, London, 1990, p456; *The Role of Force in History*, Lawrence and Wishart edition, 1968, p30) When popular protests broke out in Hesse-Cassel against breaches of the constitution by that state's ruler, Austrian troops marched in to 'restore order.' Prussia mobilised as though to intervene against Austria, but, under Russian pressure, capitulated at a conference at Olmütz in November 1850. The London Protocol of 1852 was the decision taken by a conference of Europe's great powers that Schleswig-Holstein must be indissolubly united with Denmark (translator's note).
27. Alexander II, Tsar of Russia (1855–1881), was assassinated by Narodnik terrorists (translator's note).
28. 'The fundamental principle of our policy', wrote Nesselrode in 1833 to Lieven in London, 'obliges us to put forth every effort to preserve authority wherever it exists, to strengthen it wherever it is being weakened, and, finally to rescue it wherever it is being openly subjected to attack.' This despatch was intended to be read by Palmerston, who had proved to be less tractable on the Belgian question than on that of Poland. 'Great Britain, our old friend and ally, has shared these views with us too long not to appreciate how fundamental they are.' (Martens, *Recueil des traités et conventions conclus par la Russie avec les puissances étrangères*, Volume 12, pp24–5) (author's note) Prince Kh A Lieven was Russia's ambassador in London from 1812 to 1834 (translator's note).
29. Karl Marx, 'Contribution to the Critique of Political Economy', January 1859, Lawrence and Wishart edition with an introduction by Maurice Dobb, London, 1971, pp22–3 (translator's note).
30. Napoleon III (Louis Napoleon), nephew of Napoleon Bonaparte, seized power in a coup and ruled as French Emperor (1852–1871) (translator's note).
31. Karl Marx, 'The Eastern Question', Marx and Engels, *Collected Works*, Volume 12, Moscow, 1979, p26 (translator's note).
32. Ernest Charles Jones (1819–1869) was a leader of the left of the Chartist movement, and a friend of Marx and Engels (translator's note).
33. Karl Marx, *Herr Vogt*, London, 1860, pp58–9 (*Collected Works*, Volume 17, Moscow, 1981, pp116–7: New Park edition, p101, translator's note). The articles on Palmerston were assembled in a book *The Story of the Life of Lord Palmerston*, which was prepared for publication by Eleanor Marx, but which appeared after her tragic death. There had been previously published in the pamphlet form mentioned by Marx both the third chapter, entitled 'Palmerston and Poland' and the fifth, entitled 'Palmerston, What Has he Done?'. These two works, especially the second, had been expanded when they came out

as separate pamphlets. They were published in the series *Tucker's Political Flysheets*, Volume 1, nos 1 and 2 (author's note).

34. George Canning (1770–1827) was Foreign Secretary in the government of the 'Liberal Tories' (1822–27), and briefly Prime Minister. He is often credited with constitutional principles (translator's note).
35. The Carbonari were secret groups of Italian nationalist revolutionaries, supporters of Garibaldi (translator's note).
36. Karl Marx, *The Story of the Life of Lord Palmerston*, London, 1899, pp8–9 (Marx and Engels, *Collected Works*, Volume 12, Moscow, 1979, pp347–8; Lawrence and Wishart edition, pp167–8) (translator's note).
37. I intend to deal with these articles in greater detail in another place, when I shall take a closer look at Marx's views on Palmerston's policy in relation to the Eastern Question and Britain's policy in the period of the Crimean War (I did this in *Gesammelte Schriften von Karl Marx und Friedrich Engels, 1852 bis 1862*, Stuttgart, 1917, two volumes. This publication contained both the articles on the Eastern Question and those on Palmerston) (author's note).
38. Lord Dudley Coutts Stuart (1803–1854) was an acquaintance of Prince Adam Czartoryski, and a supporter of Polish independence. In 1836, he had printed his 'Address on the Policy of Russia, Delivered in the House of Commons' (translator's note).
39. Benjamin Disraeli, later First Earl of Beaconsfield (1804–1881) was a prominent Tory politician, and then Prime Minister (1868, 1874–1880) (translator's note).
40. Count Filipp Ivanovich, Baron von Brunnow (1797–1875), was Russia's envoy (1840–54, 1858–60), and then ambassador in London (1860–74) (translator's note).
41. Arthur Wellesley, Duke of Wellington (1769–1852) defeated Napoleon at Waterloo, and was afterwards Prime Minister (1828–30) (translator's note).
42. And the Russian semi-official Professor Martens adds: 'These words of the Duke of Wellington attracted serious attention on the part of the Sovereign, who underlined them in Baron Brunnow's despatch of 29 April (11 May) 1849.' (Martens, op cit, pp253–5) (author's note) In this quotation in the text Riazanov inserts, before 'the Duke of Wellington', the words 'the convinced Tory', presumably to point out that neither Disraeli nor the Duke was a Whig (translator's note).
43. Herbert Henry Asquith (1858–1928) was Liberal Prime Minister (1908–1916); Sir Edward Grey (1862–1933), Lord Grey of Falloden, was Foreign Secretary at the same time (translator's note).
44. V Lyakhov was the Tsarist colonel in command of the troops who suppressed the Persian revolutionary movement in 1908 (translator's note).
45. NG von Hartwig (1855–1914) was Russia's representative in Persia in 1906–8 (translator's note).
46. Marx-Engels, *Collected Works*, Volume 17, Moscow, 1981, p117 (*Herr Vogt*, New Park Publications, 1982, p101. Peter I, the Great, was the modernising Russian Tsar (1682–1725) who first asserted Russian power in the Baltic region (translator's note).
47. The fact that Eleanor died before it was published must be the explanation for the carelessness with which this book was printed. Neither the place where nor the date when the work had appeared is given. Quite apart from various misprints, one of the chapters is disfigured, owing to the negligence of the publishers, by a huge omission. The articles were first published in the London *Free Press* of 16 and 23 August, 13 and 20 September, 4 October, 6 and 20 December 1856, 4, 18 and 25 February and 1 April 1857 (author's note).

Chapter Two

Marx on Russo-British Relations

Marx begins his *Revelations* by reprinting three letters from British residents and envoys at the court of St Petersburg. One of them was written by Rondeau to Walpole[1] and concerns events in 1736, when Russia was at war with Turkey. The second was from the pen of George Macartney and addressed to the Earl of Sandwich[2] in 1765, when Britain was seeking to conclude a trade agreement with Russia. The author of the third letter was James Harris (later Earl of Malmesbury), who in 1782 wrote to Grantham[3] about giving Russia the island of Minorca so as to win her over to Britain's side.

In thinking that these letters were completely unknown at that time Marx was mistaken only as regards the third of them. This had already been published by the grandson of James Harris, Earl of Malmesbury, in 1844.[4] The diplomatic correspondence of eighteenth century British ambassadors had also been used by the Prussian historian Raumer, the one of whom Marx said in his letter about Proudhon that he was 'composed of on the one hand and on the other hand'.[5] Being principally interested in the history of Prussia, Raumer extracted from these despatches those materials which threw light upon relations between Prussia and Britain, and which gave piquant details about the Russian court in the eighteenth century. The British despatches were utilised from the same standpoint in the well-known book *La Cour de Russie il y a cent ans*, published in Berlin in 1858, after Marx's work had appeared.[6] The correspondence of British diplomats with the cabinet of St James's was first published by the Russian Historical Society, beginning in 1873, in its *Sbornik*, but this publication was far from covering the whole of the eighteenth century, or from being complete.[7] We will merely mention, for the time being, that Harris' letters were completely missing from the collection – for what reason we shall see later.

Thus Marx was dealing, in the main, with material which at that time was quite unused, and which gave him access to the secrets of international diplomacy in the eighteenth century. Study of this correspondence showed, in his opinion, that British diplomacy was systematically fooled by Russian diplomacy, and that the British envoys acted as obedient tools in the hands of the St Petersburg Court. The following sarcastic description which Marx gives to the entire correspondence shows better than anything else the road by which he arrived at his conclusion:

> In perusing these documents, there is something that startles us even more than their contents, viz, their form. All these letters are 'confidential', 'private', 'secret', 'most secret'; but in spite of secrecy, privacy and confidence, the English statesmen converse among each other about Russia and her rulers in a tone of awful reserve, abject servility and cynical submission which would strike us even in the public despatches of Russian statesmen. To conceal intrigues against foreign nations secrecy is recurred to [*sic*] by Russian diplomatists. The same method is adopted by English diplomatists freely to express their devotion to a foreign court. The secret despatches of Russian diplomats are fumigated with some equivocal perfume. It is one part the *fumée de fausseté*, as the Duc de Saint-Simon has it,[8] and the other part that coquettish display of one's own superiority and cunning which stamps upon the reports of the French secret police their indelible character. Even the master despatches of Pozzo di Borgo are tainted with this common blot of the *littérature de mauvais lieu*.[9] In this point the English secret despatches prove much superior. They do not affect superiority but silliness. For instance, can there be anything more silly than Mr Rondeau informing Horace Walpole that he has betrayed to the Russian Minister the letters addressed by the Turkish Grand Vizier to the King of England, but that he had told 'at the same time those gentlemen that, as there were several hard reflections on the Russian Court, he should not have communicated them, *if they had not been anxious to see them*', and then told their excellencies not to tell the Porte

that they had seen them (those letters)! At first view the infamy of the act is drowned in the silliness of the man. Or, take Sir George Macartney. Can there be anything more silly than his happiness that Russia seemed 'reasonable' enough not to expect that England 'should pay the *whole expenses*' for Russia's 'choosing to take the lead at Stockholm'; or his flattering himself that he had 'persuaded the Russian court' not to be so 'unreasonable' as to ask from England, in a time of peace, subsidies for a time of war against Turkey (then the ally of England); or his warning the Earl of Sandwich 'not to mention' to the Russian ambassador in London the secrets mentioned to himself by the Russian Chancellor at St Petersburg? Or can there be anything more silly than Sir James Harris confidentially whispering into the ear of Lord Grantham that Catherine II[10] was devoid of 'judgement, precision of idea, reflection and *l'esprit de combinaison*'?[11] (Footnote by Marx: Or, to follow this affectation of silliness into more recent times, is there anything in diplomatic history that could match Lord Palmerston's proposal made to Marshal Soult [in 1839] to storm the Dardanelles, in order to afford the Sultan the support of the Anglo-French fleet against Russia?).[12]

On the other hand, take the cool impudence with which Sir George Macartney informs his minister that because the Swedes were extremely jealous of, and mortified at, their dependence on Russia, England was directed by the Court of St Petersburg to do its work in Stockholm, under the British colours of liberty and independence. Or Sir James Harris advising England to surrender to Russia Minorca[13] and the right of search, and the monopoly of mediation in the affairs of the world – not in order to gain any material advantage, or even formal engagement, on the part of Russia, but only 'a strong glow of friendship' from the Empress, and the transfer to France of 'her ill humour'.

The secret Russian despatches proceed on the very plain line that Russia knows itself to have no common interests whatever with other nations, but that every nation must be persuaded separately to have common interests with Russia to the exclusion of every other nation. The English despatches, on the contrary, never dare so much as to hint that Russia has common interests

> with England, but only endeavour to convince England that she has Russian interests. The English diplomatists themselves tell us that this was the single argument they pleaded, when placed face to face with Russian potentates.[14]

Marx concludes his characterisation of the English diplomats with the following harsh words:

> If the English despatches we have laid before the public were addressed to private friends, they would only brand with infamy the ambassadors who wrote them. Secretly addressed as they are to the British government itself, they nail it forever to the pillory of history; and, instinctively, this seems to have been felt even by Whig writers, because none has dared to publish them.[15]

We have already seen that Marx was mistaken. The third letter, the one that scandalised him the most, had been printed 12 years previously, and had not aroused any indignation. It is interesting, however, that David Urquhart, in the special editorial note in which he drew his readers' particular attention to Marx's article, showed himself obviously in agreement with the characterisation given by Marx, and added a number of facts from the history of Anglo-Russian diplomacy in the first half of the nineteenth century with a view to demonstrating that the British diplomats of that period were no better and no cleverer than those of the eighteenth century.

Considering that he had proved his thesis – the limitedness of eighteenth-century British diplomacy and its servile dependence on the St Petersburg court – Marx then posed the question: how far back was to be found the beginning of this 'Russian' character of British diplomacy, which became normal in the course of the eighteenth century?

Marx thought that it had begun in the time of Peter the Great, and he made this period the centre of his investigation. By way of prelude, he considered it necessary to reprint some English pamphlets which had been published in Peter the Great's time, and which had either quite escaped the attention of contemporary historians or which, in their view, did not deserve that attention. From among these pamphlets, he selected three that were directed against Russia and in defence of Sweden, in the conflict between these countries for predominance in the Baltic Sea. The first of them, *The Northern Crisis*, which appeared in 1716, exposed the general policy of Russia and pointed out the danger with which the Russification of Sweden threatened Britain and her commerce.[16] The second, *The Defensive Treaty*, published in 1717, examined Britain's policy from the standpoint of the treaty made between Britain and Sweden in 1700.[17] The third, *Truth is but Truth, As It is Timed*, published in 1719,[18] showed that the new political plans which had led to the transformation of Russia into the pre-eminent power on the Baltic Sea were in direct contradiction to the traditional policy which England had pursued throughout the seventeenth century.

In Marx's opinion, these three pamphlets were quite sufficient to refute the notion, common to all continental and British writers, that Russia's true intentions had been appreciated or suspected only at a much later period and, moreover, too late; that the diplomatic relations between Britain and Russia – and here we quote, verbatim, a thesis which comes so improbably from Marx's pen – 'were but the natural offspring of the mutual material interests of the two countries; and that, therefore, in accusing the British statesmen of the eighteenth century of Russianism we should commit an unpardonable hysteron-proteron'.[19]

Marx would have been ready to forgive them if they had merely shared the conceptions of their own time, on the grounds that 'to understand a limited historical epoch, we must step beyond its limits, and compare it with other historical epochs. To judge governments and their acts we must measure them by their own times and the conscience of their contemporaries. Nobody will condemn a British statesman of the seventeenth century for acting on a belief in witchcraft, if he finds Bacon himself[20] ranging demonology in the catalogue of science. On the other hand, if the Stanhopes, the Walpoles, the Townshends,[21] etc, were suspected, exposed and denounced in their own country by their own contemporaries as tools or accomplices of Russia, it will no longer do to shelter their policy behind the convenient screen of the prejudice and ignorance common to their time.'[22]

And all the pamphlets mentioned showed incontrovertibly, in Marx's view, that the British statesmen of the eighteenth century were absolutely blind, that they absolutely failed to notice the danger of which they were so eloquently warned by the anonymous author of *The Northern Crisis*,[23] that they, as the authors of the two other pamphlets showed, had most perfidiously sacrificed Sweden in order to please Russia, and, by ensuring the latter state's hegemony in the Baltic Sea, had fostered and nourished their own country's future foe. Furthermore, they had completely disregarded their country's commercial interests – a crime unforgivable in Britain.

Marx himself brings support to the pamphleteers: basing himself upon statistical data, he shows that by modern historians 'nothing has been more exaggerated than the dimensions of the trade opened up to Great Britain by the huge market of the Russia of Peter the Great and his immediate successors'.[24] After analysing the figures for exports and imports in the trade with Sweden and Russia between 1697 and 1760, he comes to the following conclusion:

> During the first 60 years of the eighteenth century the total Anglo-Russian trade formed but a very diminutive fraction of the general trade of England, say less than one forty-fifth. Its sudden increase during the earliest years of Peter's sway over the Baltic did not at all affect the general balance of British trade, as it was a simple transfer from its Swedish account to its Russian account. In the later times of Peter I, as well as under his immediate successors, Catherine I[25] and Anna, the Anglo-Russian trade was positively declining; during the whole epoch dating from the final settlement of Russia in the Baltic provinces, the export of British manufactures was continually falling off ... Neither the contemporaries of Peter I nor the next British generation reaped any benefit from the advance of Russia to the Baltic.

'In general,' Marx adds, 'the Baltic trade of Great Britain was at that time trifling in regard of the capital involved, but important in regard of its character. It afforded England the raw produce for its maritime stores. That from the latter point of view the Baltic was in safer keeping in the hands of Sweden than in those of Russia was not only proved by the pamphlets we are reprinting, but fully understood by the British ministers themselves.'[26]

But how are we to explain something so strange as this persistent aid rendered to Russia, if Britain was interested in not allowing the Russians to establish ascendancy in the Baltic Sea?

It turns out that there was, after all, a small group of British merchants whose interests did coincide with those of Russia, namely, the Russian Trade Company. It was this body that raised a cry against Sweden, that bombarded parliament with its petitions, and that met before the opening of parliament in 1714, 1715 and 1716 in order to prepare complaints against Sweden.

But how could these merchants have exercised such influence upon the government, that it constantly submitted to their suggestions? The point, says Marx, was that the oligarchy which after the

'Glorious Revolution' usurped power and wealth at the expense of the British people, needed, of course, to find allies, not only outside the country, but also inside it. These latter it found among what the French call *la haute bourgeoisie*, as represented by the Bank of England, the moneylenders, the state's creditors and the large-scale manufacturers. How carefully and tenderly the oligarchy looked after the interests of this class is apparent from the laws it made.

It is understandable that this oligarchy was also obliged to give its foreign policy at least the outward semblance of a policy guided by commercial interests. And this could be done all the more easily because the particular interests of one or another tiny fraction of the merchant class could always be identified with this or that measure taken by the ministry. The interested fraction would then raise a howl about 'defending the interests of commerce and navigation', and the nation would stupidly echo this howl.

Thus the foreign policy of the oligarchy remained true to itself in one respect alone: it strove at all costs to please Russia. It merely *concealed* itself behind interests of trade and industry which the cabinet could then discover *post festum*. In the period of the Great Northern War,[27] the British ministers found the needful commercial pretext for their hostile actions against Sweden in the losses which Swedish privateers were inflicting on British merchants, although the Swedes were acting in complete conformity with the international law of the time.

It might be supposed that Britain was merely following the example of Holland, which also denounced the confiscation of her vessels by the Swedes as mere piracy. And in one respect, indeed, Holland was bound, like England, by the same defensive treaty which England had concluded with Sweden in 1700, and so had no right to take any hostile measures against Sweden.

In another respect, however, Holland's position was markedly different from Britain's. Having lost her commercial and maritime hegemony, Holland had already entered upon a period of decline. Like Genoa and Venice, when the change in trade routes deprived them of their former commerce, Holland was obliged to lend to other nations the capital for which she could find no application at home. Russia proved to be an immense market of no less dimensions for her trade than for her capital and her population.

Already in the first half of the nineteenth century, Holland was Russia's principal banker. And in Peter the Great's time, she supplied Russia with ships, officers, guns and money. The Russian navy of that time could have been called, more properly, Dutch rather than Russian. The Dutch gloried in the fact that they sent the first ship from Western Europe to the new port of St Petersburg,[28] and they paid for the trade privileges they obtained from Peter with the same 'fawning meanness' that marked their dealings with Japan.

Marx was therefore much more indulgent to Holland than to Britain. If Holland's rulers were Russophil, well, there was clearly a quite different and solid foundation for this, one that was absent in the case of Britain.

Marx was so convinced of the hostile attitude of the British to the Swedes that, despite this 'solid foundation', he explained by pressure from Britain the protest made by Holland against Swedish privateers. Yet at the same time, he knew that Peter was using the Dutch to bring pressure on British diplomats in his favour.

Thus, the entire policy of Britain, and of Holland which was under Britain's influence, facilitated the rise of Russia.

But Marx had other proofs as well that the principal source of Russia's might was the persistent complicity and connivance of Britain. The whole history of Russia until the time of Peter the Great showed that without access to the Baltic Sea, modern Russia would have been unthinkable. In order to justify his idea, Marx set forth a brilliant outline of the history of the Russian state before Peter the Great.

Notes

1. Claudius Rondeau (d 1739), Consul-General (1730–1731) and resident minister (1731–1739) in St Petersburg, wrote his reports to Horace Walpole (1717–1797), the noted aristocratic politician, diarist and wit. *Revelations of the Diplomatic History of the Eighteenth Century* appears in Marx and Engels, *Collected Works*, Volume 15, London, 1986, pp25–96 (translator's note).
2. Sir George, later Earl McCartney (1737–1806) was Envoy Extraordinary at the Court of St Petersburg (1764–1767); John Montagu, Fourth Earl of Sandwich (1718–1792) was the Secretary of State who persecuted John Wilkes (translator's note).
3. Sir James Harris, Earl of Malmesbury (1746–1820) was appointed ambassador to the court of Catherine the Great in 1777; Thomas Robinson, Second Baron Grantham (1738–1786) was Secretary of State for the Foreign Department in 1782 (translator's note).
4. *Diaries and Correspondence of James Harris, First Earl of Malmesbury, Edited by his Grandson*, four volumes, London, 1844. The letter quoted by Marx is printed, but more fully, in Volume 1 on pages 528–35 (author's note).
5. *Beiträge zur Neueren Geschichte aus dem Britischen Museum*, Leipzig, 1836–1839 (author's note). 'Like the historian Raumer, the petty bourgeois is composed of "On the one hand and On the other hand"' — Marx, Letter to JB Schweitzer, 24 January 1865, *Selected Correspondence of Marx and Engels*, Foreign Languages Press edition, 1956, p192. Friedrich Ludwig Georg von Raumer (1781–1873) was the author of an account of England in 1835; Pierre Joseph Proudhon (1809–1865) was a French social theorist, one of the founders of Anarchism, the author of *The Philosophy of Poverty* (1846) against which Marx wrote his *The Poverty of Philosophy* (1847) (translator's note).
6. *La Cour de Russie il y a cent ans, 1725–1783*, consisting largely of extracts from the

despatches of the British and French ambassadors at the Court of St Petersburg, appeared anonymously, but is attributed to the historian Alexander Ivanovich Turgenev (1784–1845), a friend of Pushkin and an opponent of serfdom and the autocracy (translator's note).

7. ***Sbornik Russkogo Istoricheskogo Obshchestva***, St Petersburg, 1873–1901, 140 volumes. Volumes 39, 50 and 61 contain correspondence for the period of Peter I (1704–19): volumes 66, 76 and 80 cover 1728–39, volume 85 covers the period from 1740 to 3 March 1741, volumes 91, 99, 102, 103 and 110 cover 1741–50, and volumes 12 and 19 cover correspondence between 1762 and 1776. As the extracts were made by officials of the Ministry of Foreign Affairs, everything that might be ticklish or shocking from the standpoint of the Russian court was carefully removed. The translation into Russian is in places very bad and incorrect, sometimes deliberately so. But even in this form, these volumes provide material of the highest importance for the study of the history of relations between Britain and Russia in the eighteenth century. Since the British despatches are printed in the original language, this Russian publication is now readily utilised by British historians. Publication of the correspondence in Britain itself has been undertaken only recently. Thus, the Royal Historical Society published in 1900–1902 the correspondence of the British ambassador (John Hobart, Earl of Buckinghamshire (1723–1793), edited by Mrs A. D'Arcy Collyer. It is enough to compare this edition with the corresponding volume of the Russian edition to see how tendentiously the latter has been compiled, and how primitively from the standpoint of scholarship (author's note). The British edition is by the Royal Historical Society, Camden Series 3, Volumes 2 and 3 (translator's note).
8. 'Aroma of duplicity.' The Duc de Saint-Simon (1675–1755) wrote ***Memoirs***, which are an important source for the history of the French state at the end of the seventeenth century and the beginning of the eighteenth (translator's note).
9. 'Writings from the underworld.' Count Carl'Andrea Pozzo di Borgo (1764–1842) was a Corsican who entered the Russian diplomatic service and, as the Tsar's ambassador in London and Paris in the 1830s, became very influential in international affairs (translator's note).
10. Catherine II the Great, was the Tsaritsa of Russia (1762–1796) who carried out the first partition of Poland (translator's note).
11. 'The ability to put two and two together.' (translator's note)
12. Karl Marx, ***Revelations of the Secret Diplomatic History of the Eighteenth Century***, Marx and Engels, ***Collected Works***, Volume 15, London, 1986, pp38–40. Nicolas-Jean de Dieu Soult (1769–1851), who had been one of Napoleon's field-marshals, and presided over three ministries under Louis-Philippe, was sent to London in 1838 as France's ambassador extraordinary for the coronation of Queen Victoria (1837–1901) (translator's note).
13. The island of Minorca, in the Western Mediterranean, had been seized by the British in 1708, and its capital, Port Mahon, developed as a naval base. It was ceded to Spain in 1802 (translator's note).
14. Karl Marx, ***Revelations of the Secret Diplomatic History of the Eighteenth Century***, op cit, p40 (translator's note).
15. Ibid, p40 (translator's note).
16. ***The Northern Crisis, or Impartial Reflections on the Policies of the Czar***, London, 1716. Much importance is ascribed to this pamphlet, and it is quoted more than once in Droysen, ***Geschichte der preussischen Politik***, Volume 4, part 2, p193 (author's note).
17. ***The Defensive Treaty Concluded in the Year 1700, Between His Late Majesty, King William, of Ever-Glorious Memory, and His Present Swedish Majesty, King Charles XII***, London, 1717 (author's note).
18. ***Truth is But Truth, As It is Timed***, London, 1719 (author's note).
19. Karl Marx, ***Revelations of the Secret Diplomatic History of the Eighteenth Century***, op cit, p40; Lawrence and Wishart edition, p63. 'Hysteron-proteron' means 'putting the cart before

the horse'. Marx denies that the relations between Russia and England were determined by 'the mutual material interests of the two countries', and Riazanov sees this as contradicting Marx's own materialist conception of history (translator's note).

20. Sir Francis Bacon (1561–1626), Baron Verulam and Viscount St Albans, laid down the philosophical basis for the experimental method in the natural sciences (translator's note).
21. James, First Earl of Stanhope (1673–1721) was dominant minister during the first half of the reign of George I (1714–1721); Sir Robert Walpole, Earl of Oxford (1676–1745), was Prime Minister from 1721 to 1742; Charles, Second Viscount Townshend of Rainham (1675–1738) was the Whig politician who directed English foreign policy from 1721 to 1730 (translator's note).
22. Karl Marx, ***Revelations of the Secret Diplomatic History of the Eighteenth Century***, op cit, p56 (translator's note).
23. '***He [Peter] will then most certainly become our rival, and as dangerous to us as he is now neglected.*** We then may, perhaps, though too late, call to mind what our own ministers and merchants have told us of his designs of carrying on alone all the northern trade, and of getting all that from Turkey and Persia into his hands through the rivers which he is joining and making navigable from the Caspian or the Black Sea to his Petersburg. We shall then wonder at our blindness that we did not suspect his designs when we heard of the prodigious works he has done at St Petersburg and Reval ... As he desires that the designs with which he labours may not prove abortive, so he does not assign them a certain day of birth, but leaves them to the natural productions of fit times and occasions, like those curious artists in China who temper the mould this day of which a vessel may be made a hundred years hence.' (***Revelations of the Secret Diplomatic History of the Eighteenth Century***, op cit, p38 (author's note) (Lawrence and Wishart edition, pp75–6, 82, translator's note)
24. Karl Marx, ***Revelations of the Secret Diplomatic History of the Eighteenth Century***, op cit, p57 (translator's note).
25. Catherine I was Tsaritsa of Russia between 1725 and 1727 (translator's note).
26. Karl Marx, ***Revelations of the Secret Diplomatic History of the Eighteenth Century***, op cit, p60 (translator's note).
27. ***Post festum*** means after the occasion (Latin). The Great Northern War (1700–21) was fought between Sweden and the Russia of Peter the Great allied with Denmark, Saxony and Poland (translator's note).
28. Peter the Great founded St Petersburg in 1703 (translator's note).

Chapter Three

The Historical Development of Russia as Depicted by Marx[1]

The overwhelming influence of Russia has taken Europe at different epochs by surprise, startled the peoples of the West, and been submitted to as a fatality, or resisted only by convulsions. But alongside the fascination exercised by Russia there runs an ever-reviving scepticism, dogging her like a shadow, growing with her growth, mingling shrill notes or irony with the cries of agonising peoples, and mocking her very grandeur as a histrionic attitude taken up to dazzle and to cheat. Other empires have met with similar doubts in their infancy. Russia has become a colossus without outliving them. She affords the only instance in history of an immense empire, the very existence of whose power, even after world-wide achievements, has never ceased to be treated like a matter of faith rather than a matter of fact. From the outset of the eighteenth century to our days, no author, whether he intended to exalt or to check Russia, thought it possible to dispense with first proving her existence.

But whether we be spiritualists or materialists with respect to Russia – whether we consider her power as a palpable fact, or as the mere vision of the guilt-stricken conscience of the European peoples – the question remains the same: 'How did this power, or this phantom of a power, contrive to assume such dimensions as to rouse on the one side the passionate assertion, and on the

> other the angry denial of its threatening the world with a rehearsal of Universal Monarchy?'[2]

Some historians, Marx goes on, assert that the 'northern spectre' which frightened nineteenth-century Europe had arisen already in the ninth century, that the policy of the Romanovs is a natural continuation of the policy of Rurik and his successors, those Norsemen who, in the ninth century, came to Russia from Sweden and founded a state.[3]

Yet, in spite of the 'plausible parallelism', the policy of the first Rurikoviches,[4] says Marx, 'differs fundamentally from that of modern Russia. It was nothing more nor less than a policy of the German barbarians inundating Europe – the history of the modern nations beginning only after the deluge has passed away. The Gothic period of Russia in particular forms but a chapter of the Norman[5] conquests. As the empire of Charlemagne[6] precedes the foundation of modern France, Germany and Italy, so the empire of the Ruriks[7] precedes the foundation of Poland, Lithuania, the Baltic settlements, Turkey and Muscovy itself. The rapid movement of aggrandisement was not the result of deep-laid schemes, but the natural offspring of the primitive organisation of Norman conquest – vassalship without fiefs, or fiefs consisting only in tributes – the necessity of fresh conquests being kept alive by the uninterrupted influx of new Varangian adventurers,[8] panting for glory and plunder. The chiefs, becoming anxious for repose, were compelled by the Faithful Band to move on, and in Russian as in French Normandy there arrived the moment when the chiefs despatched on new predatory excursions their uncontrollable and insatiable companions-in-arms, with the single view to get rid of them. Warfare and organisation of conquest on the part of the first Ruriks differ in no point from those of the Normans in the rest of Europe. If Slavonian tribes were subjected not only by the sword but also by mutual convention, this singularity is due to the exceptional position of those tribes, placed between a northern and eastern[9] invasion, and embracing the former as a protection from the latter. The same magic charm which attracted other northern barbarians to the Rome of the West attracted the Varangians to the Rome of the East. The very migration of the Russian capital – Rurik fixing it at Novgorod, Oleg removing it to Kiev, and Sviataslaff [*sic*][10] attempting to establish it in Bulgaria – proves beyond doubt that the invader was only feeling his way, and considered Russia as a mere halting place from which to wander on in search of an empire in the South. If modern Russia covets the possession of Constantinople to establish her dominion over the world, the Ruriks were, on the contrary, forced by the resistance of Byzantium, under Zimiskes, definitively to establish their dominion in Russia ...'[11]

> If any Slavonian influence is to be acknowledged in this epoch, it is that of Novgorod, a Slavonian state, the traditions, policy and tendencies of which were so antagonistic to those of modern Russia that one could found her existence only on the ruins of the other. Under Yaroslav the supremacy of the Varangians is broken, but simultaneously with it disappears the conquering tendency of the first period, and the decline of Gothic Russia begins. The history of that decline, more still than that of the conquest and formation, proves the exclusively Gothic character of the empire of the Ruriks.

This empire shared, says Marx, the fate of other medieval monarchies:

> The incongruous, unwieldy and precocious empire heaped together by the Ruriks, like the other empires of similar growth, is broken up into appanages, divided and subdivided among the descendants of the conquerors, dilacerated [*sic*] by feudal wars, rent to pieces by the intervention of foreign peoples. The paramount authority of the Grand Prince vanishes before the rival claims of 70 princes of the blood. The attempt of Andrew of Suzdal[12] at recomposing some large limbs of the empire by the removal of the capital from Kiev to Vladimir proves successful only in propagating the decomposition from the South to the centre. Andrew's third successor resigns even the last shadow of supremacy, the title of Grand Prince, and the merely nominal homage still offered him. The appanages to the South and to the West become by turns, Lithuanian, Polish, Hungarian, Livonian, Swedish. Kiev itself, the ancient capital, follows destinies of its own, after having dwindled down from a seat of the Grand Princedom to the territory of a city. Thus, the Russia of the Normans completely disappears from the stage, and the few weak reminiscences in which it still outlived itself dissolve before the terrible apparition of Genghis Khan.[13] ***The bloody mire of Mongolian slavery, not the rude glory of the Norman epoch, forms the cradle of Muscovy, and modern Russia is but a metamorphosis of Muscovy.***[14]

'The Tartar yoke' destroyed all the traditions of the 'Norman' period of Russian history, says Marx, and in addition left a deep impression on the psychology of the Russian people.

> The Tartar yoke lasted from 1237[15] to 1462 – more than two centuries: a yoke not only crushing, but dishonouring and withering the very soul of the people that fell its prey. The Mongol Tartars established a rule of systematic terror, devastation and wholesale massacre forming its institutions. Their numbers being scanty in proportion to their enormous conquests, they wanted to magnify them by a halo of consternation, and to thin, by wholesale slaughter, the populations which might rise in their rear. In their creations of desert they were, besides, led by the same economical [*sic*] principle which has depopulated the Highlands of Scotland and the Campagna di Roma – the conversion of men into sheep, and of fertile lands and populous abodes into pasturage.

The conquerors did not destroy the principalities which they found in being, but confined themselves to reducing them to vassalage and obliging them to pay tribute. The 'Tartar yoke' had already lasted a hundred years[16] when Muscovy began to emerge from among the principalities which, under the Golden Horde, strove to annihilate each other by means of the most shameless bribery of their rulers and mutual denunciation:

> It was in this infamous strife that the Moscow branch won at last the race. In 1328 the crown of the Grand Princedom, wrested from the branch of Tver by dint of denunciation and assassination, was picked up at the feet of Usbeck Khan by Yury, the elder brother of Ivan Kalita.[17] Ivan Kalita I and Ivan III, surnamed the Great,[18] personate Muscovy rising by means of the Tartar yoke and Muscovy getting an independent power by the disappearance of the Tartar rule. The whole policy of Muscovy, from its first entrance into the historical arena, is resumed in the history of these two individuals.[19]

Marx then proceeds to give a graphic description of the policy of Ivan Kalita, the founder of Moscow's might:

> The policy of Ivan Kalita was simply this: to play the abject tool of the Khan, thus to borrow his power, and

then to turn it round upon his princely rivals and his own subjects. To attain this end he had to insinuate himself with the Tartars by dint of cynical adulation, by frequent journeys to the Golden Horde,[20] by humble prayers for the hand of Mongol princesses, by a display of unbounded zeal for the Khan's interests, by atrocious calumnies against his own kinsfolk, by blending in himself the characters of the Tartar's hangman, sycophant and slave-in-chief. He perplexed the Khan by continuous revelations of secret plots.

Whenever the branch of Tver betrayed a *velléité*[21] of national independence, he hurried to the Horde to denounce it. Wherever he met with resistance, he introduced the Tartar to trample it down. But it was not sufficient to act a character: to make it acceptable, gold was required. Perpetual bribery of the Khan and his grandees was the only sure foundation upon which to raise his fabric of deception and usurpation. But how was the slave to get the money wherewith to bribe the master? He persuaded the Khan to install him [as] his tax gatherer throughout all the Russian appanages. Once invested with this function, he extorted money under false pretences. The wealth accumulated by the dread held out by the Tartar name, he used to corrupt the Tartars themselves. By a bribe he induced the Primate to transfer his episcopal seat from Vladimir to Moscow, thus making the latter the capital of the empire, because the religious capital ... By a bribe he allured the Boyards [*sic*] of the rival princes into treason against their chiefs, and attracted them to himself as their centre. By the joint influence of the Mahometan Tartar, the Greek Church and the Boyards he unites the princes holding appanages into a crusade against the most dangerous of them – the prince of Tver: and then, having driven his recent allies, by bold attempts at usurpation, into resistance against himself ... he draws not the sword, but hurries to the Khan. By bribes and delusion again he seduces him into assassinating his kindred rivals under the most cruel torments. It was the traditional policy of the Tartar to check the Russian princes the one by the other, to feed their dissensions, to cause their forces to equiponderate, and to allow none to consolidate himself. Ivan Kalita converts the Khan into the tool by which he rids himself of his most

> dangerous competitors and weighs down every obstacle to his own usurping march. He does not conquer the appanages, but surreptitiously turns the rights of the Tartar conquest to his own exclusive profit. He secures the succession of his son through the same means by which he had raised the Grand Princedom of Muscovy, that strange compound of princedom and serfdom. During his whole reign he swerves not once from the line of policy he had traced to [*sic*] himself: clinging to it with a tenacious firmness, and executing it with methodical boldness. Thus he becomes the founder of the Muscovite power, and characteristically his people call him Kalita – that is, 'the purse', because it was the purse, and not the sword, with which he cut his way. The very period of his reign witnesses the sudden growth of the Lithuanian power which dismembers the Russian appanages from the West, while the Tartar squeezes them into one mass from the East. Ivan, while he dare not repulse the one disgrace, seemed anxious to exaggerate the other. He was not to be seduced from following up his ends by the allurements of glory, the pangs of conscience or the lassitude of humiliation. His whole system may be expressed in a few words: the machiavellianism of the usurping slave. His own weakness – his slavery – he turned into the mainspring of his strength.[22]

But Ivan Kalita merely laid the foundation upon which the state of Muscovy was built. The true creator of Muscovy was Ivan III:

> At the commencement of his reign (1462–1505) Ivan III was still a tributary to the Tartars: his authority was still contested by the princes holding appanages; Novgorod, the head of the Russian republics, reigned over the north of Russia; Poland-Lithuania was striving for the conquest of Muscovy; lastly, the Livonian Knights were not yet disarmed.[23] At the end of his reign we behold Ivan III seated on an independent throne, at his side the daughter of the last emperor of Byzantium, at his feet Kasan [*sic*], and the remnant of the Golden Horde flocking to his court; Novgorod and the other Russian republics enslaved – Lithuania diminished and its king a tool in Ivan's hands – the Livonian Knights vanquished. Astonished Europe, at the commencement of Ivan's reign, hardly aware of the

> existence of Muscovy, hemmed in between the Tartar and the Lithuanian, was dazzled by the sudden appearance of an immense empire on its Eastern confines, and Sultan Bayazet himself, before whom Europe trembled, heard for the first time the haughty language of the Muscovite.[24]

In order to show how Ivan III, whom Russian historians themselves depict as a coward, had been able to accomplish all these feats, Marx gives us a survey of the most important events of his reign: his struggle with the Tatars, his subjection of the Republic of Novgorod, his struggles with other appanage-holding princes, and, lastly, with Poland-Lithuania:

> Ivan rescued Muscovy from the Tartar yoke not by one bold stroke but by the patient labour of about 20 years. He did not break the yoke, but disengaged himself by stealth. Its overthrow, accordingly, has more the look of the work of nature than the deed of man. When the Tartar monster expired at last, Ivan appeared at its deathbed like a physician who prognosticated and speculated on death rather than like a warrior who imparted it.[25]

In connection with this broadly correct account – Solovyov[26] also speaks, not of the overthrow of the Tatar yoke, but of its collapse – Marx draws the following conclusion:

> The character of every people enlarges with its enfranchisement from a foreign yoke: that of Muscovy in the hands of Ivan seems to diminish. Compare only Spain in its struggles against the Arabs with Muscovy in its struggles against the Tartars ... In rising against the Horde, the Muscovite had not to invent but only to imitate the Tartars themselves. But Ivan did not rise. He humbly acknowledged himself a slave of the Golden Horde ... He thus did not conquer but filch [*sic*] strength. He does not drive, but manoeuvre [*sic*] his enemy out of his strongholds. Still continuing to prostrate himself before the Khan's envoys and to proclaim himself as his tributary, he eludes the payment of the tribute under false pretences, employing all the stratagems of a fugitive slave who dare not confront his owner, but only steal out of his reach. At last the Mongol wakes from his torpor and the hour of battle sounds. Ivan, trembling at the mere sem-

> blance of an armed encounter, attempts to hide himself behind his own fear, and to disarm the fury of his enemy by withdrawing the object upon which [?] to wreak his vengeance. He is only saved by the intervention of the Crimean Tartars, his allies.[27]

Ivan III behaved in a still more cowardly fashion during subsequent invasions:

> He caught one Tartar with another Tartar ... With the spoils of the vanquished Tartars he enchained the victorious Tartar. But if too prudent to assume, with the eyewitnesses of his disgrace, the airs of a conqueror, this impostor did fully understand how the downfall of the Tartar empire must dazzle at a distance – with what halo of glory it would encircle him, and how it would facilitate a magnificent entry among the European powers. Accordingly, he assumed abroad the theatrical attitude of the conqueror, and, indeed, succeeded in hiding under a mask of proud susceptibility and irritable haughtiness the obtrusiveness [*sic*] of the Mongol serf who still remembered kissing the stirrup of the Khan's meanest envoy. He aped in more subdued tone the voice of his old masters, which terrified his soul.[28]

Marx finds the influence of the Tatar period of Russia's history even in the phraseology of the Russian diplomacy of his own day: 'Some standing phrases of modern Russian diplomacy, such as the magnanimity, the wounded dignity of the master, are borrowed from the diplomatic instructions of Ivan III.'[29]

While emancipation from the Tatar yoke was seen by Ivan III as the first precondition for establishing a Muscovite hegemony, the second was the destruction of Russian liberty. He reduced to subjection one after the other the old city republics of Russia, Vyatka and Novgorod, and left Pskov with only the shadow of its former independence:

> It is still worthy of notice what exquisite pains were always taken by Muscovy, as well as by modern Russia, to execute republics. Novgorod and its colonies lead the dance: the republic of the Cossacks follows: Poland closes it. To understand the Russian mastication of Poland one must study the execution of Novgorod, lasting from 1478 to 1528.[30]

After putting an end to this republic, Ivan III also put an end to the last of the appanage-holding princes: 'Ivan seems to have snatched the chain with which the Mongols crushed Muscovy, only to bind with it the Russian republics. He seemed to enslave these republics only to republicanise the Russian princes.'[31]

With the same skill, Ivan III carried on his struggle with Lithuania, against which he stirred up the Emperor Maximilian, Matthias Corvinus[32] and Stephen, Prince of Moldavia, together with Mengli-Ghirei, the Crimean Khan, 'who proved as powerful a tool against Lithuania as against the Golden Horde'.[33]

Invaluable services were rendered to Ivan III by the Orthodox Church, for the strengthening of his authority:

> But to lay claim to the inheritance of Byzantium, to hide the stigma of Mongolian serfdom under the mantle of the Porphyrogeniti,[34] to link the upstart throne of Muscovy to the glorious empire of St Vladimir, to give in his own person a new temporal head to the Greek Church, whom of all the world should Ivan single out? The Roman Pope.[35]

At the Pope's court, and in his care, dwelt Sophia Paleologina, who had left for Rome with her father after the fall of Constantinople. The Pope gave her, the heiress of the Byzantine Emperor, to the prince of Muscovy, thereby consolidating the religious and political hegemony of Muscovy over the entire Orthodox East.[36]

Marx finds present already in Ivan III's policy all the basic elements of the policy of modern Russia:

> A simple substitution of names and dates will prove to evidence [*sic*] that between the policy of Ivan III and that of modern Russia there exists not similarity, but sameness. Ivan III, on his part, did but perfect the traditionary [*sic*] policy of Muscovy, bequeathed by Ivan I Kalita. Ivan Kalita, the Mongolian slave, acquired greatness by wielding the power of his greatest foe, the Tartar, against his minor foes, the Russian princes. He could not wield the power of the Tartar but under false pretences. Forced to dissemble before his masters the strength he really gathered, he had to dazzle his fellow serfs with a power he did not own. To solve this problem he had to elaborate all the ruses of the most abject slavery into a system, and to execute that system with the patient labour of the slave. Open force itself could enter as an intrigue only into a

> system of intrigues, corruption and underground usurpation. He could not strike before he had poisoned. Singleness of purpose became with him duplicity of action. To encroach by the fraudulent use of a hostile power, to weaken that power by the very act of using it, and to overthrow it at last by the effects produced through its own instrumentality – this policy was inspired by Ivan Kalita by the peculiar character both of the ruling and the serving race. His policy remained still the policy of Ivan III.[37]
>
> It is yet the policy of Peter the Great and of modern Russia, whatever changes of name, seat and character the hostile power used may have undergone. Peter the Great is indeed the inventor of modern Russian policy, but he became so only by divesting the old Muscovite method of encroachment of its merely local character and its accidental admixtures, by distilling it into an abstract formula, by generalising its purpose and exalting its object from the overthrow of certain given limits of power to the aspiration of [*sic*] unlimited power. He metamorphosed Muscovy into modern Russia by the generalisation of its system, not by the mere addition of some provinces.
>
> To resume. It is in the terrible and abject school of Mongolian slavery that Muscovy was nursed and grew up. It gathered strength only by becoming a virtuoso in the craft of serfdom. Even when emancipated, Muscovy continued to perform its traditional part of the slave as master. At length Peter the Great coupled the political craft of the Mongol slave with the proud aspiration of the Mongol master, to whom Genghis Khan had, by will, bequeathed his conquest of the earth.[38]

But although Muscovy had worked out all the basic elements of the policy of Peter the Great, and although, even before Peter, steady enlargement of territory had been the *leitmotiv* of the whole activity of the Muscovite rulers, it was only from Peter's time onward that this policy secured a firm foundation, and he alone it was who laid the basis for Russia's expansion westwards:

> Before Peter's time one of the most characteristic features of the Slavs, which strikes every observer, is the fact that almost everywhere they were settled in the heart of the continent, leaving the sea coasts to other, non-

> Slavonic peoples. Wherever Slavs touched the seaboard they were subjected to alien rule. The Russian people shared this common fate of the Slavonic race. Continent-bound, for the most part, they were unable, until Peter the Great's time, to secure any maritime outlet, except on the White Sea, which is covered with ice for three quarters of the year. The spot where St Petersburg now stands has been for a thousand years contested ground between Finns, Swedes and Russians.

All the rest of the Baltic coast which now belongs to Russia, together with the coast of the Black Sea, was acquired by Russia after Peter came to the throne. Moreover, 'as if to witness the anti-marine peculiarity of the Slavonic race', says Marx, no portion of the Baltic coast has really become Slavonic to this day, and the same is true of the Circassian and Mingrelian coast of the Black Sea.[39]

Only Peter 'broke through all the traditions of the Slavonic race'. 'It is water that Russia wants': these words, addressed as a rebuke to Prince Cantemir,[40] were the watchword of his whole life. Conquest of the Sea of Azov was the aim of his first war with Turkey, conquest of the Baltic that of his war with Sweden, and conquest of the Caspian Sea that of his foray into Persia:

> For a system of local encroachment, land was sufficient; for a system of universal aggression, water had become indispensable. It was but by the conversion of Muscovy from a country wholly of land into a sea-bordering empire that the traditional limits of the Muscovite policy could be superseded and merged into that bold synthesis which, blending the Mongol slave with the world-conquering tendencies of the Mongol master, forms the life-spring of modern Russian diplomacy.[41]

And when we are told, in explanation of the policy of Peter the Great, that no great nation can exist without a sea, that Russia could not leave the mouths of the Neva, the Don, the Dnieper and the Bug in others' hands, that Peter seized only what was absolutely necessary for the development of his country, one extremely important fact is overlooked – 'the *tour de force* by which he transferred the capital of the empire from the inland centre to the maritime extremity, the characteristic boldness with which he erected the new capital on the first strip of Baltic coast he conquered, almost within gunshot of the frontier, thus deliberately giving his dominions an *eccentric centre*.'[42]

We may confidently assert that in all Russian literature, in which the dispute about the significance of Peter the Great's reforms and actions has not ceased to this day, in which both the principal tendencies in Russian political thought, the Slavophils[43] and the Westernisers, in all their latest varieties – always distinguished by their hostile or approving attitude to Peter – it would be hard to find a more brilliant, more graphic definition of Peter's principal action, which opened the St Petersburg period of Russia's history, when, in the words of the original Slavophils, she fell victim to the decadent West, or when, from the standpoint of the Westernisers, she entered into European civilisation, than the following lines from Marx's pen:

> To transfer the throne of the Tsars from Moscow to St Petersburg was to place it in a position where it could not be safe, even from insult, until the whole coast from Libau to Tornea was subdued – a work not completed till 1809 ... 'St Petersburg is the window from which Russia can overlook Europe', said Algarotti.[44] It was from the first a defiance to the Europeans, an incentive to further conquest to the Russians ... St Petersburg, the *eccentric centre* of the empire, pointed at once to a periphery still to be drawn.
>
> It is, then, not the mere conquest of the Baltic provinces which separates the policy of Peter the Great from that of his ancestors, but it is the transfer of the capital which reveals the true meaning of his Baltic conquests. St Petersburg was not, like Moscow, the centre of a race, but the seat of a government; not the slow work of a people, but the instantaneous creation of a man; not the medium from which the peculiarities of an inland people radiate, but the maritime extremity where they are lost; not the traditionary [*sic*] nucleus of a national development, but the deliberately chosen abode of a cosmopolitan intrigue. By the transfer of the capital Peter cut off the natural ligaments which bound up the encroaching system of the old Muscovite Tsars with the natural abilities and aspirations of the great Russian race. By planting his capital on the margin of a sea, he put to open defiance the anti-maritime instincts of that race, and degraded it to a mere weight in his political mechanism. Since the sixteenth century Muscovy has made no important acquisitions but on the side of Siberia, and to[45] the sixteenth century the dubious conquests made towards

the West and the South were only brought about by direct agency on the East. By the transfer of the capital Peter proclaimed that he, on the contrary, intended working on the East and the immediately neighbouring countries through the agency of the West. If the agency through the East was narrowly circumscribed by the stationary character and the limited relations of Asiatic peoples, the agency through the West became at once illimited [*sic*] and universal from the movable [*sic*] character and the all-sided relations of Western Europe. The transfer of the capital denoted this intended change of agency, which the conquest of the Baltic provinces afforded the means of achieving, by securing at once to Russia the supremacy among the neighbouring northern states; by putting it into immediate and constant contact with all points of Europe, by laying the basis of a material bond with the maritime powers, which by this conquest became dependent on Russia for their naval stores; a dependence not existing as long as Muscovy, the country that produced the great bulk of the naval stores, had got no outlets of its own; while Sweden, the power that held these outlets, had not got the country lying behind them.

If the Muscovite Tsars, who worked their encroachments by the agency principally of the Tartar Khans, were obliged to *Tartarise* Muscovy, Peter the Great, who resolved upon working through the agency of the West, was obliged to civilise Russia. In grasping upon the Baltic provinces, he seized at once the tools necessary for this process. They afforded him not only the diplomatists and generals, the brains with which to execute his system of political and military action on the West, they yielded him, at the same time, a crop of bureaucrats, schoolmasters and drill-sergeants who were to drill Russians into that varnish of civilisation that adapts them to the technical appliances of the Western peoples, without imbuing them with their ideas.

Neither the Sea of Azov, nor the Black Sea, nor the Caspian Sea could open to Peter this direct passage to Europe. Of the four wars which fill the military life of Peter the Great, his first war, that against Turkey, the fruits of which were lost in a second Turkish war, continued in one respect the traditionary [*sic*] struggle with the Tartars. In another respect it was but the prelude to the

> war against Sweden, of which the second Turkish war forms an episode and the Russian war an epilogue. Thus the war against Sweden, lasting 21 years, almost absorbs the military life of Peter the Great. His whole creation hinges upon the conquest of the Baltic coast.[46]

Marx thought that he had found at last the solution to the problem and solved the riddle of the sphinx, which is constituted by the existence of the Russian colossus. And, along with this, he also established the origins of that Anglo-Russian slavery under the yoke of which lay the Europe of his time:

> The mere fact that the conversion of Muscovy into Russia was brought about by its transformation from a half-Asiatic inland country into the paramount maritime power of the Baltic, would it not enforce upon us the conclusion that England, the greatest maritime power of that epoch – a maritime power lying, too, at the very gates of the Baltic, where, since the middle of the seventeenth century, she had maintained the attitude of supreme arbiter – that England must have had her hand in this great change, that she must have proved the main prop or the main impediment of the plans of Peter the Great, that during the long protracted and deadly struggle between Sweden and Russia she must have turned the balance, that if we do not find her straining every nerve in order to save the Swede we may be sure of her having employed all the means at her disposal for furthering the Muscovite? And yet, in what is commonly called history, England does hardly appear on the plan of this grand drama, and is represented as a spectator rather than as an actor. Real history will show that the Khans of the Golden Horde were no more instrumental in realising the plans of Ivan III and his predecessors than the rulers of England in realising the plans of Peter I and his successors.[47]

Let us take a closer look at what this 'real history' teaches us.

Notes

1. The quotations from *The Secret Diplomatic History of the Eighteenth Century* in this chapter are on pages 108–22 of the Lawrence and Wishart edition, and Marx and Engels, *Collected Works*, Volume 15, London, 1986, pp74–96 (translator's note).
2. Karl Marx, *Revelations of the Secret Diplomatic History of the Eighteenth Century*, Marx and

Engels, *Collected Works*, Volume 15, London, 1986, pp74–5 (translator's note).
3. Marx has in mind here Fallmerayer, who, as he puts it, unconsciously followed in the track beaten by Russian historians (author's note). Jakob Philipp Fallmerayer (1790–1861) was a publicist and historian (translator's note).
4. The dynasty which ruled Russia until the death of Tsar Fyodor I (1584–1598) was called Rurikovich, from Rurik (862–879), its legendary founder. After the interlude known as 'The Time of Troubles', Mikhail Fyodorovich Romanov (1613–1645) came to the throne, founding the dynasty which ruled thereafter until 1917 (translator's note).
5. That is, Norse (translator's note).
6. Charlemagne (Charles the Great) was the Frankish king (768–814) who had himself crowned Holy Roman Emperor in AD 800 (translator's note).
7. That is, the Rurikoviches (translator's note).
8. The Scandinavians who played an important part in Russia's early history, as warriors and merchants, were called by Western writers 'Varangians'. The trade route between the Baltic and Black seas was known as 'the road from the Varangians to the Greeks'. According to legend, the first Russian state was founded by these Norsemen – hence Marx's reference to a 'Russian Normandy', which he compares to 'French Normandy.' This 'Normanist theory' of the origin of the Russian state has been strongly disputed (translator's note).
9. Riazanov has 'Southern' (translator's note).
10. According to ancient chronicles, the first of his line to rule was Rurik (862–879); Oleg (882–912) united Novgorod and Kiev into a single realm; Svyatoslav I, Prince of Kiev (945–972), invaded Bulgaria in 968–970 (translator's note).
11. Karl Marx, *Revelations of the Secret Diplomatic History of the Eighteenth Century*, op cit, pp75–6. The Byzantine emperor John I, surnamed Tzimisces (969–976), drove the Russians out of Thrace and Bulgaria in 970–973 (translator's note).
12. Andrew I Yuriyevich Bogolyubsky (1157–1174) was Prince of Vladimir (from 1157) and Suzdal (from 1169), and captured Kiev (translator's note).
13. Temujin (1162–1227), the leader of one of the Mongol clans, was proclaimed Genghis Khan, ruler of all the Mongols, in 1206, and thereafter embarked upon a programme of world conquest that took his armies as far West as Silesia (translator's note).
14. Karl Marx, *Revelations of the Secret Diplomatic History of the Eighteenth Century*, op cit, pp76–7. Riazanov's emphasis (translator's note).
15. Riazanov has 1224. In 1223, the Tatars (usually described as Mongols by Western writers) defeated a Russian army at the River Kalka, but nothing came of this for the moment, owing to the death soon afterwards of Genghis Khan. The sustained Tatar invasion of Russia began in 1237, and the establishment of the 'Tatar yoke' is now usually dated from 1243 (translator's note).
16. Riazanov inserts 'almost' (translator's note).
17. Yuri Danilovich was elevated to the position of Grand Prince of Vladimir in 1317 by Sultan Muhammad Usbeck, the Khan of the Golden Horde (1313–1342), whose sister he married; Ivan I Kalita was Grand Prince of Moscow (1328–1340) and Vladimir (1331–1340). Riazanov inserts his patronymic, 'Danilovich' (translator's note).
18. Ivan III Vasilyevich ruled Moscow from 1462 to 1505 (translator's note).
19. Karl Marx, *Revelations of the Secret Diplomatic History of the Eighteenth Century*, op cit, pp77–8 (translator's note).
20. The Golden Horde (from Turkic *orda*, a camp) was the headquarters of the Tatar Khan. The name came to be used for his subjects generally (translator's note).
21. 'A slight inclination to do something' (French) (translator's note).
22. Karl Marx, *Revelations of the Secret Diplomatic History of the Eighteenth Century*, op cit, pp78–80 (translator's note).
23. At this time, Livonia (now divided between Latvia and Estonia) was ruled by the German 'crusading' order of the Knights of the Sword (translator's note).

24. Karl Marx, *Revelations of the Secret Diplomatic History of the Eighteenth Century*, Marx and Engels, *Collected Works*, London, 1986, p80. Sultan Bajazet (Bayezid II, the Just) reigned from 1447 to 1512. He expanded his power in the Balkans as far as the estuaries of the Dniester and Dnieper (translator's note).
25. Karl Marx, *Revelations of the Secret Diplomatic History of the Eighteenth Century*, op cit, pp80–1 (translator's note).
26. SM Solovyov (1820–1879) wrote a history of Russia to which Riazanov several times refers (translator's note).
27. Karl Marx, *Revelations of the Secret Diplomatic History of the Eighteenth Century*, op cit, p81 (translator's note).
28. Op cit, p82 (translator's note).
29. Op cit, p82 (translator's note).
30. Op cit, p84 (translator's note).
31. Op cit, p84. Riazanov, or his printer, has put 'Turks' for 'Russian princes' (translator's note).
32. Matthias I Corvinus was King of Hungary, 1458–1490; Maximilian I was Holy Roman Emperor, 1493–1519 (translator's note).
33. Karl Marx, *Revelations of the Secret Diplomatic History of the Eighteenth Century*, op cit, p85. Stephen the Great was Voivode of Moldavia (1457–1504); Mengli-Ghirei, Khan of the Crimea (1468–1515) separated from the Golden Horde in 1443, and allied with Ivan III and the Sultan, fighting both Poland and Moldavia (translator's note).
34. The 'Porphyrogeniti' (those born in the purple) were the family of the Byzantine Emperors (translator's note).
35. Karl Marx, *Revelations of the Secret Diplomatic History of the Eighteenth Century*, op cit, p86. Vladimir, Prince of Novgorod and Kiev (c980–1015), made Christianity the official religion of Russia in 988, and is honoured as a saint by the Orthodox Church (translator's note).
36. Zoe, the daughter of Thomas Palaeologos, the brother of the last Byzantine Emperor, is known in Russian history as Sophia Palaeologina. As the Russian historian Kliuchevsky commented, 'as heiress to the declining house of Byzantium, the new Tsarina of Russia had transferred the supreme rights of the Byzantine house to Moscow, as to a new Tsargrad, and there shared them with her husband' (*A History of Russia*, Volume 2, p19, translator's note).
37. Karl Marx, *Revelations of the Secret Diplomatic History of the Eighteenth Century*, op cit, pp86–7. Ivan II, Ivanovich, the Red, ruled Russia during 1353–59 (translator's note).
38. Owing to negligence on the part of the publisher, this entire passage was omitted from the work when it was published as a book, *The Secret Diplomatic History of the Eighteenth Century* (Compare *Free Press*, 25 February 1857) (author's note). (Marx and Engels, *Collected Works*, Volume 15, London 1986, p87. See note to p118 of the Lawrence and Wishart edition. Translator's note).
39. Karl Marx, *Revelations of the Secret Diplomatic History of the Eighteenth Century*, op cit, p88. The paragraph is rendered there in this slightly different form: 'One feature of the Slavonic race must strike every observer. Almost everywhere it confined itself to an inland country, leaving the sea-borders to non-Slavonic tribes. Wherever they touched the sea-board, as in the Adriatic and part of the Baltic, the Slavonians had soon to submit to foreign rule. The Russian people shared this common fate of the Slavonian race ... Nor had they, before Peter the Great, proved able to conquer any maritime outlet beside the White Sea, which, during three-fourths of the year, is itself enchained and immovable. The spot where Petersburg now stands had been for a thousand years past contested ground between Finns, Swedes and Russians.' By the Circassian and Mingrelian coast, Marx means the Eastern coast of the Black Sea, occupied, before the Russian annexation, by the Cherkesses and the Georgian principality of Mingrelia (translator's note).
40. Karl Marx, *Revelations of the Secret Diplomatic History of the Eighteenth Century*, op cit, p89.

When the Turks defeated the Russians at the Pruth in 1711, Prince Demeter Cantemir of Moldavia (1710–1711), who had sided with the invaders, had to leave his country and take refuge in Russia, where he became an adviser to Peter the Great (translator's note).

41. Karl Marx, *Revelations of the Secret Diplomatic History of the Eighteenth Century*, op cit, p89 (translator's note).
42. Op cit, p89 (translator's note).
43. The best known 'Slavophil' of today, Solzhenitsyn, runs true to form in seeing the reign of Peter the Great as the time when Russia 'took the wrong road' (translator's note).
44. Karl Marx, *Revelations of the Secret Diplomatic History of the Eighteenth Century*, op cit, pp89–90. Francesco Algarotti, an Italian philosopher (1712–1764), visited Russia and wrote a widely read account of his impressions (translator's note).
45. That is, until (translator's note).
46. Karl Marx, *Revelations of the Secret Diplomatic History of the Eighteenth Century*, op cit, pp90–1 (translator's note).
47. Op cit, pp91–2 (translator's note).

Chapter Four

The Tatar Yoke and the Russian Autocracy

That 'overwhelming influence' of Russia which from the eighteenth century onward startled all thinking people in Western Europe, and which finally established itself in the first half of the nineteenth century, was no less of a mystery to Russia's intelligentsia, who experienced all too palpably the whole political weight of the Russian colossus. The constant development and consolidation of 'the state', alongside the complete passivity of 'society', transformed the entire Russian people into one compact mass which Russian absolutism threw into the scales of foreign politics with a resolution that shrank from no sacrifices. The more the contradiction between 'state' and 'society' revealed itself in the West, the more clearly did the contrast appear between the West and Russia. While the 'rulers' of Europe gazed with envy on Russian absolutism, unconstrained by any parliament, and while the democratic elements nourished hatred for it, both the former and the latter were in no doubt that the external political might of Russia was due precisely to the undivided rule of absolutism. And, on the other hand, the fact that external policy, and success therein, constituted the strongest aspect of Russia's Tsardom gave it still further strength inside the country and helped it ruthlessly to crush all attempts at opposition. While the traditional notion of state power as the demiurge of national history continued to prevail in Western Europe, in Russia this was a firmly established dogma.

One group cursed Tsardom, the other blessed it. But whether they saw it, like all Russia's history, as a completely original phenomenon, or only as one of the phases of social development which had long since been left behind by Western Europe, it was for both alike the source of Russia's entire development, that country's principal determining factor. Even today the most prominent representatives of Russian historiography draw a sharp line between Western Europe and Russia. Over there, in the West, the state was created by civil society, and it is in the latter that we have to seek the key to the historical process of its development. In Russia, on the contrary, it was the state that created civil society and the state that was the driving force of Russian history.

Let us hear, for example, what Milyukov[1] has to say:

> The point is that in our country the state had an immense influence on social organisation, whereas in the West social organisation conditioned the state structure. European society was built up, so to speak, from within, organically, from the lowest storeys to the highest. The foundation of this historical structure, the peasantry, took shape in the main during the migrations of peoples between the sixth and ninth centuries. Later, during the Middle Ages, a second storey was constructed upon this foundation – Europe's feudal aristocracy, whose strength lay in their enserfed peasantry. Finally, and only in modern times, through stubborn struggle against this second social stratum, by way of partial, small victories over the rights and privileges of particular small estates and provinces, there emerged a strong state, which slowly and gradually extended the limits of its authority. But here in Russia the historical process went in precisely the opposite direction – from the top downward. If we leave aside Kievan Russia, in which quite different conditions of historical development obtained, in North-Eastern Russia the representative of state power, the Prince, was almost the first settled inhabitant of the state. Around him everything was in movement, a whole population was coming and going ... From among this 'fluid element' of our history, as the historian Solovyov liked to describe them, there gradually emerged a small circle of personal assistants to the Prince. It was only through intense combined efforts by the government and the landowners that this element was at last firmly reduced to 'serfdom'. Thus, in our country the state power attached the landowners to itself, and the landowners attached the peasantry to themselves. This mode of construction long

> preserved for the summit of Russian society, for the ruling power, the leading role in the historical process of building the community. Not only did the Russian state not have to combat the rights and privileges of particular individuals and social groups, this state itself strove to call these social groups into existence and activity, so as to utilise this activity for its own ends.[2]

I have quoted Milyukov's own words because in Germany his essays were seen, to his surprise, as 'a Marxist history of Russian culture.' Milyukov is as little a Marxist as Lamprecht,[3] even though he has undoubtedly been influenced by Marxism. He belongs to that group of Russian historians who have ascribed great importance to the 'economic factor' in Russia's history and have done a great deal towards studying the country's socio-economic and financial history. Nevertheless, despite the big step forward, as compared with the old school of historians, for these historians too, as we have seen, the Russian state becomes, after a certain moment, in contrast to Western Europe, the principal determining factor in Russian history.

This traditional conception was shared by Russian revolutionaries as well. For them, too, it was beyond doubt that the forms of our society owed their existence to the state, that the latter had, by its arbitrary will, created our social classes, that it determined the direction taken by all social development, and that it is the principal source of the oppression and exploitation of the working classes. This thesis, and the idealisation of the order of ancient, pre-Muscovite Russia connected therewith, was professed by Bakunin and Tkachev,[4] and it formed the basis of the entire tactics and political activity of *Narodnaya Volya*.[5] Russian Tsardom was transformed into a burdensome inheritance from the past, lacking any roots in the present and merely hindering social development.

In a slightly modernised form, this thesis was incorporated in the new Social Democratic programme, which declared that 'the most important of all these *survivals* (from the pre-capitalist order) and the mightiest bulwark of all this barbarism is the Tsarist autocracy. ***By its very nature*** it is inimical to all social progress ...'[6]

Whence came this survival, which is certainly not only distinguished by amazing vitality, but is also the source of life of social classes allegedly created by it? What date can be given for its origin? What stage of pre-capitalist social relations saw the birth of this archaic product which is, by its very nature, inimical to all social progress?

The first historians of Russia answered this question as simply as the theologians answer the question of mankind's fall into sinfulness. The good-natured Slavs invited 'Germans'[7] to come and establish order in their country, and, after their political 'fall', the autocracy was established in Russia. Since that time, Russia's fate has been determined by the fate of the autocracy. Whether the Russian monarchy resulted from voluntary invitation of the Varangians by the Slavs, or, as others think, resulted from conquest, the autocracy is the primary factor in all the subsequent history of Russia. Depending on the personal qualities of particular monarchs, the autocracy either grew weaker or grew stronger, and, along with it, Russia either declined or thrived. After a period of prosperity under the first Rurikoviches, Russia's unity was broken up, owing to the mistaken policy of Yaroslav the Wise,[8] into a multiplicity of appanages, and, as a consequence of this, the country fell victim to the Tatars – only later, thanks this time to the wise policy of the princes of Muscovy, to be restored to unity under Ivan III. Since the Romanov dynasty came to the throne, and as a result of their still wiser policy, we have seen a continuous growth in Russia's power and well-being.

This primitive conception, which makes the Rurikoviches and the Romanovs no less the creators of Russia than the Hohenzollerns are made by official Prussian historiography the creators of Germany, met with protest already among the Decembrists,[9] but it continued to prevail down to the 1850s, as the official philosophy of history of Nicholas's Russia. True, under the influence of Hegel's philosophy,[10] a new tendency was observable already at the end of the 1840s, but this too, while demolishing the old legend, sought merely to rationalise Russia's princes and sovereigns, abstracting from the concrete Rurikoviches and Romanovs and, by transforming them into 'the first servants of the state', made of Russian history a process of continuous development of the idea of the state.

Whereas the first historians of Russia had endeavoured to show that the autocracy was beneficial and that Russia ought to be grateful to her autocrats, the new school set itself to demonstrate that the autocracy had been necessary and advantageous, given the external historical conditions in which Russia's history had unfolded. This view became predominant only in the 1860s, and at that time encountered opposition from the democratic tendencies, which pointed to the importance of 'the people' and 'society' in the ancient history of Russia, and saw an intense struggle between 'state' and 'people' where the above-mentioned historians perceived only an organic process of development. And the factor that they saw as helping the Muscovite princes to dispose finally of the traditions of Kievan Russia was – the Tatar invasion.

The view that the Tatar conquerors brought about a profound change in the political relations in Russian society, that they created a quite new political hierarchy, still enjoys popularity among democratic elements. In the struggle between prince and people which they see as forming the entire content of the history of Russia in the fifteenth century, the Muscovite princes emerge victorious only because they are the protégés of the Khan. According to this concept the Muscovite princes, relying as they did upon the help of the Tatars, which they utilised all over Russia, had no need of support from the boyars or the people in order to consolidate their power, and were able to engage in unhindered expansion of their territory. In the same way, contrary to those historians for whom the autocracy resulted from an organic process and who denied almost any importance to the Tatar yoke, the democratic elements saw the beginning of the Russian autocracy precisely in the Tatar yoke, which for them was an alien excrescence on the national organism. Asia triumphed, in the persons of the autocrats of Muscovy, stifling Europe, of which 'Norman' Russia had formed part. After several centuries there then began the St Petersburg period of Russia's history, which, from this standpoint, turned into a period when, especially under the influence of Peter's reforms. the process of the Europeanisation of Russia was initiated.

The chief scholarly authority on whom the adherents of this view relied was Chernyshevsky's close friend, the historian Kostomarov.[11] He set forth his ideas most completely and systematically in a monograph entitled *The Beginning of the Autocracy in Ancient Russia*, which appeared 15 years after the publication of the article by Marx we are discussing. The similarity between certain of the fundamental ideas in this work and those of Marx, where the significance of the Tatar yoke is concerned, amounts sometimes to literal coincidence, as may be seen from the following quotation:

> In the pre-Tatar period no foundations whatever had developed for Russia's future autocracy, and still less had there been any conscious striving in that direction ... With the Tatar conquest a rapid and abrupt turn took place ... Previously there had been no one ruler over all Russia: now there was the first of such rulers, in the shape of the dread conqueror, the Khan. Russia, which he had subdued by force, became his spoils of war, his property: all the Russians, from prince to peasants without excep-

> tion, became his slaves. In this servitude Russia found its unity, that unity which it had not attained in the period of freedom ... The Khans enhanced the rank of the senior prince, giving him authority and power ... This he obtained by one method only, namely, subservience to the overlord ... Servility before the conqueror was the only guarantee of tranquillity for the country ...[12]

For Marx, the Tatar invasion plays the role of an elemental factor bursting into Russian history: with one blow the Tatars swept away all the *European* elements and turned Kievan Russia into an *Asiatic* country. The Tatar yoke demoralised not only the princes but the entire people as well, transforming them into slaves. The Tatar period gave Russia both despotism and serfdom. Until Peter's time, Muscovy remained an Asiatic country.

Marx does not spare the dark colours when he describes all the vileness of the Muscovite princes, and the same is true of Kostomarov and his followers. But whereas the latter seek to distinguish between princes and people, and, while ruthlessly exposing the legends about the personal valour of Muscovy's Ivans, Dmitris and Vasilys,[13] point to stubborn resistance and heroic struggle against the Tatars, Marx denies to the Russian people the qualities which he recognised in the people of Spain. Carried away by his basic idea, he forgets that the Spaniards, too, needed more than one century in order to free themselves from Arab rule. Even Kostomarov, while demolishing with his merciless criticism the legend of the personal heroism of Dmitri Donskoy,[14] in whose time the Tatars suffered their first major defeat, when he describes the battle of Kulikovo (1380), uses the same words that are commonly employed to describe the importance of the battle of Las Navas de Tolosa (1212).[15]

Marx is absolutely correct when he points to the profound difference between 'Norman' Russia and Muscovy. Kievan Russia can no more be called the cradle of Muscovy than the Empire of the Ottos can be called the cradle of Brandenburg.[16] But it does not follow from this that one can set a sort of impassable chasm between those two periods of Russian history. It must not be forgotten that the Tatar invasion found Kievan Russia in a condition very far removed from that which it had enjoyed in its heyday in the tenth to twelfth centuries. Although it was, even at that time, situated on the highroad of the peoples, along which one flood of nomads after another poured into Western Europe, and was throughout this period obliged to fight against the Khazars, the Pechenegs and the Polovtsians,[17]

Kievan Russia succeeded in coping with these raids. Kiev was in those days a flourishing commercial city, through which passed the trade route between the Scandinavian countries and Constantinople. At that very time when Germany, which had long remained isolated from the main roads of world trade (coming close to them only to a very slight extent along the Rhine), was beginning, with the start of the Crusades and the shifting of the centre of gravity of world trade from Constantinople to Italy, to emerge from its condition of natural economy, Kievan Russia was ceasing to perform its old function of intermediary between Constantinople and Scandinavia. The products of hunting and fishing, which previously had been sent to Kiev, were now being sent through Pskov and Novgorod to the Baltic Sea, where commerce was radically changing its character precisely in the twelfth and thirteenth centuries, which saw the rapid development of the cities of Lübeck and Visby.[18] By the time of the Tatar invasion Kiev had long since lost its commercial importance, and the centre of gravity of Russia's political and economic life had moved from the south-west to the north-east.

Marx himself mentions that it was nearly a century after the Tatar invasion that Muscovy began to stand out among the other principalities. Besides its comparative security from Tatar raids, the rise of Muscovy was facilitated to a considerable degree by the fact that it lay at the intersection of two very important trade routes: from the Volga to the Western Dvina, and from Novgorod to the Ryazan region. In the fifteenth century, many European merchants, coming from Poland and Germany, flocked to Moscow to buy furs. The chief branches of economic activity in ancient times, the extractive occupations of hunting, bee-keeping and fishing, were being supplemented and supplanted by agriculture. The settled population, attached by their occupation to the soil, were increasing in numbers. In Moscow and other towns the 'suburban' – that is, commercial and industrial – population was growing.

Of course, the Muscovite prince's alliance with the Tatar Khan gave him a certain advantage, but what ultimately brought victory in the struggle between Tver and Muscovy was not the machinations and intrigues of the latter's ruler – in that respect the princes of Tver had little to learn from their rivals – but the economic preponderance of Moscow, which filled with money that 'purse' with which Ivan Kalita and his successors were able to buy from the Golden Horde their mandate as Grand Princes and the right to collect the tribute. As always where external influences are concerned, the nature and strength of these influences were determined by *internal* conditions. As the Khan's protégé the Muscovite prince was victorious, not in a struggle to strengthen absolutism, but in a competition between different princes. And he eventually became the autocrat of all Russia not in the sense of an absolute, unrestricted ruler, but in the sense of an independent sovereign.[19] The Muscovite prince was not an absolute ruler, even within his own principality, and many decades had yet to pass before he could succeed, by basing himself upon the commercial and industrial population and the 'service' estate, in disposing of the descendants of the old appanage-princes and the boyar opposition.

The Tatar menace played exactly the same role in the history of the formation of Russia as the 'Turkish menace' played in the history of the creation of Austria-Hungary, the Moorish menace in the history of Spain, the Swedish menace in that of Prussia, and so on. By making necessary a concentration of all the country's military resources, it settled the argument in favour of that part of the country which proved able to put forward the strongest force, and this argument was decided not by the personal qualities of the Habsburgs, Hohenzollerns or Rurikoviches, but by the economic and financial resources of the regions they headed. As for Russian absolutism, in this we find exactly as much specifically 'Tatar' influence as we find in, say, the absolutism of Prussia or England.

The best evidence is provided by the history of the Russian autocracy from the time of Ivan III, which was when, by general agreement, it was finally established in Russia. During the entire period of 'pre-capitalist relations', right down to the time of the great reforms, the autocracy was not at all the *primus agens*.[20] Its character, and even its outward form, underwent marked and continuous change. Just like Western Europe, Russia passed through the process of the formation of an estates-monarchy. And if in Russia this process, as also that of the replacement of the estates-monarchy, was long-drawn-out, if the reign of the absolute monarchy lasted longer than in some Western countries, this circumstance can and must be explained in the same way as the analogous development of the absolute monarchy in Prussia and Austria. The elements out of which absolutism was created in Russia were just as little the product of absolutism as the elements out of which absolutism was formed in Prussia were produced by absolutism. The development of absolutism is favoured to one degree or another by the presence of external danger, and by the existence of national or regional antagonisms, but it is inconceivable without the centralisation of economic life, without commodity production, and without money economy, just as it is inconceivable without an army or without finances.

It is so little a 'survival of pre-capitalist relations' that, on the contrary, it attains the apogee of its development only at a certain stage in the development of capitalism.

'By its very nature', it is an instrument of economic and political exploitation, and the history of absolutism in Russia, as in Western Europe, is a history of struggle by the ruling classes, and by different sections of them, to gain possession of this powerful instrument and to adapt it to their needs.

For Marx, all these internal conditions for the development of absolutism in Russia are completely invisible. Consequently, in his account there is no place for two centuries of Russia's history, from Ivan III to Peter, a period marked by a fundamental regrouping of social classes. It is enough to mention that at the beginning of this period we still find a free peasantry, whereas under Peter I this peasantry is finally reduced to serfdom. Just as in Germany, the capitalist epoch in the countryside had as its harbinger an epoch of large-scale agricultural production on the basis of serf and corvée labour. The victory of the absolute monarchy over the old hereditary nobility was bought at the expense of the free peasantry, which was put at the mercy of the new nobility. At the very time that Russian absolutism comes forward into the European arena in the full glory of its might, it finally becomes an instrument in the hands of the nobility. The eighteenth century was the age of unrestrained rule by the nobility, and the reign in which the nobles were most favoured was that of Catherine II, the devoted 'friend' of Europe's Encyclopaedists.[21]

By missing out the entire internal history of Russia from Ivan III to Peter I, Marx prevented himself from understanding Russia's external policy. How little Russia gained by the power it obtained, according to Marx, from the Golden Horde is shown by the history of Russia in the sixteenth and seventeenth centuries, when it was compelled to wage a persistent struggle in the North against Sweden, in the West against Livonia and Poland, in the South against the Crimean Tatars, and after them the Turks, and in the East once more against the Tatars. As though repeating the history of Prussia, Russian historians depict the process of the transformation of Russia into a military monarchy under the influence of these incessant wars, which devastated many regions of Muscovy incomparably worse and more systematically than the Tatar yoke had done. The Crimean Khan treated the successor of Genghis Khan most disrespectfully, and demanded tribute with no less insistence than the Khans of the Golden Horde. While at the end of the fifteenth century the Venetians, the Pope and Maximilian were still trying to draw Muscovy into participation in the fight against the 'Turkish menace', nearly 200 years later, at the end of the seventeenth century, Russia had grown so much more powerful that it could no longer be treated as a *quantité négligeable*[22] in European politics.

One of the factors that delayed the development of Russia was the same as that by which Marx explained the delay in the development of Germany after the beginning of the sixteenth century, namely, a fresh change in trade routes. It was characteristic that the fiercest struggle between Poland and Livonia on the one hand, and Muscovy on the other, for mastery of the Baltic Sea took place just when the axis of world trade was shifting from the meridian of the Baltic to the shores of the Atlantic Ocean. The decline of the Hanseatic League[23] dealt the trade of Novgorod a severer blow than that city's subjection to Muscovy. The rivalry of the Livonian towns and the Swedish merchants finished off the dying Hanseatic League. Its political importance fell together with its economic power. Domination of the Baltic passed from the Poles to the Swedes, who finally closed Russia's outlet to the Baltic Sea. Narva, which the Russians had captured in 1558, had to be given back to the Swedes in 1581. Thus, Russia, whose trade had received a strong stimulus as a result of the acquisition of Kazan and Astrakhan, was deprived of the possibility of participating independently in Baltic commerce at the very time when it annexed Siberia, and when the Volga became a wholly Russian river.

Consequently, Russia was threatened with complete economic stagnation. However, trade with Western Europe, which until then had been carried on mainly through the Baltic, now found a new outlet. This was pierced by the English, through the White Sea. The year 1584 saw the foundation of Archangel, which thenceforth became a principal centre of Russia's foreign trade, and remained so until the foundation of St Petersburg. After the English came the Dutch. For his ability to strengthen his position in the Baltic, Peter I was, in the last analysis, indebted to the English and the Dutch. If we are to speak of England's 'guilt' as the power principally responsible for promoting the rise of Russia, this crime was committed by the English long before the time of the Great Northern War. In order to understand how and why relations between England and Russia took shape in the eighteenth century, we need to acquaint ourselves with the role played by England in the 'Europeanisation' of Russia.

Notes

1. This is the same PN Milyukov (1859–1943) who became the leader of Russia's Constitutional Democrats (Cadets) (translator's note).
2. P Milyukov, *Ocherki po istorii russkoy kultury*, St Petersburg, 1898, pp115–7 (author's note).
3. Karl Lamprecht (1856–1915) was a German historian who wrote a history of Germany in which he emphasised economic factors (translator's note).

4. Mikhail Alexandrovich Bakunin (1814–1876) was a Russian revolutionary opponent of Marx, one of the theorists of anarchism; Peter Nikitich Tkachev (1844–1886) was a Narodnik active in the revolutionary movement of the 1860s in Russia (translator's note).
5. *Narodnaya Volya* (The People's Will, or The People's Freedom) was the revolutionary organisation, formed in 1879, which carried out the assassination of Tsar Alexander II in 1881 (translator's note).
6. *1903: Second Congress of the Russian Social Democratic Labour Party*, New Park Publications, 1978, pp5–6 (Riazanov's emphases) (translator's note).
7. The Russians used to apply to Germans, Scandinavians, Dutch and English alike the name now used exclusively for the Germans. The reference here is to the legend that the Russians invited the Scandinavian Rurik and his followers to organise a state in their country (translator's note).
8. When Yaroslav the Wise (1019–1054) died, he divided his realm among his three sons (translator's note).
9. The Decembrists were the group of nobles, influenced by Western liberal ideas, who attempted a military coup d'état in St Petersburg in December 1825, aiming to establish a constitutional monarchy (translator's note).
10. Georg Wilhelm Friedrich Hegel (1770–1831), the German philosopher whose dialectical theories greatly influenced Marx and Engels (translator's note).
11. Nikolai Gavrilovich Chernyshevsky (1828–1889), author of the influential political novel *What is to be Done?* (1868), was active in the revolutionary movement in Russia in the 1860s. NI Kostomarov was banished from St Petersburg and forbidden to publish for a time, owing to what the Tsarist authorities considered the subversive tendency of his historical writings (translator's note).
12. NI Kostomarov, *Sobranie sochinenii*, Volume 5, St Petersburg, 1905, pp5–95 (author's note).
13. Vasily I Dmitriyevich, the son of Dmitri Donskoy, was Grand Prince of Moscow (1389–1425) (translator's note).
14. Dmitri Donskoy, Grand Prince of Moscow (1359–1389), transferred the seat of the Grand Princedom to Vladimir, and defeated Mamai, commander of the army of the Golden Horde and son-in-law of Khan Berdibek, at Kulikovo (translator's note).
15. The Battle of Kulikovo, in which a Tatar army under Mamai was defeated by a Russian army under Dmitri Donskoy, Prince of Moscow and Vladimir, is seen as the beginning of the process of Russia's liberation from the 'Tatar yoke'. The Battle of Las Navas de Tolosa, when the combined forces of Castile, Aragon, Navarre and Portugal defeated the Caliph al Nasir's Moorish army, is seen as the beginning of the 'reconquest' of the Iberian peninsula, which was not completed until the fall of Granada in 1492 (translator's note).
16. Otto I, II, and III were 'Holy Roman Emperors' in the tenth century. Otto I, the Great, was King of Saxony (936–973) before he was proclaimed Holy Roman Emperor in 962AD. Brandenburg-Prussia, from which the emperors of the 'Second Reich' (1871–1918) arose, began to rise to power in the seventeenth century (translator's note).
17. The Khazars were a Turkic people whose state religion was Judaism, who controlled a great multi-tribal empire on the steppes during the seventh and ninth centuries AD; the Pechenegs (Patzinaks) were a nomadic Turkic people who passed across the Ukraine into the Balkans from the ninth century onwards; the Polovtsi (Cumans) followed them in the same direction, and finally annihilated them in 1091 (translator's note).
18. Visby, on the Swedish island of Gotland, and Lübeck, on the German shore of the Baltic, both members of the Hanseatic League, were closely associated at this time (translator's note).
19. The word *samoderzhavie*, usually translated as 'autocracy', originally meant 'sovereignty', in the sense of complete independence of any overlord (translator's note).
20. That is 'prime mover' (Latin. Translator's note).

21. The Encyclopaedists were French savants whose rational critique of religion was one of the stimuli for the French Revolution (translator's note).
22. '*Quantité négligeable*' here means a factor so unimportant that it can be left out of account (translator's note).
23. The Hanseatic League, a grouping of cities on or near the Baltic and North seas, dominated the international trade of Northern Europe from the fourteenth century to the sixteenth (translator's note).

Chapter Five

The Europeanisation of Russia Under the Influence of Trade with England

The tremendous role played by the colonial system as one of the chief factors in primitive accumulation often causes us to forget that the classical country of capitalism, England, had almost no colonies until the seventeenth century, and that it is only from the latter half of that century that one can speak of England as a colonial power.

At the time when the Portuguese and the Spaniards were gradually gaining control of the New World and of the trade in Asiatic products, the English were engaged in emancipating themselves from dependence on the Hanseatics, in whose hands lay all their foreign trade. In 1552, the Hanseatic League was deprived of its principal privileges in England, and almost at the same time a company was formed in London, made up of merchants and some representatives of the nobility, for the purpose of undermining the Portuguese monopoly of the trade in spices. In 1553, an expedition was fitted out to make a voyage to India by way of the North-East Passage. This expedition ended in failure. Its leader, Willoughby, was lost, with two of his ships, but the captain of the third ship, Richard Chancellor, was cast ashore on the coast of the White Sea, at the mouth of the Northern Dvina. From there he made his way to Moscow, where he was most joyfully received by Ivan the Terrible.[1]

When Chancellor returned to London, his society was given a charter conferring a monopoly of trade with Russia and with all countries which it might succeed in opening up. This was the society of 'Merchant Adventurers for the Discovery of Lands, Countries,

Isles, Not Before Known or Frequented by Any English'. It became known more familiarly as the Muscovy Company,[2] or the Russia Company, which is what Marx calls it. After the 'Merchant Adventurers of England', who had received their charter in 1505, this was the largest trading company in the sixteenth century.

In 1555, Chancellor was sent once more into Russia, where he was again received very graciously. The Russia Company was given the right to carry on trade in all kinds of goods, duty-free, throughout Russia. Furthermore, any disputes between the English merchants and the Russians were to be settled by the Tsar in person. Ivan the Terrible, who was accorded in English documents the resounding title of 'Emperor of all Russia', decided to establish direct ties with the government of England. When Chancellor returned to England, he was accompanied by an envoy from the Tsar, Osip Nepeya. Their vessel was wrecked, the rich cargo of Russian produce – wax, tallow, furs, felt and yarn – was lost, and Chancellor and most of the crew were drowned, but Nepeya managed to survive. When he reached London he was received with great honour. On his return to Russia, Nepeya was accompanied by Jenkinson, the famous traveller. With the Tsar's permission, Jenkinson voyaged down the Volga into the Caspian Sea, and on into Central Asia. After this journey of his the Russia Company began to seek freedom in trade through Russia with Persia. In 1569, the Englishmen's monopoly was confirmed, and the company was authorised to convey goods, duty-free, to Bukhara and 'Cathay'.

But hard on the heels of the English came the Dutch. As they arrived later, they received fewer favours, and often had to resort to acting as middlemen for the English. Relations between the rivals soon deteriorated, and the Dutch used every means to deprive the English of their monopoly position. They declared that England traded in other people's goods, and charged unheard-of prices for them.

Ivan the Terrible hoped that in exchange for the favours he had granted to the English he would obtain England's help in his struggle against Poland and Sweden. But Elizabeth[3] stubbornly rejected any alliance – not because she was afraid of promoting the rise of Russia, but because such an alliance would be of advantage only to Russia, and was quite valueless for England.

> In the degree that England came to the front as a commercial state, in that degree did its interests become hostile to those of Spain, the great commercial power of the sixteenth century, which dominated the western

> seaboard of the Mediterranean and strove to be the mistress of the seas. Almost everywhere English commerce strove to develop, it found the road barred by Spain ... In the sixteenth century the Spaniard was England's hereditary enemy, the prototype of everything horrible for a Briton.[4]

This antagonism between England and Spain determined the entire foreign policy of Elizabethan England. It would have been very incautious to create fresh enemies on the eve of the Armada, especially as the trading relations between Russia and England via the White Sea had already aroused strong resentment among the Baltic powers.

Eventually England's stubbornness angered the Tsar, and in 1570, after sending Elizabeth an irate letter,[5] he cancelled all the Englishmen's privileges, together with their right to trade with Persia. The Russia Company at once set up a cry, and appealed to Elizabeth to save their trade from ruin. Despite Ivan's abuse, she sent Jenkinson to Russia again, and he succeeded in getting the former favours restored – to be sure, not for long.

What angered the Tsar most was that 'commercial affairs are put first and considered more important than Our[6] affairs, although their success necessarily depends on the latter', and he threatened to transfer all trade into the hands of the Venetians and the Germans. His wrath gave place to graciousness only in 1580, when he was obliged to appeal to England for war materials needed for his war with Sweden and Poland. Elizabeth hastened to meet his request, and in the spring of 1581 13 ships laden with munitions set sail for Russia. A fresh proposal from Ivan, for an alliance against Stefan Bathory, was rejected.[7] Despite the intrigues of the Dutch, Ivan was obliged once more to confirm the privileges of the English, because he had by now finally lost all his conquests on the Baltic littoral. When, soon after this, Ivan died (1584), one of the Englishmen's sworn enemies, the *dyak*[8] Shchelkalov, who favoured the 'Germans' in trade matters (the English alleged that he took bribes from the Dutch), said to the English envoy: 'Your English Tsar is dead .'[9]

We have seen that England, while highly appreciative of trade links with Russia, firmly resisted any political alliance with that country, and looked upon it merely as a colony. The question of who dominated the Baltic was at that time of absolutely no interest to England. She was no more inclined to help Sweden than to help Russia. What was of first importance to her was trade interest, and the desire to retain the monopoly of trade with Russia through the

White Sea, where she had least to worry about competition from the Dutch and the Swedes. In 1583, Elizabeth, disregarding the insistent appeals of King Gustavus of Sweden, concluded a treaty with Denmark which provided for free access by English vessels to the mouth of the Northern Dvina, and stipulated their right, in the event of stormy weather, to unhindered entry into Norwegian and Icelandic ports.[10] The number of English ships visiting Russia increased from year to year, and in 1582 reached nine. In 1584, a new town was founded at the mouth of the Northern Dvina, and was given the name of 'New Kholmogory'[11], which in 1637 was superseded by 'Archangel'. Until the foundation of St Petersburg, this was Russia's principal commercial port, through which passed all her foreign trade. The most important commodities exported to England were furs, skins, flax, hemp, cordage, timber for masts, tallow, pitch and tar, while the English supplied Russia mainly with cloth, silken and woollen materials, haberdashery, sugar, paper and metals.

After the death of Ivan the Terrible, the position of the English deteriorated. They were obliged to pay duties, though only at half-rate, and it was not until Boris Godunov[12] came to the throne in 1602 that they recovered their complete freedom from this burden, which Boris confirmed in 1605. But every proposal for an alliance was rejected by England.

The 'Time of Troubles'[13] had a very marked effect on the Englishmen's trade turnover, and England greeted with enthusiasm the accession of Mikhail Romanov. The new government of Muscovy allowed the English to keep all their privileges. England again refused an alliance, but offered her mediation as peacemaker between Sweden and Russia, so as to ensure her right to trade with Persia, and to seek a route to India. Peace was concluded at Stolbovo in 1617.[14] The English ambassador protested against the intrigues of the Dutch envoys, who also figured as intermediaries on this occasion. The English were starting to suffer more and more from competition on the part of the Dutch, who had by then already achieved a dominant position in Baltic trade. Furthermore, opposition from the Muscovite merchants was growing stronger, and the Romanovs had to take serious account of this.

The history of England's experience with the Lombards and the Hanseatics was being repeated here,[15] though on a different scale. The merchants of Moscow were as fervently 'nationalist' as the Londoners had been, and they would not rest until the English had been stripped of their privileges.

Under Tsar Mikhail, Russia made her first attempt to obtain a subsidy through alliance with England, but managed to get no more than 40,000 thalers[16] from that source. At last the Muscovite merchants succeeded in preventing the English from receiving the right to trade with Persia duty-free. This was a first step. The revolution in England provided the desired excuse for depriving the English of all the privileges they had enjoyed for nearly a century. Those who showed most indignation against the rebel English, joining with the Muscovite merchants to incite the government against them, were the Dutch, themselves Protestants and republicans.

In 1646, the Muscovite merchants presented Tsar Alexei with a complaint against the foreign merchants, and asked him to save them from ruin. 'All the markets we have enjoyed since time immemorial have been taken over by the English "Germans", and this is why we have given up our ancient occupations, and no longer go to Archangel.' The English 'have reduced all Muscovy to famine, for they buy up, in Moscow and other towns, meat, grain and other foodstuffs, to send to their own country.' They added this argument, calculated to be particularly telling with the government: the English 'cheat the Tsar of his revenues'. The Englishmen's guilt is clinched by the fact that they cannot appeal to their charter, because these English merchants 'have broken with their king, and have been fighting against him for four years'.

However, it was only on 1 June 1649, after the execution of Charles I,[17] that a decree by the Tsar expelled all the English merchants from Moscow and his other towns. 'It has been made known to our sovereign that the English throughout your country have committed a great crime: they have killed Charles their king. For this reason you shall no longer be permitted to live in Muscovy.'

But the Tsar's anger was not so strong as to make him reject trade with England completely. The English were still allowed to come to Archangel, though they no longer enjoyed the right to trade duty-free – which was a painful blow to the Russia Company.

The Pretender to the English throne, the future Charles II,[18] asked the Tsar for financial assistance, but this was refused, and instead of the 100,000 roubles he asked for, he was sent only sables worth 15,000 roubles and 5,000 roubles' worth of grain. An attempt by Cromwell[19] to recover the privileges of the English merchants came to nothing. But even the accession of Charles II, although it brought the renewal of friendly relations with England, did not lead to restoration of the former privileges. On behalf of Charles II, the English representative in Moscow acknowledged the Tsar's decree of 1649 as a sign of special friendship with his king, and expressed the hope that, now that the latter had recovered his throne, the penalty imposed on his rebellious subjects would be lifted. Notwithstanding this servility, however, all that the English obtained, after protracted negotiations, was the right to send their merchants to Moscow in numbers not exceeding ten. Between 1664, when England received this negative reply, and the beginning of the eighteenth century, the former friendly relations changed for the worse.

To be sure, the English did not go away: they were merely obliged to pay duty on their commercial dealings. The Dutch had achieved equality with them in conditions of competition.

But Russia was now again linked with Europe by strong ties of external trade, and it was precisely in the seventeenth century, under the influence of the English and the Dutch, that the process of 'Europeanising' Russia began.

Money economy, the development of which had been checked in the sixteenth century, while the shift in trade routes had been taking place, began to make rapid progress immediately after the end of the 'Time of Troubles'. A whole series of new commercial centres arose along the main roads to Moscow, and from Moscow northward to Archangel. Six trade routes radiated from Moscow, which became 'the focus of commercial activity for all Russia. Its importance was still further enhanced because the government itself undertook trading operations, and the Tsar himself was, as one Englishman put it, the principal Russian merchant in Russia.'[20] From Moscow goods were sent via Yaroslavl, Rostov and Pereyaslavl to Vologda, where the English bought up the flax accumulated there, and where they had a depot for their own goods. From Vologda they returned to Archangel. Besides Moscow itself, central Russia saw the development of Nizhny-Novgorod, which in the eighteenth century became the entrepot for Asiatic goods brought from Astrakhan, Western European goods brought from Archangel, Siberian goods brought from Kazan, and Muscovy's own goods for despatch to the East. This town also became the place where grain was bought, and from which it was distributed throughout the North of Russia. With the help of a network of buyers-up, some large-scale merchants covered the entire country, and concentrated all its internal trade in their hands. Defending their privileges, the English declared, quite correctly, that their trade was advantageous to small traders. But that was exactly why the big merchants incited against them. These merchants wanted to be the sole middlemen between the foreign traders and Russian producers and consumers. By a new set of regulations promulgated in 1667, foreigners were allowed to trade in Russia's inland towns only if they possessed special licences from the Tsar, and then only on payment of special supplementary duties. They had imposed on them a transit duty of twenty *dengi*[21] per rouble, to be charged on imports and exports alike.

It is difficult to establish precise figures for the export trade through Archangel. In 1653, that is, in the year when trade with the English was in rather a bad way, exports amounted in value to 1,032,406 roubles of those days – a very large sum for the period.[22] The average customs revenue from Archangel came to 70,000 roubles per annum. At the beginning of Peter the Great's reign, exports through Archangel were already worth three million roubles.

The seventeenth century saw the implantation of industry in Russia with the help of the Dutch, the English and the Hamburgers. In the 1630s, a Dutch capitalist named Venius was given the right to build an ironworks near Tula. It was thus that the famous factories of Tula began. In 1670, a company was formed, headed by the Hamburg capitalist Marselis and the Dutch capitalist Akema, with a similar licence to establish ironworks on the Vaga, at Kostroma, and on the Sheksna.

The merchants who had looked so jealously on the privileges of foreign traders now urged the government to grant privileges to foreign industrialists. 'Whatever industry is set up by the English will likewise be set up by the men of Muscovy. If the English discover ore and make iron therefrom, this will mean no loss to us, but only profit.'

In the second half of the seventeenth century, Moscow became a centre to which thronged masses of craftsmen, technicians, adventurers and charlatans. By the middle of the century, according to Olearius,[23] there were already as many as a thousand Protestant households in Moscow – mostly English, Scottish and Dutch. The 'German Liberty'[24] was German in name only, the English and Scots being most prominent in it. That same revolution which had given the Muscovite government the excuse to deprive the English of their privileges had brought to Moscow many who were unhappy with Cromwell's rule – Drummonds, Hamiltons, Dalziels, Crawfords, Grahams, Leslies and Gordons. In this atmosphere, Peter acquired not only European culture, but also sympathy with the Stuart dynasty.

And it was not in Peter's time, but earlier, that there began the process of political centralisation, when a number of reforms in the military and fiscal spheres were introduced. The development of a money economy made it possible to commute many taxes and duties in kind into monetary payments. The meetings of the Zemsky Sobor,[25] which had played such a striking role in the sixteenth and seventeenth centuries, were suppressed. Reform of provincial and municipal administration began. The distinctive forms that were assumed by this process of formation of an absolute monarchy do not disguise the identity of its basic features with the corresponding process in Western Europe, as Kautsky describes this in his *Thomas More*:

> It was natural that the new political central power should cluster round the person of the local prince, and that he should form the head of the centralised administration and army. His interests and the interests of commerce were the same ... Commerce needed the army to assert its interests, both at home and abroad ... But the new polity not only needed the prince as supreme captain. It also needed him as chief of the political administration. The feudal administrative apparatus was in process of dissolution, the bureaucracy was as yet in its infancy. Political centralisation, which was an economic necessity for commodity production at the incipient stage of the capitalist mode of production [so as to facilitate economic centralisation – and which, in its turn, evoked and intensified political centralisation], needed at the outset a personal head strong enough to maintain the unity of the administration against the discordant elements, especially the nobles. This strength only the army captain possessed. The uniting of all the resources of the military and administrative apparatus, on the one hand, and princely absolutism on the other, was an economic necessity for the period of the Reformation and long afterwards.[26]

State absolutism was just such an economic necessity in Russia. In Peter the Great it found its personification: by virtue of his energy and his dedication to the idea of the state he can take his place alongside the classical representatives of this type. And it was only because Marx did not notice that Peter was essentially a product engendered by European capitalism that he could see in him merely a transformed Tatar.

The question as to whether Russia belonged to Asia or to Europe had already been settled irrevocably by the end of the seventeenth century, and the godfathers and tutors of Russia were the most powerful commercial and industrial countries at that time – England and Holland.

Notes

1. Livonia, Poland and Sweden were unwilling to allow weapons or technicians to reach Russia. Not long before Chancellor's arrival, an attempt to bring into Russia several dozen craftsmen, printers and doctors had met with failure. The Emperor Rudolf II behaved no better (author's note). Rudolf II was Holy Roman Emperor from 1576 to 1612; Ivan IV, Vasilyevich, the Terrible, ruler of Russia (1530–1584), was proclaimed Tsar in 1547 (translator's note).
2. Chancellor's first visit to Moscow was in 1553–54, in the expedition commanded by Sir Hugh Willoughby. The Muscovy Company was formed in 1555 (translator's note).
3. Elizabeth I ruled England (1558–1603) as the last of the Tudor monarchs (translator's note).
4. Karl Kautsky, *Thomas More und seine Utopie*, Stuttgart, 1907, pp237–8 (author's note). (English translation, *Thomas More and His Utopia*, London, 1927, pp187–8. Translator's note).
5. 'And we had thought that you had been ruler over your land, and had sought honour to yourself and profit to your country, and therefore we did pretend those weighty affairs between you and us. But now we perceive that there be other men that do rule, and not men, but boors and merchants, the which seek not the wealth and honour of our Majesties, but they seek their own profit of merchandise. And you flower in your maidenly estate like a maid ...' Ivan could not find a worse insult (The Tsar's letter was dated 24 October 1570. The contemporary official translation is taken from *Early Voyages and Travels to Russia and Persia*, Hakluyt Society, Volume 2, 1886, p296. Ivan actually calls Elizabeth 'a typical old maid') (author's note).
6. That is, the Tsar's (translator's note).
7. Stefan Bathory, King of Poland (1575–1586), fought against Russia, in alliance with Sweden, in the Livonian War (1558–1583) which ended in Russia's defeat (translator's note).
8. A *dyak* was one of the Grand Prince's official secretaries in pre-Petrine Russia (translator's note).
9. Kostomarov, *Ocherki torgovli mosk. gos. v XVI i XVII st.*, in *Sobranie sochinenii*, Volume 8 (St Petersburg, 1906), p284 (author's note).
10. The King of Denmark ruled at this time over Norway and Iceland, and claimed authority over the seas between them, through which the English ships had to pass on their way to Archangel. However, the King of Sweden at this time was not named Gustav, but John III (1568–1592). The Swedes were opposed to anything that might strengthen Russia (translator's note).
11. Kholmogory was the small settlement at the mouth of the Northern Dvina when the English first arrived (translator's note).
12. Boris Godunov effectively ruled Russia during 1598–1605 (translator's note).
13. The 'Time of Troubles', at the end of the sixteenth century and the beginning of the seventeenth, was a period of palace revolutions, peasant revolts and foreign (Polish and Swedish) invasions which ended only with the accession of the first Romanov Tsar in 1613 (translator's note).
14. At the Treaty of Stolbovo, by taking Ingria and Karelia, Sweden cut Russia off completely from the Baltic Sea (translator's note).
15. In the later Middle Ages, English merchants fought to oust the foreign (Italian and German) merchants who had dominated England's external trade so long as the country remained too backward to bring it under 'native' control (translator's note).
16. *Yefimki* has been translated here as 'thalers'. Coins minted from the silver mined at Joachimsthal in Bohemia (Czech Jachymov) were called *joachimiki* in Poland, from which the Russians made their word *yefimki*. In Germany, they were called *Joachimsthaler*, or *thaler*, for short, from which comes our word 'dollar' (translator's note).

17. Charles I, Stuart, ruled England (1625–1649) until he was overthrown in the English Civil War (translator's note).
18. Charles II, Stuart (1660–1685), was restored to the English throne after Cromwell's death, when he brought the country into alliance with the France of Louis XIV (1643–1715) (translator's note).
19. Oliver Cromwell ruled England, later with the title of Lord Protector, from 1649 to 1658 (translator's note).
20. Kostomarov, *Ocherki torgovli mosk. gos. v XVI i XVII st.*, in *Sobranie sochinenii*, Volume 8 (St Petersburg, 1906), p284 (author's note).
21. The *denga* was a silver coin, 200 of which made up one rouble which, until Peter's reforms, was not a coin, but only a unit of account (translator's note).
22. According to Klyuchevsky's calculations, in 1651–1700 the rouble was worth 17 times as much as its present value (author's note).
23. Adam Olearius (1603–1671) was a German diplomat and traveller who visited Russia in the 1630s and wrote a description of the country (translator's note).
24. The 'German Liberty' was the suburb of Moscow where Westerners had to live (translator's note).
25. The Zemsky Sobor (Assembly of the Land) was a sort of primitive parliament, or Estates-General (translator's note).
26. Karl Kautsky, op cit, pp17–18 (author's note). English translation, pp15–16. The phrase here given in square brackets is omitted in this translation (translator's note).

Chapter Six

The Importance of Russian Trade for England

But trade relations between Russia and England were very important for England, too. In the second half of the sixteenth century, this trade was, along with piracy and the slave trade, one of the principal sources of 'primitive accumulation'. When the Hansa's monopoly over the Baltic Sea was broken, commercial preponderance there passed to Holland, and remained with her until the eighteenth century. England's attempts to grasp the heritage of the Hansa ended in failure, and the Eastland Company, which received its charter in 1579, was unable during a whole century to overcome the Dutch competition. According to Child, the Dutch trade at the end of the seventeenth century was ten times as great as the English.[1]

But the Russia Company played a large role in another respect as well. It organised the whale-hunting around Spitsbergen.[2] In this sphere, too, there was competition from the Dutch, who were not slow to follow the English. The Russia Company looked on the Arctic Ocean as its own property. If it allowed anyone else to take part in whale-hunting, this was only in return for the payment of a big duty. The Dutch, maintaining here, as elsewhere, the principle of *mare liberum*,[3] fitted out a war fleet to protect the capital they had invested. Exploiting their superior power, the Dutch inflicted heavy losses on the Russia Company, which had to conclude an agreement with the recently founded East India Company. Relations between England and Holland became especially strained in 1617 when, as we have seen, the English and the Dutch both acted as intermediaries in the conclusion of peace between Sweden and Russia. The antagonism between the Dutch and the English, which under

Cromwell led to an open rupture,[4] was nourished in the first half of the seventeenth century, both by rivalry in colonial trade and by a struggle for mastery of the Northern and Russian markets. Trade with Russia brought in profits that were no less colossal than those from colonial trade. Under Alexei (1645–76), exploitation of the splendid forests of mast timber along the river Yug[5] was leased to a foreign company which loaded four ships with this timber. Wood that cost them between 25 and 30 kopecks was sold abroad for four or five roubles. When the Dutch managed to oust the English by kindling the anger of Russian monarchists against 'regicides', within a few years they had about 200 agents in Archangel alone.

This was how those 'British interests' were created in Russia which called for diplomatic protection. Just as in the Netherlands, Germany and the Scandinavian countries, it was, in the main, members of the Company of Merchant Adventurers of England who served as England's diplomatic agents, so in Russia these agents were members of the Russia Company. The English intermediary at the peace conference at Stolbovo was also a member of the governing board of this company, one Meyrick.[6] 'The colonial system ripened trade and navigation as in a hothouse. The "companies called Monopolia" (Luther)[7] were powerful levers for the concentration of capital. The colonies provided a market for the budding manufactures, and a vast increase in accumulation which was guaranteed by the mother country's monopoly of the market.' (Marx)[8]

In the England of 1550–1650, a dominant role was played by monopolistic companies whose principal sphere of activity still lay in Europe. Behind them stood the flourishing woollen industry. If England was able already by the beginning of the eighteenth century to claim commercial supremacy, this was due, even then, to her industrial supremacy. The East India Company still played, until the end of the eighteenth century, a very minor role compared with the Merchant Adventurers of England, who provided the English woollen industry with an outlet, first through Antwerp, and later through Hamburg, and with the Russia Company, which organised the exports to Russia.

It is quite understandable that the Russia Company should have wielded great influence, and should have been able to 'raise a cry'. That its 'cry' was listened to very attentively we have seen through the whole story of the relations between England and Russia. It is enough to recall that among the members of the Russia Company, as of the Hamburg Company, were many representatives of the 'gentlefolk'. While in the list of members of the Hamburg Company we find Robert Sidney, Earl of Leicester,[9] the Earl of Carlisle,[10] Lord

Churchill, Lord Ashley,[11] etc, in the first charter of the Russia Company we find among the names of its founders the Marquis of Winchester, the Earl of Arundel, the Earl of Bedford and the Earl of Pembroke.[12]

But in the first half of the seventeenth century the Russia Company's 'cry' was not so powerful as to drown the 'cries' of the representatives of other 'British interests'. While relations between this company and the Hamburg Company continued to be friendly, already at the end of the sixteenth century new companies had arisen whose interests were far from coinciding with those of the Russia Company. Let it be recalled that the Company's prosperity depended, unlike that of the Hamburg Company, not only on the exportation of English manufactures to Russia, but also on the success of its whale-hunting, and on its transit trade in Persian silk across Russia. Naturally, its interests clashed with those of the Eastland Company, founded in 1579 to carry on trade in the Baltic Sea, which did not, of course, observe the strict prohibition on trading with Russia through Narva, and those of the Turkey Company, founded in 1581 and launched immediately into organising the purchase of raw silk in Persia. Though the competition from the first-named company proved to be harmless, that from the second increased steadily all through the seventeenth century – incidentally, because the execution of Charles I made not the slightest impression on the Turkish Sultans.[13] But this was competition only in one sphere, in the trade in raw silk, a sphere in which both the Russia Company and the Turkey Company soon encountered a more dangerous rival, namely, the East India Company. Although, as we have seen, the Russia Company had not given up hope, even in the eighteenth century, of getting hold of the Persian silk trade, it was obliged already by the end of the seventeenth century to concentrate on trade in products of Russian origin, especially because the whale-hunting business, which had become less and less profitable owing to the decline in the number of whales, ceased to possess any special importance for it after the foundation in 1670 of the Hudson's Bay Company, in North America. The Russia Company began to be threatened from that direction likewise with competition in the trade in naval stores. In 1699, it was decided that the Commissioners of Customs should present to both Houses during each session of Parliament a report on the quantity of naval stores that would be imported into England from Russia. Anderson[14] thinks that this was because the government at that time had in mind promoting the importation of naval stores from North America.

Such, then, was the position of the Russia Company as the eighteenth century opened. The year 1699 saw an end to the everlasting altercations with the so-called 'interlopers', that is, those Englishmen who, attracted by the profitable trade with Russia, carried on their commercial activity without the Company's permission, being unwilling to pay its high entrance-fee. In this year the fee was reduced to £5, which meant that the trade practically ceased to be a monopoly. The Company continued, as before, to represent the interests of the Russia trade, and to fight for them, both in the City and in Parliament.

However, as we have seen, it was not the only company. Besides its 'cry' there rang out the 'cries' of other interested companies or groups of merchants and industrialists. There can be no doubt that all these groups strove to influence the government to favour their interests, trying to make its policy serve them. But, the more complex became the sphere of commercial and industrial interests, the wider and more numerous were external dealings and the more involved relations with other countries, so the more stubborn and bitter inevitably became the struggle between these different groups. That one of them was most likely to triumph whose particular interest corresponded at a given moment with the general direction of foreign policy, which, *à la longue*, was determined by the general interests of 'national' trade as a whole.

Under Elizabeth, the whole of foreign policy was determined by the antagonism between England and Spain. Hence the constant alliance with the Netherlands. Relations with France were generally friendly, insofar as France continued to wage her time-honoured struggle against the Habsburgs of Spain.

In the first half of the seventeenth century, an antagonism flared up ever more strongly between England and Holland, and in Cromwell's time this led to a protracted war. At the end of the seventeenth century, during the War of the English Revolution,[15] France again became the hereditary enemy which she had been at the time of the Hundred Years' War.[16] Holland, in the words of Frederick II, became a mere longboat towed behind the British man-of-war.[17] France's allies were England's enemies, and vice-versa. The so-called system of the balance of power was governed by the antagonism between, on the one hand, France and the powers in tow to her, and, on the other, England, Austria and Holland.

Russia had no place in either of these combinations. Whereas at the end of the fifteenth century the Turkish menace had led Venice, the Pope and the Emperor Maximilian to make an unsuccessful attempt to draw Russia into European affairs, now, on the contrary, Russia herself was obliged – and the more insistently as the end of the seventeenth century approached – to seek alliance with European powers.

Russia's immediate enemies were now Poland, Sweden and Turkey. But in all three of these countries French influence was predominant, with France seeking to use them against the Habsburgs. So long as England's foreign policy was not determined by antagonism with France, an alliance between England and Russia was a political impossibility. This was eventually understood by the Muscovite diplomats, and they ceased to pester England. Not being at home in the political relationships of Western Europe, in 1687 they proposed an alliance to Louis XIV, but were told, categorically, that 'between France and the Emperor there is perpetual enmity, and between the Sultan and the King, on the contrary, perpetual peace and enduring friendship prevail'.

Russia took part in the Holy League against the Turks,[18] but she was treated as a third-rate power. Right down until the Great Northern War she was left out of account in Western Europe's political combinations.

At the beginning of the eighteenth century, when the War of the Spanish Succession coincided with the Great Northern War,[19] the state of affairs altered. An alliance between England and Russia became possible. But was this possibility transformed into actuality, as Marx supposed? Was it the case that the oligarchy which held power in England after 1689, together with the Russia Company, systematically supported Russia and helped her to crush Sweden? Real history has already shown us that it was not the Tatar Khans who created absolutism and Peter, that it was Anglo-Dutch capital that 'Europeanised' Muscovy, and that England was as 'guilty' of creating Muscovy as of creating Japan. Let us now see whether it is true that real history reveals the British statesmen of the eighteenth century to have been systematic accomplices of Peter I.

Notes

1. Sir Josiah Child (1630–1699), President of the Court of Directors of the East India Company, wrote, in *A New Discourse of Trade* (1693), of 'the Dutch, who have no Eastland companies, yet have ten times the trade to the Eastern parts as [sic] we have ...' (p83) (translator's note).
2. Spitsbergen is now usually shown on maps under its Norwegian name, Svalbard (translator's note).
3. The Dutch at this time took the line that all seas should be 'free' to all nations alike (translator's note).
4. A reference to the first Anglo-Dutch War, 1652–53 (translator's note).
5. The Yug is a tributary of the Northern Dvina (translator's note).
6. Sir John Meyrick (d 1632) acted as agent of the Muscovy Company in Russia (1567–1600) and was England's ambassador in Russia from 1601 (translator's note).

7. Martin Luther (1483–1546) was the German monk who began the Protestant Reformation (translator's note).
8. Karl Marx, *Capital*, Volume I, Penguin edition, 1976, p918 (translator's note).
9. Robert Sidney, Earl of Leicester (1563–1626) was a member of the East India and North West Passage companies (translator's note).
10. The same man who in 1664 tried unsuccessfully to obtain a renewal of the English privileges in Russia (author's note). Charles Howard, First Earl of Carlisle (1629–1685) was Ambassador Extraordinary to Russia, Sweden and Denmark, 1663–64 (translator's note).
11. John Churchill, First Duke of Marlborough (1650–1722), repeatedly defeated the armies of Louis XIV. His wife was a confidante of Queen Anne, and he became fabulously rich, building Blenheim Palace; Anthony Ashley Cooper, First Earl of Shaftesbury (1621–1683) led the opposition during the reign of James II (translator's note).
12. William Paulet, First Marquis of Winchester (1485–1572) was Elizabeth's Lord Treasurer; Henry Fitzalan, Twelfth Earl of Arundel (1512–1580) was Lord Steward and a member of the royal council; Francis Russell, Second Earl of Bedford (1727–1785) was a privy councillor and diplomat; William Herbert, First Earl of Pembroke (1506–1570) was Steward of the Royal Household (translator's note).
13. On 18 August 1648, Ibrahim I had been removed 'by legitimate means', and executed. He was the first Sultan to suffer such a fate (author's note). Ibrahim I (1640–1648) was overthrown by a revolt of the Janissaries after a period of misrule (translator's note).
14. Adam Anderson, *An Historical and Chronological Deduction of the Origins of Commerce ...* (1801), Volume 2, p644 (translator's note).
15. The War of the English Revolution, also known as the War of the Grand Alliance, the War of the League of Augsburg and the Nine Years' War, lasted from 1689 to 1697, when it was ended by the Treaty of Ryswick. The campaign in Ireland which included the Battle of the Boyne (1690) was a 'side-show' of this war (translator's note).
16. The Hundred Years War (1337–1453) was a dispute fought intermittently between the kings of England and France over the succession to the French crown (translator's note).
17. Frederick the Great uses this phrase in his *Histoire de mon temps* (translator's note).
18. The 'Holy League' of Austria, Venice, Poland and Russia waged war against Turkey between 1683 (when the Turks were repulsed from Vienna) and 1699 (translator's note).
19. The War of the Spanish Succession, in which France was opposed by Britain, Holland, Austria and other powers, lasted from 1701 to 1714: the Great Northern War between Sweden and Russia lasted from 1700 to 1721 (translator's note).

Chapter Seven

The Great Northern War

Marx is perfectly right to ascribe such great importance to the Great Northern War in relation to the rise of Russia. In the struggle for political ascendancy in the Baltic, power passed, in turn, from the Hansa to Poland, to Denmark, and to Sweden. In 1617, Russia finally lost hope, for the time being, of obtaining an outlet to the West. In the second half of the seventeenth century, Sweden almost succeeded in making the Baltic Sea into a Swedish lake. In 1700, the relative lengths of coastline belonging to the countries around the Baltic were, if we take Denmark's share as 1: Germany, 2, Sweden, 10, Russia, 0. Thus, the Great Northern War was essentially a duel between Sweden and Russia: whoever was for Sweden was against Russia, and vice versa. As a result of the Great Northern War, Sweden lost her predominant position in Northern Europe. Political hegemony in the Baltic passed to Russia, which was to retain it until the last quarter of the nineteenth century.[1]

Marx is right, too, when he says that the Great Northern War was a turning point, in the sense that it was only after this war that Russia became a European power. Only after she had acquired a solid point of support in the West could she begin her expansion towards the South and the East, so as, after gathering fresh strength, to resume her *Drang nach Westen*,[2] and, beginning in Catherine II's time, to play the role of ruler of Europe's destiny.

This is how the Russian historian Solovyov describes the significance of the Great Northern War:

> The steppe and Eastern period of Russian history came to an end, and the maritime and Western period began. For the first time, the Slavs, after their usual retreat

> before the German tribes towards the East and the steppes, returned to the West and forced the Germans to yield to them part of the coast of the 'Northern Mediterranean', which now ceased to be German.[3]

The only difference is that what the one welcomes, the other curses.

Even better does Marx depict the consequences that followed from the transference of the capital from Moscow to St Petersburg. If he ascribes the success of this move to the personal initiative of Peter, that is because he has completely ignored the entire internal process that took place in seventeenth-century Russia which prepared the conditions needed for it. St Petersburg at last took the place of Archangel. After Peter's decree ordering that all goods for export be sent to St Petersburg, exports from Archangel declined by almost the same amount (2,049,000 roubles) as those from St Petersburg increased (2,135,000 roubles). The total sum of exports from these two cities remained the same. Peter had merely shifted the channel by which Russian goods found their way to the West. This time, too, economics proved stronger than politics. The attempt that was made after Peter's death to move the capital back to Moscow did not succeed. The window into Europe had finally been opened.

But whereas Russian historians are convinced that England systematically obstructed Peter in his struggle with Sweden, Marx, on the contrary, affirms that Peter was able to overcome Charles XII[4] only thanks to England. Whereas Martens compares England's conduct in the period of the Great Northern War to her conduct during the Crimean War, seeing in both instances only a desire to harm the interests of Russia, Marx follows this example with this difference alone, that *he* sees England's conduct in the *opposite* light. The Russian historians, having explained England's policy by reference to commercial interests, are in no way embarrassed by the fact that England was risking her extensive commercial interests in Russia: to Martens, what she feared was the strengthening of Russian influence on the Bosphorus. Marx blames England for having – for the sake of what he considers the insignificant interests of some merchants, who covered with their complaints the criminal conduct of her ministers – raised up for herself a powerful enemy on the Bosphorus. Both the Russian historians and Marx alike look at the events of the early eighteenth century through the prism of the sympathies and antipathies of the second half of the nineteenth. It would be possible to adduce a great number of quotations to show that other contemporary historians too, both Western European and Russian, still continue to evaluate the events of the Great Northern War from these two points of view.

In 1900, that is, almost simultaneously with the re-issuing of Marx's work, there appeared in Volume 10 of the *Transactions of the Royal Historical Society* an article on the same subject. It was the text of a paper read to the society entitled 'Notes on Diplomatic Correspondence Between England and Russia in the First Half of the Eighteenth Century'.

The author, Mrs D'Arcy Collyer, considered it necessary to mention, at the start, that she was dealing with material which had not previously been worked upon at all: 'So far ... as I was able to discover, the detailed action of the British government in these early diplomatic relations with Russia could be studied only in the manuscripts of the Record Office and of the British Museum ...' (p143) What conclusions did she draw from her study of these documents which she offered for the attention of the learned body? They coincided so closely with Marx's that they sometimes seem to repeat them word for word.

In order to understand the 'real history' of relations between England and Russia, it is necessary not to lose sight of the fact that the Great Northern War coincided chronologically with the War of the Spanish Succession. At the same time as a coalition against Charles XII was being contemplated in the North, a new coalition was being prepared in the South against Louis XIV. Both of these wars were waged within the borders of Europe. But whereas in the War of the Spanish Succession what was being decided, together with the question of the domination of the Mediterranean, was that of the domination of the Atlantic Ocean, the main highway of world trade in the seventeenth century, and so the question of who was to have commercial preponderance and domination in the New World, in the Great Northern War what was being decided was the question of preponderance in the Baltic Sea, which had become, to an even greater extent than the Mediterranean, a mere by-road. The time when the Baltic, on the one hand, and the Mediterranean, on the other, were the principal reservoirs of European trade had long passed. What was a question of life and death for the Baltic powers – which of them was to be dominant in the Baltic Sea – was for England and the great powers of Europe of merely local interest. Holland, which had profited by the decline of the Hansa to acquire commercial preponderance in the Baltic, and England, which had appeared there in Holland's wake, sought only to ensure that the Sound[5] remained open, and, depending on that situation, each supported now Denmark, now Sweden. The countries round the Baltic, like Russia, were for them merely so many objects of commercial exploitation. Politically, Sweden and Poland followed the lead of

France which, from time to time, giving them a substantial tip for their trouble, would set them on either Turkey or the Habsburg Empire. For the theoreticians of Europe's balance of power, Sweden was no more a European power than Russia was.

In the very midst of the War of the Spanish Succession one publicist wrote:

> The reader, one would think, need not be told that Europe here is to be taken in a strict sense, for those nations of Europe who are concerned in the present war with France, on one side or the other; without concerning ourselves with the affairs of Sweden or Muscovy, Hungary or the Turks, which, though it is true they are in Europe, yet as this is the governing part of Europe, it has been a word legitimated to this part by the custom of the times.[6]

The facts very soon compelled a change in this conception. It turned out that the interests of England, France and Austria were so strongly affected by the Great Northern War that one could as little separate the North of Europe from the West as separate the East from the North. Something that had long been accomplished in the sphere of economics had to be given recognition in that of politics. The European powers might wish as much as they liked for the return of those times when Russia belonged to Asia, but their desires were just as impotent as the fervent endeavour of the opposition to Peter to wrest Russia away from Europe.

> How tenacious were the established political conceptions of the day is shown by the fact that the appearance of an influential new power, in the shape of Russia, made at first no impact on the idea of the balance of Europe. European political thought found a way of evading the problem. Just as the internal balance of the German group of states had been linked with the general balance of Europe in such a way that a special balance of Germany had been constructed, and the preservation of the balance of Europe made dependent on the preservation of this balance, so now there arose the idea of a balance of the North, to be linked in the same way with the interest of preserving the balance of Europe (Kaeber, op cit, p78).

This desire was, of course, strongest of all in France. There they cherished the hope of realising it after Peter's death, and they had not abandoned that hope even by the middle of the eighteenth century. But other European powers dreamt of it, too – especially those whose interests conflicted with the interests of Russia. These hopes influenced the policy of the European powers at the court of St Petersburg right down to the time of Catherine II. Until the end of the War of the Spanish Succession, however, England was wholly absorbed in the struggle with France, and for her the question of relations with Sweden was decided only in connection with that struggle. Sweden must not be allowed to form an alliance with France, and Turkey must be restrained from going to war with Austria. All the efforts of English and Dutch diplomacy were concentrated on these tasks.

On 9 July 1698, France concluded a defensive alliance with Sweden – this time in the face of strong opposition from the anti-French party. But in 1700 William III,[7] acting for both England and Holland, succeeded in concluding a similar alliance with Sweden – that alliance to which Marx refers so frequently. At this time, relations between Sweden and Russia were friendly. Charles XI not only allowed Peter to buy 600 guns in Sweden, but also promised to make him a present of 300 more, and this was duly done after he died.[8] That was during the war with Turkey.[9] There were no grounds for fearing a war between Sweden and Russia. Sweden's superiority in strength was beyond any doubt.

With what disdain the chief European powers looked on Russia was shown at Karlowitz, where in 1699 England and Holland acted as principal intermediaries in bringing about peace between Austria, Venice, Poland and Russia, on the one hand, and Turkey on the other. This was Russia's first experience of participation in a European coalition. The Russian ambassador complained bitterly to Holland and England that they concerned themselves exclusively with the interests of Austria, and showed more regard for Venice than for Russia. But England and Holland needed to set Austria's forces free for the coming war with France. The congress at Karlowitz – the first at which Russian diplomats encountered those of Europe – showed how ignorant these Asiatics were, compared with the Europeans, and how 'piously' the European powers fulfilled their obligations.[10] Only in the period of the Great Northern War did Russia's diplomats learn to exploit the differences between the European powers, and their immediate 'instructors' in this high art, as in military matters, were the Swedes.

But perhaps England, in spite of everything, acted in quite the opposite way – failed to fulfil her obligations to Sweden, and instead helped Russia? Once again, real history gives us the answer.

We have seen that even the Muscovite diplomats did eventually get to understand that, in spite of all the advantages England gained from trade with Russia, there was no prospect of persuading her to agree to a political alliance. We have seen how the attempt to form an alliance with France ended in fiasco. Russia's participation in the coalition against the Turks showed that Austria, too, had need of her only insofar as she could be made use of against Turkey.

But allies were needed. After Carlisle's unsuccessful embassy in 1664, when the Dutch agitated so zealously against the privileges of the Russia Company, the English resolved to take advantage of the first favourable opportunity to recover their former monopoly in Russia. This opportunity was presented by Peter's visit to Holland and England. In October 1697, English envoys headed by Lord Pembroke (a scion of the same noble house as the Pembrokes who had founded the Russia Company)[11] approached Peter with a joint letter in which, after mentioning that 'the English, more than any other people in Europe, have traded and worked with Russia with great benefit and profit to both sides', requested that 'the English merchants be given back the right of residence they enjoyed for so many years, together with their usual privileges, free of tax'. In short, they wanted to re-establish in Moscow the former English Steelyard.[12] On top of this, they asked for the grant of a tobacco monopoly.

Despite all his goodwill towards the English, the autocrat Peter could not restore the privileges that had been taken away in 1649, but they did receive a monopoly of the importation of 'the nicotine-bearing herb commonly called tobacco'. Local cultivation of tobacco was to be permitted only in Little Russia,[13] and its introduction thence into other provinces of Muscovy was forbidden, on pain of confiscation. In 1702, the English obtained the monopoly of the trade in flax and its export from Russia, despite a strong protest from Russian merchants.

In exchange for these favours, Peter received only courtesy and an old frigate given him in 1697 by William III. England remained deaf to all his proposals. In 1704, one Whitworth was sent to Russia as an envoy extraordinary.[14] It was his task to assure Peter that, *in the event of peace being concluded between Russia and Sweden*, Queen Anne[15] would not neglect his interests. The real purpose of his mission was to obtain new privileges for the English. They wished to add further monopolies to their control of flax and tobacco. In particular, he was to petition 'that they may be permitted to buy and export pitch and tar and other naval stores for the use of this our kingdom'.[16]

Whitworth was received with exceptional ceremony. Peter wished by this reception to emphasise how highly he valued good relations with England. But Whitworth, for his part, behaved haughtily. He rebuffed a proposal that England mediate between Sweden and Russia; he declined to accept Peter's assurances that he did not intend to build warships in the Baltic; and when it was put to him that Narva and St Petersburg could develop trading connections with England, he replied that the Swedes would not allow English ships to enter those ports. However, he warned his own government that 'no applications being made to the Russians except on this account (that is, the grievances of English merchants or the English commercial interests), they are apt to suspect we have great want of their commodities, but little esteem for their force and friendship'.[17]

And, in fact, Peter and his assistants did soon come to realise this. Whitworth in Russia and the English government in London provided him with two striking lessons on the matter. The first was the order given, in the interests of the English tobacco monopoly, for the English craftsmen who had been teaching the Russians how to process tobacco to leave Russia immediately, and for all the materials used in this instruction to be 'discreetly' destroyed. After seeing to the fulfilment of the first part of this order, the English ambassador proceeded to carry out the second. This is how he described his exploit:

> The same evening I went to the workhouse together with Mr Parsons, my secretary, and four of my servants. We spent the best part of the night in destroying the several instruments and materials, some whereof were so strong that they obliged us to make a great noise in pulling them to pieces ...' He would have liked to save some of the materials for other uses, 'but my orders were too precise, and no time was to be lost, nor durst I then let anything be carried out for fear of suspicion, and I hear the burgomasters are most vexed at this loss.[18]

Yet Peter I still stayed silent. Whitworth himself explained this indulgence by the Tsar's desire that England should undertake mediation between Russia and Sweden and help him to obtain an honourable peace.

Let us see how the Russian ambassador was treated in London. At the end of 1706, Peter sent thither A.A. Matveyev,[19] his ambassador in the Hague. The ambassador's task was to explain how advantageous for the English it would be for Russia to obtain convenient harbours on the Baltic coast: 'Russian goods will be sent to England safely and quickly, several times a year, and not as happens now from Archangel; and these Russian goods would be cheaper, for the Baltic ports are nearer to Moscow and the other principal cities, and there is easy access to them by waterways.'[20] Nor was that all. As Peter now appreciated that other arguments were needed if he was to impress the English government, he offered, through Matveyev, to join the 'Grand Alliance' against Louis XIV. In addition – and this was fresh evidence of the 'Europeanisation' of Russian diplomacy – Matveyev was instructed to discover whether he could bribe any of the English ministers, and Marlborough in particular.[21] Peter was agreeable, if need be, to giving up all his conquests in the Baltic region, even Narva, with the sole exception of St Petersburg: 'There can be no thought of yielding that.'

But the English ministers led Matveyev by the nose and fed him with 'sweet and barren words'. Several months went by. With the arrival of Marlborough the situation changed. Peter agreed to let him have one of the Russian principalities – he could chose Kiev, Vladimir or Siberia – and an income, guaranteed for life, of 50,000 thalers.

Obliged, at last, to speak plainly, the English ministers told Matveyev that they could not offer their mediation between Sweden and Russia. Professor Martens, who was familiar with the schemings of 'perfidious Albion', explains this attitude as due to the fact that 'the English government did not wish to contemplate the possibility that Russia might become a Baltic power'. But, according to Matveyev, Marlborough and Godolphin[22] said to him: 'Can we, for the sake of mere commercial gains from Muscovy, irritate the King of Sweden now that he is so powerful, and while we are at war with France?'

These negotiations were taking place when Charles XII was at the height of his power, when he had just concluded the Peace of Altranstädt and become 'the arbiter of Europe',[23] and was preparing, on the pretext of protecting the Protestants, to descend like a new Gustavus Adolphus[24] upon the Habsburg Empire – and when France, on the one hand, and the 'Grand Alliance', on the other, were exerting all their efforts to win the Swedish king to their side. And Marlborough had just returned to London from his visit to Charles XII's camp, where he and the Emperor had managed only with great difficulty to calm down the Swedish king. In order to deprive him of any pretext for intervening in the affairs of the Empire, a promise had been given that full satisfaction would be granted to the Silesian Protestants. To propose mediation to Charles XII for the conclusion of peace between him and Russia, even on such favourable conditions as Peter offered, at the very moment when the Swedish king, after crushing the King of Denmark and Augustus, was getting ready to teach Peter a second lesson like that administered at Narva[25] – why, such a proposal could be made only by naive 'Asiatics' who had forgotten that England had other commercial interests besides those connected with Russia.

Matveyev was particularly dissatisfied with the Russia Company. 'I wasted a great deal of time waiting on those boors the English merchants, but they, except for a certain Stales, not only failed to help me, but did not even answer me.' His dissatisfaction reached its apogee, however, when, as he was preparing to leave on 21 July 1708, the Sheriff ordered that he be detained on account of a debt of £50, and the bailiffs, after beating him mercilessly, threw him into a debtors' prison, from which he was released only when the merchant Stales stood surety for him.

It is hardly surprising that our poor 'Asiatic', after receiving such a lesson in refined European behaviour, was delighted when, on 30 July 1708, he at last left London, and no longer had to have dealings with this 'Christ-hating people, filled with rascally impiety'.[26]

Notwithstanding its contempt for Russia, even the English government was alarmed. But it quickly regained its composure when Whitworth replied from St Petersburg that 'points of honour are not so nicely distinguished here', and that 'the Muscovites are dangerous only to those who fear them, and the best way to make the Russians see reason is not to give way to them'.

On 28 September (9 October) 1708 the Swedish general Lewenhaupt was defeated at Lesnaya,[27] and on 27 June (8 July) Charles XII himself was defeated at Poltava. To the account of the battle which Peter sent to his people, he added the postscript: 'This has laid the cornerstone for St Petersburg.' And it really was the cornerstone for the entire edifice of his state and policy. 'From this time on,' Ranke adds, 'Russia began to lay down the law in Northern Europe.'[28]

The situation changed at once. When Peter made his triumphal entry into Moscow, he was greeted with the most flattering expressions by that same Whitworth. Recalling the sixteenth-century English tradition, he hailed Peter with the title of 'Emperor', and gave him such pleasure thereby that, despite all Whitworth's exploits in Russia, he received from the Tsar the gift of his portrait, set in diamonds. From a Saul whose conduct would have satisfied even David Urquhart, he had been transformed into Paul.[29]

On 5 February 1710, Whitworth apologised on behalf of Queen Anne for the insult offered to Matveyev, and, presenting a copy of an act which had just been passed by Parliament concerning the privileges of members of the diplomatic corps at the Court of St James's, he explained to Peter that it was not possible to punish all those who had offended Matveyev. Having been convinced that 'because of the defect, in that particular, of the former established constitutions of her kingdom', Anne could not deal with her subjects in the way he had dealt with the rebel Streltsy,[30] Peter decided to remain satisfied with the apology. Professor Martens, who still, 200 years later, burns with fury at 'perfidious Albion', explains thus this compliance on the Tsar's part: 'The great reformer did not think it possible to sacrifice the higher political interests of Russia to the justified feeling of indignation evoked by Matveyev's experiences in London.' Peter had still not lost hope that England would act as mediator for the conclusion of peace with Sweden. On 9 (20) August, an agreement was signed between England and Russia by which 'His Tsarist Majesty has decided, for the convenience of maritime commerce, to put all buoy, lighthouse, pilotage and anchorage dues on an equal basis with the British nation'.[31]

Did Peter's victory at Poltava make the same impression on the English ministers as on Whitworth? Did the new fact of Russia's military superiority over Sweden enter their consciousness? No. And the opinion they held to was strengthened by Peter himself when, through his insistent demand that Charles XII be expelled from Turkey,[32] he became involved in another war. Only at the end of 1711 did he succeed in extricating himself from this misfortune, by sacrificing Azov and Taganrog,[33] and abandoning to the mercy of the Turks the Slavs who, counting on Peter's aid, had risen in revolt.

In this episode of the Great Northern War, we encounter for the first time the characteristic features of Russia's new policy of conquest, or that constant 'mistake' of which she was accused by Russian patriots – inability to concentrate on one task at a time and a tendency to complicate the solution of one problem by bringing up others, or, to express oneself less euphemistically, her excessive greed. Throughout the whole of the eighteenth and nineteenth centuries, the Eastern Question was entangled with the Swedish and Polish questions and, to the great dissatisfaction of Russia's realistic politicians, hindered the forward march of Russia to the West, compelling her each time to make needless concessions, now to 'sly and arrogant' Prussia, now to 'ungrateful' Austria.

But in this episode we also observe another, no less interesting phenomenon. While Marx's bugbear, the Russia Company, despite all its Russophilia, proved unable to promote an alliance with Russia, its competitor, the Turkey Company, although its attention was focussed mainly on struggling against French influence at Constantinople, sounded the alarm very early on against Russia – much earlier than did the writers of the pamphlets discovered by Marx.

We have seen already how Russia was treated at the Congress of Karlowitz. Left unsatisfied, Peter made only a truce with the Turks, the terms of which were to be finally settled in Constantinople. The Russian ambassador Ukraintsev was received with the same pomp as Menshikov was 150 years later.[34] But he made an incomparably greater impression: he arrived in Russia's first naval frigate and honoured the Sultan with a salute of 40 guns. The Turks were no less impressed by this than were the members of the Turkey Company.

Whereas in the seventeenth century diplomatic dealings between Russia and England were conducted in most cases through members of the Russia Company, this situation ceased to apply already in the eighteenth, even though the frequent complaints by British ambassadors about the failure to receive their salaries show the material dependence of these diplomats on the British merchants in Russia, that is, on that same Russia Company. In Turkey the position was even simpler. ***Right down to 1803***, the British diplomats posted there were on the payroll of the Turkey Company. The first British envoys to Turkey were actual members of that company. And whereas until the eighteenth century their chief competitor in the Levant trade was France, from the first years of that century the Turkey Company began a campaign against Russia. It influence was already felt at the Congress of Karlowitz. W. Miller, the author of a very interesting article entitled 'Europe and the Ottoman Empire before the Nineteenth Century', is wrong in supposing that this anti-Russian influence made its appearance only in 1711, at the time of Peter's Turkish campaign:

> It is worth noticing [he says] that on this occasion the influence of England was, for the first time, used against Russia. Since the formation of the Russian navy, the English Levant Company, which, in the beginning of the eighteenth century, had all the trade of the Near East in its hands, had become alarmed at the rivalry of Russian merchants, and the English ambassador at Constantinople, in opposing for this reason the return of his Russian colleague, drew the attention of the Porte to the dangers of a political and religious propaganda by Russian agents among the Sultan's subjects.[35]

The details concern the history of the Eastern Question, but we cannot refrain from mentioning here that it is precisely in this circumstance that it is possible to find the key to understanding the policy of 'perfidious Albion' in the Near East in the eighteenth century, and of the independent position which British ambassadors took up in Constantinople. They frequently confronted the Cabinet in London with *faits accomplis*, and while they were not always in a position, any more than the Russia Company was, to push through their own policy – now anti-Russian, now anti-French – they nevertheless constituted a big factor in Britain's foreign policy, and contributed not a little to intensifying the contradictions in it as British trade interests became more complex.

After extricating himself with great difficulty from the Turkish war, Peter, showing the same impetuosity with which he had rushed to the Pruth,[36] now hurled himself westward. The War of the Spanish Succession was not yet over. In order to spare themselves fresh complications in the North, England, Holland and the German Empire issued on 10 March 1710 a declaration, aimed against Peter, regarding the maintenance of neutrality in all the territories of the German Empire – which, of course, included Pomerania. Justifying this action by the need to create a diversion in his war with Sweden, Peter invaded Pomerania.[37]

On 17 April 1711, Emperor Joseph I died. His successor was to be Charles, the Pretender to the throne of Spain.[38] The Tories, who had triumphed over the Whigs, used this occasion to make peace with France, on 8 October 1711.[39]

By the beginning of 1714, the War of the Spanish Succession was ended. Britain now had her hands free.

But, while Marx was certainly mistaken in his view of British policy before 1714, was he perhaps right about the period after that date? True, Peter had already established himself on the Baltic coast, he had seized Finland, he had occupied positions in Germany; true, Charles XII, with an obstinacy that contemporaries found hard to understand, stayed stuck in Turkey. But if Britain had listened to the voices that were warning her of the new 'Russian menace', and had gone to the aid of Sweden, as she was obliged to do by the defensive alliance of 1700, Russia would have been hurled back into the depths of Asia.

What do we see? Precisely in 1715 Britain allies herself with Russia and starts up afresh the war with Sweden. This is what Marx says about it:

> During the year 1715 a northern alliance for the *partition*,

> not of Sweden proper, but of what we may call the Swedish Empire, had been concluded between Russia, Denmark, Poland, Prussia and Hanover. That partition forms the first grand act of modern diplomacy – the logical premise to the partition of Poland. The partition treaties relating to Spain have engrossed the interest of posterity because they were the forerunners of the War of Succession, and the partition of Poland drew an even larger audience because its last act was played upon a contemporary stage. However, it cannot be denied that it was the partition of the Swedish Empire which inaugurated the modern era of international policy. The partition treaty was not even pretended [*sic*] to have a pretext, save the misfortune of its intended victim. For the first time in Europe the violation of all treaties was not only made, but proclaimed the common basis of a new treaty. Poland herself, in the drag[40] of Russia, and personated by that commonplace of immorality, Augustus II, Elector of Saxony and King of Poland, was pushed into the foreground of the conspiracy, thus signing her own death warrant, and not even enjoying the privilege reserved by Polyphemus to Odysseus – to be the last eaten.[41] The participation in this partition treaty threw England within the orbit of Russia, towards whom, since the days of the 'Glorious Revolution' she had more and more gravitated. George I, as King of England, was bound to a defensive alliance with Sweden by the treaty of 1700 ... However, as Elector of Hanover he declared war against Sweden, which he waged as King of England.[42]

We shall not dwell on all the errors committed by Marx in this exposition, his unquestionably wrong estimation of these events, and the contradictions with his own article on the Schleswig-Holstein question. His basic mistake was the same as that made by Peter, when the Tsar became angry with Britain because, regardless of the alliance made between him and George I, she refused to help him in his struggle with Sweden. Having made an anti-Swedish alliance with George I in the latter's capacity as Elector of Brunswick-Lüneburg, an alliance which was essentially a renewal of the alliance already secured with Hanover in 1710, Peter was convinced that he had at last succeeded in achieving an alliance with Britain.

Here we observe one of the most curious episodes of world history: a number of 'autocratic' sovereigns conclude an alliance with a little German principality in full certainty that they can dispose of Great Britain just as they have disposed of the Lüneburger Heide.[43] George I himself, to whom had fallen in his old age such a tasty titbit as the British throne, had no great confidence that he would keep it for long, and, together with his loyal Hanoverians, he tried hard to feather his nest while the going was good, and acquire a few new possessions in Germany – in particular, Bremen and Verden.[44] This was the sole aim that he pursued with the persistence of a well-to-do peasant seeking to add an extra plot of land to his farm. He was as much at sea in the conflict between parties that went on in Britain as were the other autocrats, his colleagues. All he knew was that there was a Pretender who was out to take the throne of Britain away from him, that there was a party in Britain which helped this Pretender, and that he had therefore to support the other party, and he was sincerely astonished when that other party proved unable to render him such a small service as sending a couple of dozen frigates to the Baltic Sea to fight the Swedes.

The British ministers, aware of the Tory opposition at their backs and, at the same time, convinced of the need to maintain the House of Hanover (meaning all that the 'Glorious Revolution' had achieved), tossed about between George, who had to be granted some indulgences, and Parliament, for which they had to try to find some decent pretexts to cover with a constitutional veil the concessions they made to the ministers of Hanover.

Throughout the duration of the Great Northern War, Britain never declared war, either on Sweden or on Russia, and officially remained neutral. But whether George was at war with Sweden, as in 1719, or allied with her against Russia, he invariably exasperated his allies, because he could never fulfil the obligations he undertook. It would be difficult to say when he did most harm to Sweden – when he was her enemy, or when he was her ally.

In 1715, a British fleet began to cruise in the Baltic. But George, Elector of Hanover, could give orders to the British admiral only in his capacity as King of Great Britain, and Great Britain was not at war, either with Sweden or with Russia. So long as George had not quarrelled with Peter he was able to offer him some satisfaction, and one fine day Peter found himself commanding his fleet on manoeuvres in which, together with the Danish fleet, the British and Dutch fleets also participated. But, after escorting British merchant vessels into Baltic harbours, the British admiral had to return to London, and it was only in secret, in flagrant violation of his official instructions, that he was able to leave a few frigates behind for George in the latter's capacity as Elector of Hanover.

Peter soon realised that George, as King of Great Britain, was of no use to him whatsoever, and when he grabbed Mecklenburg he was even amazed that George, who had looked on calmly while he raged among other German territories, now suddenly sent him a protest. The former friends became so estranged that George contemplated seizing Peter's person. An expedition to Scania (Schonen) failed even in the preparatory stage. The allies did not trust each other. The Danes suspected Peter, and not without justification, of intending to establish himself permanently in Denmark and take control of the Sound. Peter, complaining that his allies were not fulfilling their obligations, did not hurry to fulfil his own, and it was only with great difficulty that he was got out of Denmark.

However, Charles XII (or rather, his advisors Görtz and Gyllenborg,[45] the Swedish envoys in London) now decided to save himself from the unwanted intervention of George of Hanover as King of Great Britain. The Swedish King, that bulwark of Protestantism in Germany, entered upon negotiations, through his advisors, with the Jacobites and with the Spanish minister Alberoni,[46] with a view to toppling George I from his throne. Furthermore, resolving to exploit Peter's animosity against George, the Swedes approached him, while the Russian minister at the Hague, Kurakin,[47] engaged in talks with Alberoni.

This complicated game broke down when, at the beginning of 1717, the Swedish ambassador in London, Gyllenborg, was arrested, together with several Tories. The British government lost no time in publishing Gyllenborg's correspondence, in which, incidentally, there were found letters from Peter's personal physician, Areskin.

But Gyllenborg's papers revealed other secrets, too. The future leader of Sweden's 'Hats'[48] was not only a talented diplomat, he also wielded a brilliant pen. In pamphlets which appeared simultaneously in French and English, this diplomatic Gil Blas,[49] who had with one hand been trying to restore the Stuarts to power in Britain, eloquently explained to the British with the other that they ought, in the interests of Protestantism, to support Charles XII, and, in their own commercial interests, to halt the advance of the Russians and help the Swedes to recover their lost dominions.

These pamphlets had started appearing in 1715, when Charles XII returned home from Turkey and Görtz's activities began. Besides the first two pamphlets, reprinted by Marx, there were others, most probably written by Gyllenborg. The arguments they develop are so similar to those of the pamphlets *The Northern Crisis* and *The Defensive Treaty* that it is difficult to resist the supposition that they, too, came from the pen of Gyllenborg or his assistants.

All these pamphlets turn around one question. British and Dutch merchants had hastened to form trade links with St Petersburg and Narva. In order to hinder this development, Charles XII placed the ports in question under blockade, and began to intercept British and Dutch ships. The situation became still more acute when Peter issued a decree by which all goods hitherto sent to Archangel had to be exported through St Petersburg.

Understandably, neither the British nor the Dutch merchants had any wish to wait until Charles XII had recovered his former possessions. And now, here were these pamphlets seeking to demonstrate that they had no right to do what they were doing, that the interests of Protestantism took precedence over those of a few merchants, and that on this question there could be no differences between honest Tories and honest Whigs, all of which was accompanied by a constant refrain about the increasing power of Russia.[50]

But who were the British merchants who were raising this cry? Marx had a ready answer: the Russia Company. However, until Peter closed the port of Archangel it was the *Eastland* Company that suffered worst from the Swedish privateers. The Eastland Company is often confused with the Russia Company. The latter, however, at first gained, and gained in two ways. It held a monopoly of the exportation from Russia of those goods of which Britain had special need at the time. Some of these goods were obtained from Sweden, but, with the growth of the Swedish navy, the export from that country of materials required for shipbuilding was subjected to serious difficulties. A company (the Tar Company of Sweden) was organised and given a monopoly in the export of tar and other shipbuilding materials. As far back as 1703, the English parliament had had to introduce bounties on the export of these materials from the American colonies, but this had not helped much up to now. And, as one of the pamphlets said, seeking to frighten the English with the excessive strength of Peter: 'The Tsar is unquestionably the absolute master of three-quarters of all the tar in the world, of all the hemp, of the best masts and of all the other goods we have been used to obtaining from the North.'[51]

That the Russia Company could not be particularly pleased with Peter's conquests on the Baltic coast – at least in the initial stage – is clear from the following argument: 'You yourself acknowledge that if, by the terms of peace, the Tsar retains any port on the Baltic Sea, then the Archangel trade will naturally fall off, to the prejudice of thousands of our people.'[52] This explains why the Russia Company's members received Matveyev so coldly.

But after 1715, the competing companies joined forces and,

together with the Dutch, vehemently demanded 'freedom of trade' with St Petersburg and Narva. And when a pamphleteer said to the Dutch that 'you, of course, are as ready to trample on this doctrine [that is, freedom of trade] as you were to trample on the cross in Japan',[53] they calmly replied that 'it matters little to Holland whether Sweden or the Tsar owns the provinces on the East of the Baltic Sea'.[54]

Marx himself admits that at this time the Baltic trade was particularly important by virtue not of its dimensions but of its nature. It was a period when a revolution was taking place in shipbuilding that was comparable to that which marked the first half of the nineteenth century. The construction of galleys was dying out; they were becoming as anachronistic as the sailing ship is today. The shipyards of Britain, Holland and France competed in turning out large sailing vessels with two, three or four decks. East India frigates (the 'Great Eastern'[55] of those days) were emerging from the yards more and more frequently. The manufacture of sails and ropes called for enormous quantities of flax and hemp. An ordinary vessel required for its sails up to 10 000 yards of canvas, 24 inches wide. Ireland was forcibly transformed into a country producing sailcloth. Canvas was brought out of Germany through Hamburg. Tar, pitch, potash (in which sails were boiled) and timber for masts were also needed in vast quantities. In short, these naval stores were at this time as important for Britain's industry and trade as cotton was to become in the nineteenth century. An interruption in the supply of them meant that work in the shipyards came to a standstill.[56]

The 'Asiatic' Peter, whose skill at shipbuilding is so enthusiastically described by the pamphlet *The Northern Crisis*, understood this, too, and very well, just as he had at last understood that it was by stirring up public opinion against the Hanoverian king that he could best exert influence on parliament. He had mastered the lessons of Görtz and Gyllenborg. And this truth had been learnt, also, by such true Muscovite diplomats as Kurakin.

When, in 1718, Charles XII was killed by a bullet fired either by a Dane or by a hireling of the Swedish oligarchy, and all danger of attack from Sweden disappeared, and when George I hastened to conclude an alliance with Sweden, Kurakin wrote from London:

> If they open hostilities against us, we can show parliament and the people the justice of Russia's cause and the wrongness of the king and his ministers. We must approach the leaders of the Tory Party, and, through them prevent in Parliament the success of the proposals

> emanating from the Court: we must urge the British merchants who are interested in trade with Russia to put forward their representations, in the form of exchanges of letters: and we must publish anonymously in Britain information that will show the public what the ultimate aims of the ministry are, in the direction of encroachment on English liberty, and also what harm will be done to the Baltic trade, and so forth.

Peter I and his ministers in the role of defenders of English liberty! However, while slavishly copying the procedures of their Swedish mentors, the 'Asiatics' excelled them in practicality. On 18 June 1719, Peter published a declaration addressed to all the courts of Europe, but intended primarily for Britain and Holland, in which he guaranteed 'freedom of trade', and also a declaration specially for the benefit of British merchants trading within the borders of the Russian state. In this second declaration he wrote:

> For this reason His Tsarist Majesty graciously announces to the British merchants who are at present residing in Russia that, although His Majesty is distressed by the above mentioned aid which has been given to the Crown of Sweden against His Majesty, he does not hold the British people responsible, but only the Hanoverians and their party. All the British merchants residing in Russia can therefore rely, as before, upon His Majesty's gracious protection and on freedom of trade, and the said merchants can be sure that they will have nothing to fear in Russia as a result of the intrigues of the Hanoverian interest ...

In spite of this, relations between Russia and Britain grew worse by the day. In 1719, Sweden's side was taken, not only by Hanover, but also by Britain. After persistently refusing during the first half of the Great Northern War to mediate between Russia and Sweden, Britain now no less persistently offered her mediation in favour of Sweden, and backed her offer by sending into the Baltic a squadron under Norris's command.[57] Since Britain nevertheless did not declare war on Russia, the presence of this 'honest broker' did no good. In full view of the British fleet, Russian troops landed in Sweden and rampaged there no less vigorously than in Pomerania.

It must be remembered that, although relations between Britain and Russia worsened to such a degree that, on 23 November 1720, the Russian ambassador was asked to leave London within eight days, war was nevertheless not declared. Not George of Great Britain, but George of Hanover was at open enmity with Peter. Despite all the outward similarity between the operations of the British fleet in the Baltic at this time and its operations during the Crimean War, on this occasion there could not be only a 'sham war' against Russia, because officially there was no war at all. Such a 'sham war' with Russia, the causes of which lay not in the Russophilia of British statesmen, as Marx supposed, but in the contradictory commercial interests of Great Britain, which involved her from time to time in war with Russia, but also compelled her to spare her principal supply of raw materials and safeguard the interests of the Baltic trade, we encounter for the first time only in the period of the Seven Years' War.

But George of Hanover, in his capacity as King of Great Britain, and George of Great Britain, in his capacity of Elector of Hanover, deceived not only Marx, and not only the author of the third pamphlet he reprinted, which was obviously of Hanoverian origin; he continues to this day to confuse historians of that period. Where Marx saw Russophilia, the anti-Hanoverian opposition in Britain saw servility to Hanover. Contemporary historians try very hard to sort out all this muddle: some see in it subordination to the interests of Hanover, others explain it by deep Machiavellian calculations on the part of the British ministers, endeavouring to establish a political balance in Northern Europe, while a third group – notably the British historian Chance – seek to show that Britain acted in solidarity with Hanover only when her commercial interests required this to be done. But they all find the same difficulty in distinguishing Britain from Hanover, and often forget that George was the cook in Britain and the coachman in Hanover[58] – that, throughout the duration of the Great Northern War, Britain did not fight, either against Sweden or against Russia.

However, we have forgotten – as Marx also did – another personage who played, if not an elevated role, at least a profitable one amid all this confusion. This was the German 'Ivan Kalita', as one Russian historian calls Frederick William I.[59] It was the loftiest considerations of state, of course, that made him take a hand in the partition of the Swedish Empire. 'It was to the King's advantage to be allied with the most powerful, able and vigorous ruler of the North.'[60]

By guaranteeing Peter's conquests, Frederick William obtained a guarantee of his own acquisition of Stettin.[61] This great German patriot, who had sworn not to rest so long as one Swede remained on German soil, calmly accepted Peter's rule over Mecklenburg. 'In this matter,' says Ranke, 'Frederick William was much less resolute than Denmark or Hanover.'

The rivalry of the last-mentioned state was more fearful to him than the requisitions of the Russians. Peter's friendship was more advantageous. But he fell into a tragic situation when George quarrelled with Peter. Behind George of Hanover stood George of Great Britain. War between Russia and Britain seemed inevitable: 'Finding himself under strong pressure from both East and West, on the one hand preparing to seize once and for all an extensive territory, but on the other fearing to give up his alliance with Russia, Frederick William became so upset that, as a result of all these waverings, which hurled him from one extreme to the other, he at last took to his bed.'[62]

But fear of the alliance between George I, King of Great Britain, in his capacity as Elector of Hanover, on the one hand, and Sweden, on the other, overcame his fear of Peter. On 17 August 1719, Frederick William concluded an alliance with Hanover, and with Britain. The promissory note for Stettin that he held now bore, besides Peter's endorsement, also that of Britain.

In 1720, it became clear even to Sweden that George could put at its disposal only his Hanoverian troops, or, in other words, nothing at all. After agreeing to George's proposal to give satisfaction to Denmark and Prussia so as to isolate Peter, and after satisfying George himself, Sweden was left, completely exhausted, alone against Russia. After losing all hope of mediation by Britain, which was now preoccupied with the collapse of the South Sea Company,[63] Sweden was obliged to make peace with Peter on much worse terms than could have been obtained earlier.

Peter quarrelled so violently with Britain's statesmen that diplomatic relations between Britain and Russia were resumed only long after his death. That same Britain which, in Chancellor's letter, had called Russia's first Tsar 'Emperor of All Russia', and which, through Whitworth, had hailed him 'Emperor' after Poltava, officially recognised the imperial title for the ruler of Russia only in 1742.

However, despite all his resentment against Britain's statesmen, Peter did not interfere with his country's trade with Britain. That would have meant harming exports, and consequently reducing revenue. But he did decide to strike a blow at imports from Britain, that is, at the British cloth industry.

After recovering from his fever, or after losing his fear of being deprived of Stettin, Frederick William again became reconciled with Peter: 'In 1724 Prussia received the right to supply cloth to the whole Russian army. And Britain, through her political rivalry with the

Tsar, closed the Russian market against herself until 1730, and then tried in vain to reconquer it.'

Prussia's friendship with Russia lasted a long time. While Denmark, Russia, Sweden and Germany licked the wounds inflicted by the long war, 'Prussia only became stronger and more self-assured with every year that passed.'[64]

But this Great Northern War left Germany with the heritage of the Schleswig-Holstein question, which gave Russia her first excuse to play the role of arbiter in Germany. If we are to believe Bunsen, Prussia's ambassador in London, 'that heavy yoke under which Russia held Austria and Prussia until 1848 had its beginning in 1717'.[65]

Thus, 'real history' shows that British statesmen had as little to do with the rise of Russia as had the Tatar Khans. The true responsibility lay with European capitalism, which made the Romanovs its conquistadores, just as it made the Hohenzollerns its commercial travellers.

Notes

1. Length of the coastal borders of the Baltic countries:

	1700	1800	1900
Denmark	1	1	1
Germany	3	2.5	5
Sweden	10	7	7
Russia	0	3.5	10

This table, which graphically illustrates the increase in Russia's frontage on the Baltic Sea, is taken from H Kirchoff, *Seemacht in der Ostsee*, Kiel, 1907, p9 (author's note).

2. Riazanov here adapts the well known expression *Drang nach Osten*, used for Germany's 'striving towards the East' (translator's note).
3. Solovyov, *Istoriya Rossii*, Volume 17, p387 (author's note). Solovyov here uses 'German' in the Russian meaning which embraces all the Germanic peoples, the Swedes included (translator's note).
4. Charles XII was a noted warrior king of Sweden (1697–1718), the opponent of Peter the Great in the Great Northern War (translator's note).
5. The Sound is the strait between Sweden and the Danish island of Sjaelland, with Malmö on one side and Copenhagen on the other. It was the principal link between the North Sea and the Baltic before the Kiel Canal was opened in 1895 (translator's note).
6. *The Balance of Europe*, London, 1711, pp25–26, quoted by E Kaeber, *Die Idee des europäischen Gleichgewichts in der publizistischen Literatur von Sechzehnten bis zur Mitte des Achtzehnten Jahrhunderts*, Berlin, 1907, p78 (author's note). The original pamphlet is ascribed to Daniel Defoe (translator's note).
7. William III of Orange was Stadtholder of Holland before he became King of England (1689–1702) (translator's note).
8. Charles XI of Sweden (1660–1697) died in 1697 and was succeeded by Charles XII (translator's note).
9. Meaning the war of the 'Holy League', 1683–99 (translator's note).

10. The Congress of Karlowitz, 1698–99, ended in a treaty which added important territories to Austria, Venice and Poland. Russia made only a truce with Turkey, and the peace treaty between these powers was not signed until 1700 (translator's note).
11. Pembroke and his colleagues were in Holland in connection with the treaty of Ryswick, which ended the War of the English Revolution, and approached the Tsar before he moved on from Holland to England (translator's note).
12. 'Steelyard' was originally an English mistranslation of *Stalhof*, 'sample house', the Hanseatic League's depot in London (translator's note).
13. 'Little Russia' was the name used at this time for part of the Ukraine (translator's note).
14. He arrived in Moscow in February 1705 (author's note). Charles, Baron Whitworth (1675–1725) was the English Envoy Extraordinary in Russia between 1704 and 1710 (translator's note).
15. Queen Anne ruled Britain (1702–1714) as the last of the Stuart line (translator's note).
16. *Sbornik Russkogo Istoricheskogo Obshchestva*, Volume 39, 1884, p3 (author's note).
17. F de Martens, *Recueil des traités et conventions conclus par la Russie avec les puissances étrangères*, Volume 9 (10), St Petersburg, 1892, pp9–10 (Original English text of Whitworth's despatch of 23 May [3 June] 1705 from *Sbornik*, Volume 39, op cit, p100) (author's note).
18. Whitworth to Secretary Harley, 18 (29) July 1705, in *Sbornik*, Volume 39, op cit, p138 (author's note). Robert Harley, First Earl of Oxford (1661–1724), along with Churchill and Godolphin, dominated the government of Queen Anne. The ***burmisterskaya palata*** was the central financial department which administered the suburb of Moscow where foreign merchants lived (translator's note).
19. Andrei Artamanovich Matveyev (1666–1729) was Peter the Great's ambassador to Holland from 1699 to 1712 (translator's note).
20. Solovyov, *Istoriya Rossii*, Volume 15, p195 (author's note).
21. Peter had already heard of the high price demanded by the famous general, and added to the ambassador's instructions a note in his own hand: 'I don't suppose Marlborough will come down to this, since he is extremely rich, but offer him about 200 000, or even more.' (Solovyov, op cit, p195, author's note).
22. Sidney, Baron Godolphin of Rialton (1684–1706) was Lord Treasurer, and Marlborough's son-in-law (translator's note).
23. By the Peace of Altranstädt (1706), Peter's ally Augustus II, Elector of Saxony and King of Poland, submitted to the demands of Charles XII, who had already crushed Peter's other ally, Denmark. He renounced the Polish throne in favour of the Swedish King's protégé, Stanislas Leszczynski (translator's note).
24. Gustavus II, Adolphus, King of Sweden (1611–1632) inflicted a massive defeat on the imperial forces at Breitenfeld (1631), and then began an advance deep into Germany (translator's note).
25. Charles XII had beaten Peter at Narva in 1700, despite the Russians' fivefold superiority in numbers (translator's note).
26. The incident is described in detail in Solovyov, op cit, pp318–9 (author's note).
27. General Adam Ludvig Lewenhaupt (1659–1719) was defeated at Lesnaya on 9 October 1708 (translator's note).
28. Ranke, *Die grossen Mächte* (*Sämtische Werke*, Volume 24, p18) (author's note).
29. This Whitworth, one of the outstanding diplomats of his time, was the author of a book about Russia in 1710 in which, with great perspicacity, he explains the Russians' military victories by their 'passive valour', the power of endurance of the Russian peasants (author's note). (*An Account of Russia As It was in the Year 1710*, by Charles, Lord Whitworth, Strawberry Hill, 1758, p40, translator's note)
30. In 1698, the old-style Russian soldiers called *Streltsy*, who were opposed to Peter's 'Westernising' reforms, had rebelled against him, but were defeated, and Peter had over a thousand of them executed (translator's note).

31. Martens gives the text of this agreement in the contemporary German translation (Volume 9, pp21–3) (author's note).
32. After his defeat at Poltava, Charles XII fled to Turkish territory, from where he continued to defy Peter (1709–14) (translator's note).
33. Peter the Great built Taganrog on the north of the Don estuary following his capture of Azov in 1696, but had to cede it back to the Turks at the Treaty of Adrianople in 1713 (translator's note).
34. Emelian Ignatevich Ukraintsev (1641–1708) was a professional diplomat, and envoy to Poland and Turkey; Prince Alexander Sergeyevich Menshikov (1787–1869) was commander of Russia's forces in the Black Sea region on the eve of and during the Crimean war (translator's note).
35. *English Historical Review*, July 1901, p456 (author's note).
36. Angered by the Sultan's hospitality to Charles XII, Peter invaded Moldavia, which was then under Turkish suzerainty. At the River Pruth, his army was surrounded and threatened with annihilation, and Peter had to accept humiliating terms of peace, as mentioned above (translator's note).
37. Part of Pomerania (in Polish, Pomorze) had been annexed by Sweden during the Thirty Years War (1618–48) (translator's note).
38. Joseph I was Holy Roman Emperor, 1705–1711. Charles VI, his successor as Emperor (1711–1740) was also pretender to the crown of Spain (1700–1713) during the War of the Spanish Succession (translator's note).
39. Although preliminaries of peace between Britain and France were agreed in October 1711, the actual treaty was not signed (at Utrecht) until 1713. Britain, fearing that Charles VI would be too powerful as Emperor *and* King of Spain, abandoned her Habsburg ally and recognised the Bourbon candidate to the Spanish throne. The Emperor fought on alone for a time, but had to give up in 1714 (translator's note).
40. That is, tow (translator's note).
41. Polyphemus was the cyclops in the Odyssey who had trapped the Greek sailors in a cavern and planned to eat them one by one (translator's note).
42. Karl Marx, *Revelations of the Secret Diplomatic History of the Eighteenth Century*, Marx and Engels, *Collected Works*, Volume 15, London, 1986, pp41–2. George I was Elector of Hanover (1698–1727) and King of England (1714–1727) (translator's note).
43. 'Lüneburg Heath' is the plain in Lower Saxony, between Hanover and the River Elbe, where lay the Electorate of Brunswick-Lüneburg (translator's note).
44. Annexation of Bremen and Verden would give Hanover an outlet to the North Sea (translator's note).
45. George Heinrich, Freiherr von Görtz (1668–1719) was financial and diplomatic adviser to Charles XII; Count Carl Gyllenborg (1679–1746), later Chancellor and leader of the Hats, worked with him in the absence of Charles XII in Turkey (translator's note).
46. Cardinal Giulio Alberoni (1664–1752), the King of Spain's chief minister (1716–19), sought to restore the fallen power of Spain. Not confining himself to diplomatic intrigues, he tried to recover Sicily and Sardinia, but the British Navy put an end to his ambitions by destroying the Spanish fleet off Cape Passaro (1718) (translator's note).
47. Alexander Borisovich Kurakin (1676–1727) was Peter the Great's ambassador at the Hague and in Paris (translator's note).
48. In the 1730s, a party arose in Sweden who called themselves 'the Hats', from the three-cornered hat worn by officers and gentlemen, in opposition to the policy of Chancellor Horn (1664–1742), who favoured alliance with Britain. They nicknamed his adherents 'the Caps', and themselves favoured alliance with France (translator's note).
49. Gil Blas is the eponymous hero of an eighteenth-century French novel by Lesage: he is an amusing rogue and adventurer (translator's note).
50. All these pamphlets were published in De Lamberty's collection of *Mémoires pour servir à l'histoire du XVIIIe siècle*, Volume 9, Amsterdam, 1735. They include the *Lettres d'une*

personne de distinction de Rotterdam à un ami à Amsterdam and the *Lettre d'un ami à Dantzick à un ami à Amsterdam* (author's note).

51. *Mémoire d'une personne intéressée et sensible au commerce de la mer Baltique*, in Lamberty, op cit, p663 (author's note).
52. Ibid, pp224–5 (author's note).
53. Ibid, p232 (author's note). It was alleged against the Dutch that, in order to curry favour with the rulers of Japan, who were suspicious of Christian missionary activity, their merchants had consented literally to trample on crucifixes in the presence of their 'heathen' hosts (translator's note).
54. Ibid, p242 (author's note).
55. The 'Great Eastern', an iron steamship built at Millwall in 1858, was one of the wonders of the world at that time. She laid the first telegraph cable across the Atlantic in 1865 (translator's note).
56. 'If the Baltic convoy miscarried', Townshend wrote in 1715, 'such a scarcity of naval stores must ensue as would disable His Majesty from fitting out a fleet next spring upon any event' (J Chance, 'England and Sweden in the Time of William III and Anne', *English Historical Review*, October 1901, p684) (author's note).
57. Admiral Sir John Norris (1660–1749) was sent to the Baltic in 1709–21 to blockade ships supplying France with grain, causing diplomatic protests from Sweden (translator's note).
58. The crowns of Britain and Hanover were not separated until 1837. The accession of a woman (Victoria) to the British throne meant that the connection had to be broken, because the law of Hanover, like that of other German states, did not allow a female monarch to reign (translator's note).
59. Frederick William I, Elector of Brandenburg and King of Prussia (1713–1740) was of the House of Hohenzollern, the German Imperial house after 1871 (translator's note).
60. L Ranke, *Zwölf Bücher preussischer Geschichte*, Leipzig, 1874, p12 (author's note).
61. By the Treaty of Stockholm (1720), Frederick William acquired the Baltic port of Stettin (Polish Szczecin), the most important place in Pomerania (translator's note).
62. Ranke, op. cit, p27 (author's note).
63. The reference is to the collapse of the 'South Sea Bubble', the speculation mania which developed around a company granted by the British government a monopoly of trade with South America and the Pacific islands. When it failed, thousands were ruined and charges of corruption were brought against ministers and officials (translator's note).
64. JG Droysen, *Geschichte der preussischen Politik*, Volume 4, Leipzig, 1869, p193. The German historian shows amazing ability to slip out of the most impossible situations in which he finds himself through the need to defend the quite undignified policy of Prussia, and no less amazing is his invariable readiness to discover in every unexpected change of direction a profound historical significance (author's note).
65. The year 1717 saw the conclusion of an alliance between Russia and the Duke of Mecklenburg, cemented by the marriage to the Duke of Peter the Great's step-niece and guaranteed by the stationing of Russian troops in Mecklenburg. This alliance came to be seen as marking the beginning of Russian interference in German affairs, especially in the Duchy of Holstein, which adjoined Mecklenburg (translator's note).

Chapter Eight

The Anglo-Russian Alliance in the Eighteenth Century

That part of Marx's work which was published gave a more or less detailed analysis of Anglo-Russian relations in the period of the Great Northern War only. So far as the last three quarters of the eighteenth century are concerned, Marx confined himself, in what was printed, to publishing letters by three British ambassadors and extracts from a single manuscript. It seemed to him, however, that these documents fully demonstrated his principal thesis.

We have already seen how, carried away by his fundamental idea, Marx lost his way in the labyrinth of the 'secrets' and intrigues of international diplomacy at the beginning of the eighteenth century. Instead of analysing the whole international-historical situation of the time, which shows clearly how subordinate was the importance of the Great Northern War compared with the struggle for power in the Atlantic Ocean, he causes England to behave at the beginning of the eighteenth century as though all her thoughts should have been concentrated on conflict with Russia. 'Real history' shows that in this matter Marx was mistaken, as he was also in casting all the blame for a Russophil policy on the Whigs, since, if one can speak of definite Russian sympathies held by any English party at the beginning of the eighteenth century, then that party was, as we have seen, the Tories.

The foreign policy of the Whigs continued to be determined by the antagonism with France, against whom England came into collision in the Levant, in America and in Asia. But England could settle accounts with France only if she succeeded in finding allies against France on the Continent. She could then, using her superiority on the seas, strike blows at France in every corner of the world. Consequently, her attitude to other powers continued to be determined, in the main, by the relations between France and those powers. If, for a time, as happened after the end of the War of the Spanish Succession, when France had to abandon any aggressive policy, England's relations with that country were 'friendly', she thereby took up a hostile or cool attitude toward France's regular antagonists – which meant Austria above all.

When Karl Vogt, in his ***Studies in the Contemporary Situation in Europe***, claimed that 'Britain has never been able to harmonise with Austria for long', Marx replied:

> Indeed! The common struggle of England and Austria against Louis XIV lasted with brief interruptions from 1689 to 1713, that is, almost a quarter of a century. In the War of the Austrian Succession (1740–1748) England fought for about six years together with Austria against Prussia and France. It was not until the Seven Years' War (1756–1763) that England became the ally of Prussia against Austria and France, but as early as 1762 Lord Bute[1] left Frederick the Great in the lurch and put forward proposals for the 'partition of Prussia', first to the Russian minister Golitsyn,[2] and then to the Austrian minister Kaunitz[3] ... Protestant England has antipathies towards Catholic Austria, liberal England towards protectionist Austria, solvent England towards bankrupt Austria. ***But emotional factors have always been alien to English history***.[4]

And those same material interests which linked England with Austria also linked her with Russia: with one essential difference, to be sure, which retained its importance throughout the eighteenth century. There was direct antagonism between Russia and England only in relation to Turkey, and from the end of the eighteenth century this was supplemented by direct antagonism in Asia, on account of India. In every other part of the world, however, Russia and England clashed only insofar as Russia was for or against France, for Austria or against her. It was depending on this circumstance that British and Russian interests either coincided or clashed in Sweden, Poland and even Turkey, where direct antagonism with Russia was, until the last quarter of the eighteenth century, of secondary importance compared with the Anglo-French antagonism.

We have also seen that into British foreign policy from 1714 onward a new factor entered, namely, the House of Hanover, which brought in confusion by obliging the Whigs, at first, to take account of the interests of the Georges of Hanover, which did not always coincide with those of the Georges of Great Britain. By paying this price, the Whigs safeguarded the gains of the 'Glorious Revolution' – freedom from the hegemony of France. Around the House of Hanover were concentrated the defenders of the privileges of the Bank of England, the state's creditors, who at the very name of Stuart clutched their pockets in terror, and also the influential shareholders of the East India Company, etc. Reluctantly, they made concessions to the Hanoverians, bringing down on themselves the thunders of the anti-Hanoverian opposition, that is, the Tories, who constantly argued that the Whigs' Hanoverian policy was harmful to England's trade with Russia. Despite the Whigs' desire to be involved as little as possible in continental affairs, they were compelled to show some consideration to the interests of Hanover.

While the principal reason for the rupture between Peter and George was the former's occupation of Mecklenburg, the guarantee which Denmark received from Britain for her possession of Schleswig-Holstein necessarily served as an additional apple of discord, so long as there was a danger of an attack on Denmark by Russia in the interests of the Duke of Holstein, the husband of one of Peter the Great's daughters.[5] When in 1731 he was eliminated from the succession, under Anna Ivanovna,[6] one cause of enmity between Britain and Russia disappeared. That same year saw a reconciliation between Austria and Britain: Austria gave Britain satisfaction in the matter of the Ostend Company, whose competition irritated both the British and the Dutch East India companies, while Britain recognised the Pragmatic Sanction.[7] A new factor was thus created which facilitated *rapprochement* between Britain and Russia, as the latter was at that time closely allied with Austria. And in 1731, Britain took the first step towards resuming diplomatic dealings with Russia, by appointing Rondeau as resident minister.[8] The 'cry' of the Russia Company had at last been harkened to. As Rondeau himself wrote, his main aim was 'to be the instrument of reviving so valuable a branch of our trade as our woollen manufacture is, in a country where it has languished for some years'.[9] Through him an interesting memorandum on the state of trade with Russia was submitted by the Russia Company on 7 October 1732:

> The subjects of Great Britain export two thirds of all the hemp exported, more than half of all the hides exported, the same proportion of flax, more than three-fourths of

> all the linen and full that proportion of iron, all the potash, most of the rhubarb, a great part of the isinglass, bristles, wax, etc ... Notwithstanding our exports to England are very near if not full as large as in former years, yet our imports from England are less than they were ten years ago at the least one half ...

Until 1724, Russia bought cloth for soldiers' uniforms from Britain, but since then the Prussians had conquered this market. If steps can be taken to recover it for Britain, 'we make no doubt of seeing immediately a check to the progress of the Prussians in their woollen manufactures, and in no long time see the exportation of their woollen goods entirely dropped'.[10]

This fact – the continuing growth in Russia's exports to Britain and the decline in Britain's exports to Russia between 1716 and 1730 – was known to Marx. For him, it provided another example of the stupidity of the British ministers, who were exchanging, for Russia's benefit, their country's more profitable trade with Sweden for a less favourable trade with Russia.

But we have already seen that, while exports to Russia were particularly important for Britain's clothing industry, imports *from* Russia were of first-rate importance for British shipbuilding, that is, for that industry the development of which was the *sine qua non* of Britain's commercial supremacy.

Britain and Russia were on very bad terms between 1719 and 1731, but just as Britain could not do without the goods she obtained from Russia, so Russia could not do without her exports to Britain. For Russia, this was a matter, not merely of economic, but also of financial necessity, since to sacrifice that trade would mean sacrificing her customs revenue, which consisted mainly of duties on exports.[11] A rupture would damage only British manufacturing industry and benefit only its Russian counterpart. If it be added that the strictly protectionist tariff established by Peter in 1724 was replaced in 1731 by a liberal one, we can understand what an uproar the opponents of the Whigs' Hanoverian policy felt they had to promote in Britain. A rupture would have meant the final loss of the Russian market to their competitors.

In 1734, a trade treaty was concluded between Russia and Britain which conferred on the latter the most-favoured-nation status that Prussia had enjoyed since 1726. And, very soon, Rondeau was able triumphantly to inform the British ministers that he had persuaded the Russian government to purchase 40,000 yards of army cloth from British merchants, 'which has greatly distressed the Prussians'.

But commercial *rapprochement* was far from signifying political *rapprochement*. The old story was repeated. Seeing how keen the British were to obtain a trade agreement, the Russian diplomats decided to exploit the opportunity to conclude an alliance with Britain. But, despite all their importunity, the London Cabinet stubbornly rejected this proposal. Alliance with Russia would, at that time, entail only sacrifices, whereas a trade treaty would bring nothing but gain.

Politically, Russia still remained a second-class power which was not in a position to contribute much. After Peter's death, she was wholly absorbed in a struggle between the supporters and the opponents of his reforms, and if she played any role at all in foreign policy, it was as Austria's ally.

The situation changed only after the War of Polish Succession,[12] and Russia's new war with Turkey, closely connected therewith, which began in 1735. The unexpected successes of the Russian forces led by Münnich and Lacy[13] made all the greater impression because the Austrian forces fighting alongside them suffered one defeat after another.[14] Although eventually, when Austria, without warning her ally, made a separate peace with Turkey, Russia had to give up most of her conquests, her military prestige was now greatly enhanced.

Britain came forward with an offer to mediate when the war, which had begun mainly on the initiative of Osterman,[15] showed signs of resulting in a complete triumph over Turkey. And this offer was all the more suspicious in that it came from the British ambassador in Constantinople, Fawkener.[16] When Turkey recovered herself after her first defeats, Britain responded very unwillingly to Russia's proposal that she mediate, and peace was actually concluded through the mediation of France.

It was at *this* time, at the beginning of the 1740s, that Russia first emerged as an equal member of the Concert of Europe.

In 1741 [*sic*], the War of the Austrian Succession began. Austria, which had come out of her last war with Turkey weakened and humiliated, had now to confront, in Germany itself, a dangerous rival in the shape of Prussia. The influence of France predominated in Sweden, Poland, Turkey and Western Germany. In those conditions, Russia's alliance acquired great importance:

> It is understandable that at present St Petersburg or Moscow, depending on where the Emperor's court was, should have become the focus of European diplomatic activity – the arena where ministers of different European courts competed with one another in trying

> either to coerce or to persuade the Russian government to help Maria-Theresa, and thereby maintain the balance of power in Europe.[17]

For the first time in 200 years, instead of Russia asking Britain for an alliance, Britain made this proposal to Russia. Only then, in the instructions to the British envoys in St Petersburg, do we begin to hear, more and more frequently, that Russia and Britain are natural allies. Carteret informed the Russian envoy in London:

> His Majesty the King desires nothing more ardently than friendship with her Imperial Majesty [Elizabeth].[18] We are well aware of the weight of Russia in the affairs of Europe. Many are seeking the friendship of your court, but no alliance will be so much in conformity with the interests of Russia as an alliance with the maritime powers,[19] that alliance which Peter the Great strove for in order to maintain the balance of Europe. [Carteret omitted to refer to the fact that the Tsar did not always succeed in his striving.] I hope that her Majesty will not depart from these great principles. No other country sends to Russia so many ships in ballast, in order to take on cargoes of your goods, as Britain does. Other countries may send you ships laden with wine and other vanities, but no trade will bring you such profit as your trade with us.

In 1742, the first defensive alliance was concluded between Britain and Russia. But while, under the terms of this treaty, Britain refused to recognise as a *casus foederis* a war between Russia and Turkey, Russia, on her part, accepted as a *casus foederis* only a war *within Europe*.[20] It was this article that drew the principal attacks of the opposition in Britain, who claimed that the treaty was of value only for George of Hanover. In 1747, Britain and Russia made another pact, by which Russia undertook to despatch a corps of 30,000 soldiers to the Rhine. These were the first Russian soldiers to appear in the heart of Germany.

Even the Seven Years' War[21] could not disrupt this alliance, despite the Treaty of Westminster of 16 January 1756, by which Britain pledged herself to expel by force any non-German army that set foot on German soil. Britain confined herself to paying Frederick a subsidy: apart from that, once convinced of France's helplessness, she left him to the whim of fate. She did not interfere with Russia.

The British ambassador, Keith,[22] remained in St Petersburg and did all he could to embroil France with Austria and Russia. Russian troops ruthlessly devastated East Prussia, Pomerania and the Mark, and Britain did not lift a finger to honour her obligations.

But our historian forgot that, without her imports from Russia, Britain would not have been able to wage her war at sea – that, despite all her endeavours to transform North America, through export bounties, and Ireland, through cruel repression, into workshops for the production of the naval stores she needed, Britain could not manage without these Russian materials. How well Frederick the Great realised this can be seen from the fact that when Peter III of Russia[23] wanted to do a service to his idol and prevent Britain from 'betraying' the Prussian king, he wrote to the Russian ambassador in London, at the dictation of Count Goltz:[24]

> And above all make Britain understand that if Russia were to deprive her of these goods: hemp, mast timber, iron and hempseed oil, which the British cannot do without, she would be reduced to utter ruin.

A few days after the despatch of this instruction to Count Vorontsov, Peter III was overthrown, and the threat was not put into effect.

Here we meet again that typical phenomenon which we observed when Britain was waging a sham war against Russia in alliance with Sweden. Exports from Russia to Britain not only did not decline but, on the contrary, increased, while exports from Britain to Russia in 1760 were even less than in 1730. Marx deduces from these figures the same conclusion as before, namely, that friendship with Russia was harmful to British commercial interests, because exports from Britain to Russia fell steadily until 1760: but this is no less mistaken than his previous deduction. Whenever there was any coolness between Russia and Britain, exports from the latter to the former gradually declined, but exports from the former to the latter continued steadily to increase.[25]

Besides this principal factor, a certain role was also played, of course, by another material consideration, which is mentioned by Mehring: 'No English minister could interfere with the Baltic trade. When Pitt[26] took overall control he made no attempt to conceal from Frederick the fact that he could never count on seeing that stipulation of the Treaty of Westminster carried out.'[27]

Mehring only forgot that when, in 1757, Frederick's affairs were going better, and Britain attempted, by means of a special declaration, to recall that she could not allow any power to bring its troops into Germany, she received the same answer that Peter I and Catherine I had given, namely, that although Russia made no distinction between British interests and Russian interests, she would cease to do so the moment that Britain attacked her fleet. However, Mehring is right when he says that the damage done to the Baltic trade was fatal to the ministry. Consequently, Britain took the first opportunity to leave Frederick II to his fate.

Only now do we come to the moment when Russia began to play that role in European politics which for a long time to come was to make her the arbiter of Europe. 'Never were things more favourable to the plans for the aggrandisement of Tsardom than in 1762 when, after murdering her husband, the "great whore" Catherine ascended the throne. All Europe was split up into two camps by the Seven Years' War.'[28]

After smashing the colonial might of France in America and India, Britain found herself in a state of 'splendid isolation'. Having quarrelled with her 'ancient ally',[29] and having just treated Frederick like a squeezed lemon, Britain now clung to her 'natural ally', Russia; but Catherine responded the more coldly to this courtship the more fiercely the conflict between the two parties flared up in Britain and the more strained relations became between Britain and her American colonies. This circumstance affected the entire diplomatic correspondence of the British ambassadors in a particular way. Being obliged to make concessions to Russia, they sought to reduce their scope by indulging in the basest flattery of 'the Semiramis of the North'.[30] And this they did the more fervently – something which escaped Marx's notice – because they knew very well that their official correspondence was opened, that even a letter in cipher often reached its destination only after a copy of it was in the hands of the Russian government. The more difficult Britain's situation, the cooler became Russia's attitude. The more concessions Britain made, the more certain became Russia's conviction that, by bringing pressure to bear on Britain, it would be possible to get still more from her. Catherine agreed to a defensive alliance – she would not even hear of an offensive one, saying that *ce terme d'offensive la répugnait*[31] – but only on condition that Britain agreed to regard a war between Russia and Turkey as *casus foederis*, and also that Britain contributed financial support to Russian policy in Sweden and Poland. The letters from Macartney[32] and Harris belong to this period, one being written at the beginning of it and the other at its end. Both writers were gifted and unscrupulous British diplomats; they both, in obedience to insistent demands from London, showered the court of St Petersburg with compliments, and they both, in their secret communications, described unsparingly the foulness and barbarism with which the atmosphere of that court was saturated. They not only were *not* blind worshippers of Catherine, they both, and especially Harris, left a striking and savage description of the St Petersburg of that epoch. When it was learnt in St Petersburg that Macartney was to be reappointed ambassador to Russia, the authorities there protested, and Harris, who had to operate in the most unfavourable conditions – when Britain was at war not only with the American colonists but also with France and Holland – eventually gave up and asked to retire.[33]

Despite the 'cry' of the Turkey Company, or, what amounted to the same thing, that of the British representatives in Constantinople, and despite the ever louder howling of the East India Company, Britain, while not accepting a Russian war with Turkey as a *casus foederis*, not only failed to protest against Russia's first Turkish war, not only shut her eyes to the fact that the Russian fleet sent into the Mediterranean was actually commanded by British officers,[34] and crewed, through the good offices of the British Admiralty, by British sailors, and not only assisted this fleet throughout its voyage, but also imposed a firm veto when she learnt that France wished to go to Turkey's aid and destroy the Russian expedition. When the news of the signing of the Treaty of Kuchuk-Kainardji[35] reached St Petersburg, Catherine, who was at a court ball, expressed her desire to see at her card table only cheerful faces, and invited thither, along with the Danish ambassador, the ambassador of Britain.

When Frederick II, glowing with 'friendship' for Catherine and counselling her to appease Austria at the expense of Poland, carried out the first partition of Poland along with her and Maria-Theresa (who wept bitterly about it),[36] Britain showed concern in this connection only over her trading privileges in Danzig,[37] and, when by an edict of 11 May 1774 Frederick II guaranteed these privileges, she said 'Amen!'.[38]

But none of this helped the camarilla which, with brief intervals, supported the 'personal regime' of George III.[39] It is hard to conceive how far the British ministers in London went in their servility towards Russia. What could be more cynical than the reply given to the Russian ambassador in London, that the British government was unable to send money to Sweden because the British ambassador in Stockholm (Goodricke) could be trusted with anything except money?[40]

Desiring wholeheartedly to create fresh difficulties for the British, Catherine accepted their concessions as her due, and, by way of thanks, proceeded to organise such difficulties. Every new defeat suffered by the British King in his conflict with his rebel subjects brought her sincere joy, and she refused George's request that she send an auxiliary corps of 20,000 men to America: that task she left to the German princes. In 1779, she advised Simolin, in London, to keep to 'vague generalisations only', and prepared her 'armed neutrality' of 1780, which was directed exclusively against Britain.[41] She evaded Harris's protests by asking, artlessly, what harm could come to Britain from this '*nullité armée*'?

George III and his ministers, who were unwilling to contemplate any mediation by a foreign power 'between Us and our rebellious subjects' offered Minorca to Catherine in 1781, and when North's ministry was replaced by that of Fox,[42] the new government at last agreed to treat a Russian war with Turkey as a *casus foederis*: but Catherine remained adamant. At this time, the best diplomats of the *ancien régime*, even in Austria, France and Prussia, were convinced that Britain's power was on the point of inevitable collapse.

Britain answered Catherine's stubborn rejection of her overtures by making an alliance with Prussia in 1784. This was a formal revolt by the two 'slaves' against their master. But Pitt's first attempt, in 1791, to declare war on Russia in defence of Turkey[43] revealed how strong were the material interests binding Britain to Russia. The leader of the opponents of war with Russia was Fox. He made a powerful speech against Pitt in the House of Commons.

'Fox spoke like an angel,' wrote the Russian ambassador in London, S.R. Vorontsov. 'He proved that this accursed armed neutrality, on account of which there is so much raging against Russia, was the work of the Court of Berlin, and that the Court of Sweden also had a big hand in it ... He made plain how just is the Empress's cause in this war, and how important are the links between our country and Britain, and in the end he won over several of Pitt's friends, who made speeches on the same lines as his.' And Vorontsov added, in the same letter: 'In a few days' time the Russia Company will make representations to the ministry about the dangers that war would mean for trade.'[44]

Thus, the Whigs headed the campaign in favour of Russia. But whose 'cry' rang out to supplement the nightingale-like speeches of Fox? The 'cry' of the Russia Company that we know about.[45]

But we should make the same mistake as Marx if we were to forget what powerful material interests stood behind these 'accomplices' of Russia, and whose class interests determined this policy.

The friendship was the same, but its material basis had changed, not only as compared with the sixteenth century, or with the beginning of the eighteenth, but even as compared with 1760. Britain was now in the midst of the Industrial Revolution, and, alongside a section of the City of London, and alongside Norwich and Wakefield, the agitation was headed by Leeds and Manchester. Russia, which before 1760 had been important, as regards British exports, only to the woollen industry, was now becoming a market for the cotton industry. As regards Russia's exports to Britain, it continued to be, mainly, a supplier of naval stores, but, at the same time, it was turning into a supplier of raw materials for Britain's large-scale industry. And although, at the end of the eighteenth century, Vorontsov and other henchmen of Catherine still believed that cessation of trade between Russia and Britain would affect the latter most, the experience of the Continental System[46] was to show them that this was an illusion very harmful to Russia's commercial interests.

And, beginning in 1815, the year of the new Corn Laws, and also of the annexation by Russia of the Grand Duchy of Warsaw,[47] the principal supplier of grain to the British market, the literature of the Free Traders hymned without restraint the alliance between Britain and Russia, that 'old' and 'natural' ally who would never leave her friend breadless.

Thus, the material basis of friendship between Russia and Britain had changed. They that tease each other love each other. The Russia Company, which had long since lost any importance as a trading company, continued unwaveringly to sing the benefits of alliance with Russia. On the eve of the abolition of the Corn Laws, which Russia awaited with particular impatience, Robert Peel,[48] in a brilliant speech at the annual dinner held by the Russia Company, expressed the desire that the Russian Tsar and gendarme of Europe would visit Britain. He ended his speech with a toast 'to eternal friendship between Great Britain and Russia'. And even when, at last, against the will of nearly all of Britain's statesmen, war broke out between the two countries, it proved to be, at the start, only a sham war.[49]

Even the Tories, who, at the time of the Younger Pitt, had assumed the special role of defenders of the interests of Turkey against Russia, and followed jealously Russia's advance in Central Asia, were obliged to reckon with this fact. And the 'heroic' epoch of the anti-Jacobin war showed them that even such a Russophobe as Pitt did not hesitate to enter into alliance with Russia when what was at stake was the 'highest good' of capitalist society.

Notes

1. John Stewart, Third Earl of Bute (1713–1792) was Prime Minister during the first five years of the reign of George III, and negotiated the treaty that ended the Seven Years War (translator's note).

2. Dmitry Alexeyevich Golitsyn (1734–1803) served as ambassador to France and the Netherlands (1768–98) (translator's note).
3. Prince Wenzel Anton von Kaunitz-Rietberg (1711–1794) was Maria-Theresa's chief minister (translator's note).
4. Marx-Engels, *Collected Works*, Volume 17, Moscow, 1981, pp135–6: *Herr Vogt*, New Park Publications, pp121–2 (Riazanov's emphasis) (translator's note).
5. At the same time as she supported the claim of the Duke of Holstein to Schleswig-Holstein, Russia also supported his candidacy to the throne of Sweden. This was a fresh cause of conflict within Sweden, where a 'Russian' party now confronted an 'Anglo-French' one (author's note).
6. After Peter the Great's death in 1725, he was succeeded by his wife, as Catherine I. When she died, in 1727, Peter's grandson came to the throne, as Peter II, but he died in 1730, and was succeeded by Anna Ivanovna, Peter the Great's niece, who ruled until 1740 (translator's note).
7. Austria, which ruled at this time over what is now Belgium, set up in 1722 an 'East India Company' of her own, generally called the Ostend Company, but after a few years was forced by Anglo-Dutch pressure to dissolve it. The Pragmatic Sanction was the Emperor's decree of 1713 appointing his daughter Maria-Theresa as his successor, contrary to the rule against female succession to the Habsburg throne: he had to bargain with the other powers to get them to accept it (translator's note).
8. Claudius Rondeau had been consul-general in Russia since 1730 (translator's note).
9. *Sbornik Russkogo Istoricheskogo Obshchestva*, Volume 66, pp176–7 (author's note). Why British cloth exports were so important to the 'landed interest' which then formed the governing caste is explained by Lord Crowther-Hunt: 'When England's main export was woollen manufactures there was no real division between a landed and a commercial interest. The landed men who produced the wool wanted to see the cloth exports of the country increase just as much as did the merchant classes who made their profits from this branch of the export trade.' (NC Hunt, 'The Russia Company and the Government, 1730–42', *Oxford Slavonic Papers*, Volume 7, 1957) (translator's note).
10. *Sbornik Russkogo Istoricheskogo Obshchestva*, Volume 66, pp515–8 (author's note).
11. This was why, in 1736, when Britain sent her fleet into the Baltic to defend Denmark, the Russian government again published a declaration reassuring British merchants (author's note).
12. The War of the Polish Succession (1733–38) broke out when in 1733 the Polish diet elected as king again Stanislas Leszczynski, who had been placed in power by Charles XII after his defeat of Russia at Narva (1704–1709). Russia intervened to replace him with Peter the Great's ally, Frederick Augustus of Saxony (translator's note).
13. General Burkhard Christoph von Münnich (1683–1767) commanded Russian troops in Poland, the Crimea and Bessarabia; Field Marshal Peter Petrovich Lacy (1678–1751) fought in Poland as well as during the Turkish War of 1735–39 (translator's note).
14. It is to this period that Rondeau's letter quoted by Marx belongs. This letter is now included in *Sbornik Russkogo Istoricheskogo Obshchestva*, Volume 80, pp13–19 (author's note).
15. Andrey Ivanovich, Graf von Osterman (1686–1747) dominated Russian foreign policy between 1725 and 1740 (translator's note).
16. Sir Everard Fawkener (1684–1758), a friend of Voltaire, was appointed ambassador to the Sublime Porte in 1735, and was criticised for trying to mediate in the war between Russia and Turkey (translator's note).
17. Solovyov, *Istoriya Rossii*, Volume 21, p201 (author's note). Maria-Theresa, Empress of Austria (1740–1780) was having considerable difficulty at this time in establishing her right to the throne during the War of Austrian Succession (translator's note).
18. John Carteret, First Earl of Granville (1690–1763), an opponent of Walpole, was first minister during 1742–44, and directed England's foreign policy during the War of the

Austrian Succession; the Tsaritsa Elizabeth ruled Russia from 1741 to 1762 (translator's note).

19. The expression 'the maritime powers' was used to mean Britain and Holland (translator's note).
20. A *casus foederis* is an event which will cause a treaty's provisions to be applied. Russia and Britain both wished to exclude from the scope of the treaty conflicts in which they themselves had no interest: Russia did not want to become involved in a war with France and her allies arising from Anglo-French rivalry in America or India, while Britain saw no advantage in helping Russia strengthen her position in the Black Sea region (translator's note).
21. The Seven Years' War, 1756–63, in which Austria, France and Russia confronted Britain and Prussia, arose out of Anglo-French colonial rivalry, together with the striving of Prussia, under Frederick the Great, to take Silesia from the Empress Maria-Theresa. This war consummated the 'diplomatic revolution' by which Austria and France, adversaries since the sixteenth century, now became allies (translator's note).
22. Robert Keith (d 1774) was Britain's envoy in Russia from 1757 to 1762 (translator's note).
23. Peter III became Tsar in 1761. He was a great admirer of Frederick the Great, and tried to reverse Russia's foreign policy in Prussia's favour. However, in 1762 he was overthrown and replaced by his wife, who became Empress as Catherine II (translator's note).
24. Here Riazanov has misread his source. Martens says (op cit, p215) of Peter III's instructions to the ambassador, that they were so pro-Prussian that 'one might suppose them to have been written' at the dictation of Count Bernhard von der Goltz (d 1795), Frederick's minister in St Petersburg (translator's note).
25. 1730 – £258,802; 1760 – £576,265. I deliberately use Marx's own figures (author's note).
26. William Pitt the Elder, later Earl of Chatham (1708–1788) was Prime Minister during the British victories in the Seven Years War (translator's note)
27. Franz Mehring, *Die Lessing-Legende*, p169 (author's note). The English translation is taken from F Mehring, *Absolutism and Revolution in Germany, 1525–1848*, New Park Publications, 1975, p100 (translator's note).
28. F Engels, *Die auswärtige Politik des russischen Zarentums*, in *Die Neue Zeit*, 1890, p150 (author's note). English version, 'The Foreign Policy of Russian Tsardom', *Time*, April 1890, p361; Marx and Engels, *Collected Works*, Volume 27, Moscow, 1990, p21; Paul S Blackstock and Bert E Hoselitz, *Karl Marx and Friedrich Engels: The Russian Menace to Europe*, 1953, p32 (translator's note).
29. By Britain's 'ancient ally' the House of Habsburg is meant, the Emperors and rulers of Austria (translator's note).
30. Semiramis (Sammuramat), queen regent in Assyria in the ninth century BC, was in later legend a warrior queen whose private life bore some resemblance to that of Catherine II (translator's note).
31. *Diaries and Correspondence of James Harris*, Volume 1, p169 (author's note).
32. Sir George Macartney was Britain's envoy in St Petersburg in 1764–67 (translator's note).
33. Macartney's letter which Marx published was not included in his correspondence as published by the Russian Historical Society, although a reference to this letter is given. Even though the letters published by the Society were carefully 'screened', many sharp and well-aimed characterisations are to be found in them. As for Harris' letter, we have already noted that it had been printed already in 1844. Marx did not observe that, in this letter, Harris gives a brief *résumé* of his five years' work at the court of St Petersburg, with a view to showing how pointless it would be for him to stay there any longer. It was significant that his correspondence – or rather, extracts therefrom – could appear only in that year. For the author of *La Cour de Russie il y a cent ans*, Harris's letters served as the principal source of his description of the court of St Petersburg – a description which certainly cannot be called 'Russophil' (author's note).

34. Two British admirals, Elphinstone and Greig, were with the Russian fleet which destroyed the Turkish fleet at Chesme, off Chios in 1770 (translator's note).
35. The Treaty of Kuchuk-Kainardji concluded the Russo-Turkish War of 1768–74. By it, the Sultan recognised the independence of the Crimea (soon to be annexed by Russia), ceded Azov and Kerch to Russia, opened the Black Sea to Russian commercial navigation, and gave Russia a protectorate over Moldavia and Wallachia ('the Danubian principalities', later to become the Kingdom of Romania) (translator's note).
36. The first partition of Poland was carried out in 1772. Frederick the Great remarked sarcastically about the Austrian Empress: 'Her tears were provoked by the memory of how the Poles under John III Sobieski (1674–96) had saved Vienna from the Turks in 1683.' (translator's note)
37. That is, present-day Gdansk (translator's note).
38. W Michael, ***Englands Stellung zur ersten Teilung Polens***, Hamburg, 1890 (author's note).
39. George III was King of England from 1760 to 1820, and, to begin with, attempted a personal form of government, but after a mental breakdown due to porphyria his ministers took over the administration, and his reign ended with a regency (translator's note).
40. Solovyov, ***Istoriya Rossii***, Volume 28, p199 (author's note). Sir John Goodricke was Britain's representative in Sweden from 1758 to 1773 (translator's note).
41. In the League of Armed Neutrality, Russia, Sweden, Denmark, Prussia, Spain, Holland and France joined together to prevent the British Navy from exercising the right it claimed to search their ships for war materials being conveyed to the American rebels (translator's note).
42. Frederick, Lord North of Kirtling and Baron Guildford (1732–1792) was George III's chief minister (1770–82) until replaced for a short time by Charles James Fox (1749–1806), a notable orator and a Whig politician (translator's note).
43. This episode is known in diplomatic history as 'the Ochakov crisis', from the Turkish fortress on the Black Sea coast taken by the Russians during their war with Turkey in 1787–91. The British Prime Minister, William Pitt the Younger (1759–1806) demanded that Russia return Ochakov to the Turks (translator's note).
44. ***Arkhiv Knyazya Vorontsova***, Volume 9, p190. Catherine asked Vorontsov to buy for her a marble bust of the 'great orator', and placed this in her palace of Tsarkoye Selo, between busts of Demosthenes and Cicero (author's note). Demosthenes (383–322BC) was the last great Athenian orator to defend the freedom of the Greek city states against the Macedonian conquest; Marcus Tullius Cicero (106–43BC) was the last of the great Roman orators, who spoke up for the republic against the dictatorship (translator's note).
45. How little the history of this company is known can be seen from the fact that the authors of a book specially devoted to the trading companies – G Cawston and AH Keane, ***The Early Charter Companies*** (1896), pp32–59 – were sure that the Russia Company 'died of inanition towards the close of the eighteenth century'. Yet JR McCulloch wrote of it as still existing in 1852 (***A Dictionary, Practical, Theoretical and Historical, of Commerce and Commercial Navigation***, 1852, p1125), and Schmoller confuses it with the Eastland Company (author's note). Gustav Friedrich von Schmoller (1836–1917) was a well-known German historian (translator's note).
46. Hoping to strangle Britain by cutting off her foreign trade, Napoleon ordered the countries subject to him to cease commercial relations with her. British historians call this attempted blockade 'the Continental System'. At first, Russia, then allied with France, joined in the boycott, but soon the shortage of manufactured goods and the loss of outlets for agricultural produce led the Tsar to resume normal trade relations with Britain. The resulting quarrel with Napoleon led to his Moscow campaign of 1812, and his consequent downfall (translator's note).
47. After his victories over Prussia and Austria, Napoleon constructed a 'Grand Duchy of

Warsaw' out of parts of Prussian and Austrian Poland. When Napoleon was defeated, this territory was annexed by Russia (translator's note).

48. Sir Robert Peel (1788–1850) was leader of the Tory Party and Prime Minister from 1841 to 1846 (translator's note).
49. Despite the incompetence and unwillingness to wage all-out war shown by the Allies in the Crimean War, the defeats inflicted on Russia had far-reaching effects, both on her international prestige and her internal stability. Marx contrasts, in an article from 1855, the significance of Russia's defeat at Narva in 1700 with that of her defeat at Inkerman in 1854: 'Narva was the first great disaster of a rising nation which knew how to turn even defeats into means of victory. Inkerman appears almost as the certain indication of a decline in that hot-house development which Russia had undergone since Peter the Great. The artificially accelerated growth, and the tremendous effort of maintaining with semi-barbaric means the semblance of a brilliant civilisation, seem to have already exhausted the nation, and to have inflicted upon it some kind of consumption. The Battle of Inkerman is for the Russian infantry what the Battle of Rocroi was for the Spanish infantry.' (Karl Marx, 'In Retrospect', *Neue Oder-Zeitung*, 4 January 1855; Marx and Engels, *Collected Works*, Volume 13, Moscow, 1980, p559). The defeat inflicted on the Spaniards by the French at Rocroi in 1643 had marked the end of Spain's military preponderance in Western Europe and the beginning of the end of her political ascendancy (translator's note).

Chapter Nine

Russia's Foreign Policy and the Revolution

The fact that in his polemic against Vogt in 1860 Marx refers to his work on diplomatic relations between Russia and Britain in the eighteenth century, and mentions its principal conclusion, shows that he still, at the beginning of the 1860s, held to his old opinion. Russia's internal development between the time of Peter I and that of Alexander II fell outside his field of vision. He did not observe the evolution undergone during this period by Russian absolutism, and overlooked the economic development of Russia and its close connection with that of Britain. He overlooked the fact that Russia was one of the principal colonies of capitalist Britain in the sixteenth to eighteenth centuries; that in the eighteenth century imports from Russia formed the basis for the prosperity of Britain's shipbuilding industry, and, consequently, of her commercial hegemony during the entire period of manufacture; and that in the nineteenth century, right down to the 1860s, Russia was a workshop supplying raw materials for Britain's large-scale industry, and grain to feed its helots. In short, he overlooked the fact that the commercial subjection and exploitation of the bourgeois classes of a number of European nations by the despot of the world market, Britain, had as one of its necessary conditions the aid of the despot of Russia.[1]

For him absolutism continued to be unchanging. In that same work, *Herr Vogt*, he wrote:

> The emancipation of the serfs ... is simply intended to perfect autocratic rule by tearing down the barriers which the big autocrat has hitherto encountered in the

> shape of the many lesser autocrats of the Russian nobility, whose might is based on serfdom, as well as in the shape of the self-administering peasant communes, whose material foundation, common ownership of land, is to be destroyed by the so-called emancipation.

Furthermore, indeed, 'the emancipation of the serfs, as the Russian government sees it, would increase the aggressive power of Russia a hundredfold'.[2]

A different opinion had been expressed even then by Engels, and in Marx's words I see a hidden polemic with him. Engels wrote, in his pamphlet *Savoy, Nice and the Rhine*:

> In the meantime we have obtained an ally in the form of the Russian serfs. The contest that has now broken out in Russia between the ruling and the oppressed classes of the rural population is already undermining the entire system of Russian foreign policy. That system was only possible so long as Russia had no internal political development. But that time is past. Industrial and agricultural development, fostered in every way by the government and the nobility, has reached a point where the existing social conditions can no longer be endured. Elimination of these conditions is a necessity, on the one hand, but an impossibility without violent change, on the other. With the Russia that existed from Peter the Great to Nicholas, the foreign policy of that Russia collapses as well.[3]

And Engels turned out to be right. He already at this time showed quite correctly that the main reason for Russia's domination of Europe lay in the fundamental maxim of Catherine II's entire foreign policy – in the fact that Russia left the other states of Europe, so far as possible, to maul and weaken each other – and he also pointed correctly to the chief factor that was bound to undermine the source of this power to pursue an unchanging, single minded foreign policy, namely, the internal political development of Russia.

Already the revolt of the Decembrists had provided a sinister portent. And the steady growth of the revolutionary movement in Russia increasingly revealed that Russia was losing her principal advantage, which enabled her still, in 1848, to gaze with sovereign contempt on all Europe, on the 'decadent West'.

My tongue could never find a name,
Bad enough for another's shame,
I thought it black and I blackened it,
It was never black enough to fit,
And I blessed myself and acted proud,
And now I too am under a cloud.[4]

Awareness that Russia, 'when she ate and drank, was feeding two', namely, absolutism and revolution, poisoned the life of Nicholas I throughout his reign, and it was precisely this that made him act the hangman at home and the gendarme in all Europe, and precisely this that constrained his foreign policy.

In the 1860s, just when, with the help of Germany and Britain and the connivance of France and Austria, rebel Poland had been finally crushed – that Poland which in 1795–96, in 1831 and in 1859 had been a heavy ball tied to the feet of the Russian colossus, hindering its freedom of movement – a revolutionary movement began in Russia: it was the birth time of the 'illegitimate son' of Asiatic Russia and European capitalism. Thereafter the foreign policy of Russian absolutism was at last deprived of its fatal constancy. Even though fresh splits and squabbles in Western Europe (especially the split that followed the Franco-Prussian War, which resulted in much greater mutual alienation among the Western European peoples than the split following the Seven Years' War) gave new strength to Russian absolutism, the need continually to reckon with the revolutionary movement inside the country checked it halfway on every occasion. Moreover, what had previously been the principal *end* of Russia's foreign policy was now transformed into a *means*. Carrying on the traditional aggressive foreign policy became the only way to hold back the outbreak of revolution inside the country.

Wars of conquest were now undertaken, not at times when Western Europe was enfeebled by revolution or war, but when they were required by 'internal political development'. Yet fulfilment of the minimum programme of that very revolution which Russia's rulers sought by this means to avoid was the necessary condition for success in a policy of conquest. War revealed more and more clearly the whole insolvency of Russia's 'order'. This was why the foreign policy of Tsardom, having lost along with its mutability one of its principal advantages, was now, *as a result of this internal contradiction*, suffering bankruptcy at every step it took.

It was Engels who first, not only in European but also in Russian literature, exposed all these contradictions. Already in his brilliant critique of Narodnik superstitions, written in reply to Tkachev,[5] he pointed out the class essence of Russian absolutism, and its dependence on definite socio-economic relations. And when this internal economic development brought an urban proletariat onto the scene, when Russian Social Democracy was born, Engels, in an article written specially for the first Social Democratic journal to appear in the Russian language, gave a brilliant sketch entitled 'The Foreign Policy of Russian Tsardom'.

He showed that, despite Russia's rapid progress since Peter the Great's time, despite the growth in her influence in Europe, it was only under Catherine II that she began to play the role of arbiter of Europe's destinies. He also showed that the undoubted successes of Tsardom's foreign policy were based not so much on the outstanding abilities of Russia's diplomats as on the general conditions in the European political situation that favoured it, and which Russia would have been able to exploit even better had it not been for Poland, that 'thorn in Russia's flesh'. And, developing the idea which he had expressed as far back as 1859, he further showed that Russia's internal development was bringing nearer and nearer the day when the Russian people would take a hand in determining Russia's foreign policy, and when preoccupation with its own affairs would deprive Tsardom of any desire to engage in such activities as the conquest of Constantinople, India and world domination.

Engels proved to be a good prophet. He correctly defined the essence of the problem. But at the same time the old schema of the foreign policy of European democracy which had been taken over, in its main features, by Marx and Engels – on this side, Western Europe, on that side, Asiatic Russia: here, revolution, there, the centre of European reaction, absolutism – was more and more losing its significance. Traditional notions were powerful, and it was only with difficulty that international Social Democracy altered its views on a whole number of 'problems' posed by bourgeois society. Just as the democratic movement had done, it operated, in the sphere of foreign policy, with petrified concepts of revolutionary and reactionary races and states, and failed to notice the historical process which was changing the social nature of a particular government and the class composition of the people which had 'deserved' that government.

However strange to us may sound Marx's diatribes against the Anglo-Russian slavery into which Europe had fallen again after 1848, they do include the recognition that there was in Europe another centre of reaction besides Russian absolutism, namely, a bourgeoisie which had renounced its own historical mission – European capitalism, which with its capital upheld Russian absolutism.

Never did this fact find such striking expression as in 1905. The history of 1848 was stood on its head. The revolution that began in 1848 had advanced from West to East, and halted at the Polish frontier: now it was knocking at the door of Western Europe. The Tsar, who had in 1848 been a threat to the democracy of the West, was now himself a prisoner of the Russian proletariat.

Engels had again proved to be a good prophet:

> Therefore, on the day when this main fortress itself passes into the hands of the Revolution, then the last spark of self-assurance and security will die in the reactionary governments of Europe. They will then be thrown back on their own resources and will soon discover what a difference that makes. Perhaps they may be in a position to order out their armies to restore the authority of the Tsar – what an irony of history![6]

And that irony found embodiment in reality. In St Petersburg at that time a persistent rumour circulated – and the reactionary press not only did not deny this, but triumphantly repeated it – that the German Emperor was concentrating his forces on the Polish frontier.

And just as Marx and Engels and the German proletariat turned their gaze, with passionate yearning, towards the West, awaiting the outbreak of social revolution in Britain, so did the Russian revolutionaries, the Russian proletariat, in their heroic struggle against absolutism, place their hopes on social revolution in the West. But no help came, and the proletariat fell exhausted by the battle with absolutism: after expending all the revolutionary energy it had accumulated over many years, the Russian proletariat was vanquished.

Woe to the vanquished! But when, over the fresh corpses of the fighters, amid the sound of more gallows being erected every day, flabby Philistines and sobered-up politicians, with the cold indifference of gelatine, recite to the proletariat the list of its mistakes, and lament, like so many crows: 'The revolution is dead!', it is necessary to say: 'All right, the Russian proletariat made mistakes, it made mistake after mistake, but its biggest mistake was that its revolution was a *national* one, whereas behind absolutism stood *international* capital.'

If the revolution of 1848 suffered defeat because it was smashed against Russian absolutism and because it was not followed by revolution in Britain, the Russian revolution was doomed to defeat, to a large extent, because it remained national, because in the rest of Europe the revolution did not budge. If the revolution does not turn into an international revolution, then 'it is, and if it wishes to be final it will remain, a pious wish'.

Just as in 1848, the proletariat of the most progressive bourgeois state in Europe is today still too weak to prevent its bourgeoisie from pursuing their reactionary foreign policy. Just as in those days, the Tsar makes a show of his 'close' friendship with Britain. And just as, then, the British bourgeoisie did not prevent the Tsar from tyrannising in Hungary, it now, hand in hand with the Lyakhovs, in the interests of Russian absolutism in Russia and of British absolutism in India, is murdering freedom in Persia.

November 1908

Notes

1. Yet he had already written in *Zur Kritik* 'that the Russians long ago grasped that money is a commodity is demonstrated not only by the English corn imports from 1838 to 1842, but also by the whole history of their trade' (Marx, *Zur Kritik der politischen Ökonomie*, p188). And the Russians' teachers in this matter were the British. (author's note) (English translation, *A Contribution to the Critique of Political Economy*, 1971, p177 n, translator's note)
2. Marx and Engels, *Collected Works*, Volume 17, Moscow, 1981, pp140–1; , New Park Publications, p127 (translator's note).
3. Frederick Engels, 'Savoy, Nice and the Rhine', 1859, Marx and Engels, *Collected Works*, Volume 16, Moscow, 1980, pp609–10 (translator's note).
4. From Goethe's *Faust, Part One*, 'At the Well' (Louis MacNeice's translation, 1951, p119). Margarethe, who has always disdained unmarried mothers, is now herself pregnant by Faust (translator's note).
5. *Soziales aus Russland*, 1875, printed in the symposium *Internationales aus dem 'Volksstaat'*, 1894 (translated into Russian by Vera Zasulich, *F Engels o Rossii*, Geneva, 1894) (author's note). ('Russia and the Social Revolution Reconsidered', in Paul S Blackstock and Bert E Hoselitz, *Karl Marx and Friedrich Engels: The Russian Menace to Europe*, 1953, pp229–41; 'Introduction to the Pamphlet on Social Relations in Russia', Marx and Engels, *Collected Works*, Volume 24, London, 1989, pp100–104). Vera Ivanovna Zasulich (1849–1919) was one of the pioneers of Socialism in Russia, a member of the League for the Emancipation of Labour and of the Menshevik faction of the Russian Social-Democratic Labour Party (translator's note).
6. Riazanov quotes from the German version of Engels' article, published in *Die Neue Zeit*, Volume 13 (1890), and this is the basis of the English translation in Blackstock and Hoselitz, where the passage quoted appears on page 55. The English version of the article, published in *Time*, April-May 1890, differs somewhat, with the last sentence of Riazanov's quotation reading (p544): 'The German Emperor might perhaps be tempted to sending an army to restore the authority of the Tsar – than which there could be no better way to destroy his own authority.' (cf Marx and Engels, *Collected Works*, Volume 27, Moscow, 1990, p48 and n) In Germany, where the Anti-Socialist Law did not expire until the end of September 1890, greater discretion was doubtless felt to be necessary (translator's note).

Marx and Engels and the Polish Question

D. B. Riazanov

Introduction

It is well known how prominently the call for the restoration of an independent Poland figured in all the programmes of Europe's democrats after the July Revolution. Sympathy for the oppressed Poles was combined with hatred for the principal member of the 'Holy Alliance', Russian Tsardom, and the re-establishment of Poland was seen as the best means of weakening 'barbarous Russia' and consolidating the triumph of the new revolution that was on its way.

However sharply proletarian democracy, as expressed in the writings of Marx and Engels, was counterposed to bourgeois democracy, nevertheless the demand for the restoration of an independent Poland was borrowed by it, along with other political demands, from the bourgeois political programme. The only difference was that the two founders of scientific Socialism strove to reinforce this demand with fresh arguments, and also, from the very outset, to oppose the illusions of the Polish revolutionaries.

It would be a mistake, though, to think that their views on the Polish question remained unchanged throughout the period when they were carrying out their joint theoretical work, that is, from 1844 until the death of Marx in 1883, and, if we include the subsequent views of Engels alone, until his death in 1895. Their views on this matter changed, just as did their position on other matters. We must also take into account, what is often forgotten, the fact that the views of Marx and Engels did not always coincide; that those views which are regarded as common to both men were the result of conflict between them; and that the reason why, on many questions, their views did not always coincide was that Marx and Engels approached them from different premises, both scientific and practical.

I am going to try, for the first time, to bring together the views of Marx and Engels on the Polish question – both the views expressed in common and also those statements that they each made separately on one occasion or another in the course of 40 years, many of which have remained unknown till now. The task I have undertaken is purely narrative, refraining from any criticism, even when the views of Marx and Engels obviously call for this. The purpose of my work is solely to present the question in as exhaustive a way as possible.

I

After the Polish rising of 1830–31, which prevented a campaign by the 'Holy Alliance' against revolutionary France, just as the rising of 1794 had disrupted the combined offensive of the absolutist powers, Poland remained apparently quite calm right down to 1846. Nevertheless, it was for the Polish revolutionary émigrés a period of internal conflict and self-criticism. Particular attempts at promoting a fresh revolt in Poland failed to come off. But day by day the gulf grew wider between the aristocratic section of the Polish émigrés, who ascribed enormous importance to help from the West European governments, and the democratic section, who sought to draw closer to the democrats of Western Europe.[1]

The places where the Polish émigrés first concentrated were all in France: Paris, Poitiers and Besançon. Later, a section of them moved away, either voluntarily or because they were expelled by the French government, to London and Brussels. In Brussels lived the famous Polish historian Joachim Lelewel, who met Marx and Engels there in 1845.[2] In London we find Ludwik Oborski,[3] who in the 1840s took part in all the demonstrations held in the British capital, and maintained close friendships both with Chartists and with members of the German Communist Workers' Association, especially Karl Schapper.[4]

It was in Portsmouth that appeared the first Polish revolutionary organisation, *Lud Polski*, to include in its programme the abolition of private property. But by far the greatest influence was wielded by the Polish Democratic Society (*Towarysztwo Democratyczne Polskie*), which was very active at that time. It had been founded in 1832, to oppose the aristocratic section of the émigrés led by Czartoryski.[5] The Polish democrats saw the egoistic tendencies of the aristocracy as the chief reason for the failure of the Polish revolution. They considered that the salvation of Poland lay not only in an armed uprising, but also, along with this, in a radical and democratic revolution. They therefore wished to appeal to the people, to the peasantry, and, accordingly, they included in their programme a demand for the emancipation of the peasants and their landholdings from feudal oppression. The Society carried on through its agents an active propaganda along these lines in all three parts of Poland.[6]

Under the influence of its sections working in Prussia and Austria, the society decided in 1845 to prepare for another rising. A plan of military operations was to be worked out by General Mieroslawski,[7] a member of the Society's leadership. In December 1845, he set out for Poznan and Cracow, and on 24 January 1846 a national government was set up in Cracow, which on 22 February issued a manifesto promising the peasants equality of rights, together with free ownership of the land they had worked for centuries.[8]

As is well known, this rising ended in failure. Mieroslawski was arrested in Poznan on 12 February 1846. In Russian Poland, the rising found expression only in an outbreak in Siedlce which was suppressed. In Galicia, the peasants themselves helped to put down the rising. The last remnant of the old independent Poland, the free republic of Cracow, was annexed by Austria.[9]

But this rising aroused once more the sympathy of Europe's democrats for unhappy Poland. It served as a prologue to the revolutionary movements which filled the year 1847, and culminated in the revolution of 1848. The definitely social character of the rising, which distinguished it favourably from that of 1830–31, the attempt to appeal to the people themselves, which ended so tragically, now won fresh sympathies for the Poles among the working class as well. It can be said that it was only after the Cracow revolt that the restoration of Poland became one of the fundamental principles of the foreign policy of the working class in Britain, France and Germany. What had previously resembled the sympathy felt for the oppressed Greeks, which was mainly something that moved a few ideologues or, platonically, the educated strata of society, now became the common demand of the working class which was beginning to struggle for emancipation. Thus, the restoration of Poland, together with the struggle of the Italians and the Hungarians for their national independence, became a matter of practical interest for the international democratic movement.

This is the reason why, from 1847 onward, the Polish question was invariably an item on the agenda of every important international gathering of European democrats. Just as in London the already mentioned Oborski joined the international organisation called the Fraternal Democrats, so in Brussels Polish émigrés – Lelewel, Lubliner[10] and others – took part in the formation of the Association Démocratique, whose chairman was Jottrand,[11] with Marx and Imbert[12] as his deputies (November 1847).[13]

On the instructions of this society, Marx delivered to the Fraternal Democrats in London an address of sympathy when he and Engels went to London to take part in the congress of another international society, only a few months before the foundation of the Communist League. Marx carried out his task at the meeting held by the Fraternal Democrats on 29 November 1847 to commemorate the Polish rising of 1830: it was on this occasion that he and Engels spoke publicly for the first time about the Polish question and its importance for the European proletariat.[14] In his speech, Marx examines the Polish question as part of the general struggle of the peoples for liberation, which he links with a radical change in property relations, and comes out as an international Communist who looks for the achievement of this liberation to a social revolution:

> For peoples to be able truly to unite, they must have common interests. And in order that their interests may become common, the existing property relations must be done away with, for these property relations involve the exploitation of some nations by others: the abolition of existing property relations is the concern only of the working class. It alone has also the means for doing this. The victory of the proletariat over the bourgeoisie is, at the same time, victory over the national and industrial conflicts which today range the peoples of the various countries against one another in hostility and enmity. And so the victory of the proletariat over the bourgeoisie is at the same time the signal of liberation for all oppressed nations.
>
> The old Poland is lost in any case, and we would be the last to wish for its restoration. But it is not only the old Poland that is lost. The old Germany, the old France, the old England, the whole of the old society is lost. But the loss of the old society is no loss for those who have nothing to lose in the old society, and this is the case for the great majority in all countries at the present time. They have, rather, everything to gain by the downfall of the old

society, which is the condition for the establishment of a new society, one no longer based on class antagonisms.

Of all countries, England is the one where the contradiction between the proletariat and the bourgeoisie is most highly developed. The victory of the English proletarians over the English bourgeoisie is, therefore, decisive for the victory of all the oppressed over their oppressors. Hence Poland must be liberated, not in Poland, but in England. So you Chartists must not simply express pious wishes for the liberation of nations. Defeat your internal enemies, and you will then be able to pride yourselves on having defeated the entire old society.[15]

Engels spoke on different lines: unlike Marx, he appeared as a German democrat desirous to show why German democrats had a special interest in the liberation of Poland. In the second part of his speech, however, he spoke in the same spirit as Marx:

> Allow me, dear friends, to speak here today, as an exception, in my capacity as a German. For we German democrats have a special interest in the liberation of Poland. It was German princes who derived great advantages from the division of Poland, and it is German soldiers who are still holding down Galicia and Posen. The responsibility for removing this disgrace from our nation rests on us Germans, on us German democrats above all. A nation cannot become free and at the same time continue to oppress other nations. The liberation of Germany cannot therefore take place without the liberation of Poland from German oppression. And because of this, Poland and Germany have a common interest, and so Polish and German democrats can work together for the liberation of both nations.
>
> I also believe that the first decisive blow which will lead to the victory of democracy, to the liberation of all European nations, will be struck by the English Chartists. I have lived in England for a number of years now and openly aligned myself with the Chartist movement during this period. The English Chartists will be the first to rise because it is precisely in England that the struggle between the bourgeoisie and the proletariat is the most intense. And why is it the most intense? Because in England, as a result of modern industry, of the intro-

> duction of machinery, all oppressed classes are being merged together into a single great class with common interests, the class of the proletariat; because, as a consequence, on the opposite side all classes of oppressors have likewise been united into a single class, the bourgeoisie. The struggle has thus been simplified, and so it will be possible to decide it by one single heavy blow. Isn't this so? The aristocracy no longer has any power in England; the bourgeoisie alone rules, and it has taken the aristocracy in tow. But the whole great mass of the people stands opposed to the bourgeoisie, united in a formidable phalanx, whose victory over the ruling capitalists draws nearer and nearer. And you have to thank machinery for this elimination of opposed interests which previously divided the different sections of workers, for this levelling of the living standards of all workers. Without machinery no Chartism, and although machinery may temporarily worsen your position, it is nevertheless machinery that makes our victory possible. But not only in England; in all other countries it has had the same effect on the workers. In Belgium, in America, in France and in Germany it has evened out the position of all workers, and daily continues to do so more and more; in all these countries the workers now have the same interest, which is the overthrow of the class that oppresses them – the bourgeoisie. This levelling of living standards, this identification of the party interests of the workers of all nations is the result of machinery, and so machinery is an enormous historical advance. What follows from this for us? Because the condition of the workers of all countries is the same, they must also fight together, they must oppose the brotherhood of the bourgeoisie of all nations with a brotherhood of the workers of all nations.[16]

This meeting on 29 November 1847 was not the only one at which Marx and Engels spoke about the Polish question before the February revolution. Almost on the eve of that revolution they both addressed a meeting held by the *Association Démocratique* in Brussels on the second anniversary of the Cracow rising, or, more precisely, of the manifesto issued by the Polish national government. This fact has hitherto remained unknown to all the biographers of Marx and Engels, as well as to Louis Bertrand, who in his book mentioned above devotes many pages to the *Association Démocratique*.

The meeting was organised with the help of the Polish democrats Lelewel and Lubliner. It was addressed by the Belgian Senault, by Marx, Engels and Lelewel, and by the workers Katz, Pellering and Wallau. The speeches of the last three have not survived, but we have all the others.[17]

Marx's speech on this occasion was constructed quite differently from the one he had made in London. He wants to explain to his listeners the significance of the Cracow rising. He stresses the necessary connection between political and social questions. The glorious example set to all Europe by the Cracow rising he sees in the fact that it linked together the cause of national liberation with the cause of democracy and the emancipation of an oppressed class. For this very reason, the liberation, not of feudal Poland, but of a democratic Poland, becomes a matter of honour for all European democrats.

Engels, for his part, shows that the failure of the Cracow rising was a victory for democratic Poland over the old aristocratic Poland: that the Poles' struggle against their oppressors must be preceded by a struggle among the Poles themselves.

Consequently, he criticises the rising of 1830, which was more conservative in character. One member of the government alone, Lelewel, understood that the revolution could be made popular only if the privileges of the aristocracy were abolished and the peasants freed from serfdom, with at the same time a change in the disgraceful situation of the Jews. Only the Cracow rising made the cause of Poland the cause of all peoples, and it transformed it from a subject of sympathetic phrases into a practical question for all democrats. Germany, especially, should rejoice at this, since in democratic Poland she has acquired a sure ally, having the same interests as herself. For the first condition for the liberation of Germany and Poland alike is the political revolutionising of Germany, the downfall of Prussia and Austria, and the thrusting back of Russia beyond the Dniester[18] and the Dvina.

It was in the spirit of these speeches that Marx and Engels declared in *The Communist Manifesto*, which appeared at this time: 'In Poland they [the Communists] support the party that insists on an agrarian revolution as the prime condition for national emancipation, that party which fomented the insurrection of Cracow in 1846.'[19]

II

Only familiarity with both their speeches in Brussels enables us to understand fully the position of Marx and Engels on the Polish question during the revolution of 1848.

They maintained the same principles as before, merely citing more arguments from history and doing this in a polemical form, against the representatives of the bourgeois parties in the Frankfurt Parliament, in their articles in the *Neue Rheinische Zeitung* which Mehring brought together under the general heading of 'The Debates at Frankfurt on the Polish Question'.[20]

> A French historian has said: *Il y a des peuples nécessaires* – there are *necessary nations*. The Polish nation is undoubtedly one of the necessary nations of the nineteenth century. But for no one is Poland's national existence more necessary than for us Germans.
>
> What is the main support of the reactionary forces in Europe since 1815, and to some extent even since the first French Revolution? It is the Russian-Prussian-Austrian Holy Alliance. And what holds the Holy Alliance together? The partition of Poland, from which all the three allies have profited.
>
> The tearing asunder of Poland by the three powers is the tie which links them together: the robbery they jointly committed makes them support one another.
>
> From the moment the first robbery of Polish territory was committed, Germany became dependent on Russia. Russia ordered Prussia and Austria to remain absolute monarchies, and Prussia and Austria had to obey. The efforts to gain control – efforts which were in any case feeble and timid, especially on the part of the Prussian bourgeoisie – failed entirely because of the impossibility of breaking away from Russia, and because of the support which Russia offered the feudal-absolutist class in Prussia.
>
> Moreover, as soon as the allies attempted to introduce the first oppressive measures, the Poles not only rose to fight for their independence, but simultaneously came out in *revolutionary* action against their own internal social conditions.
>
> The partition of Poland was effected through a pact between the big feudal aristocracy of Poland and the three partitioning powers. It was not an advance, as the ex-poet Herr Jordan[21] maintains, it was the last means the big aristocracy had to protect itself against a revolution, it was thoroughly reactionary.
>
> Already the first partition led quite naturally to an

alliance of the other classes , that is, the nobles, the townspeople, and to some extent the peasants, both against the oppressors of Poland and against the big Polish aristocracy. The constitution of 1791 shows that already then the Poles clearly understood that their independence in foreign affairs was inseparable from the overthrow of the aristocracy and from an agrarian reform within the country.[22]

The big agrarian countries between the Baltic and Black Seas can free themselves from patriarchal feudal barbarism only by an agrarian revolution, which turns the peasants who are serfs or liable to compulsory labour into free landowners, a revolution which would be similar to the French Revolution of 1789 in the countryside. It is to the credit of the Polish nation that it was the first of all its agricultural neighbours to proclaim this. The first attempted reform was the Constitution of 1791; during the uprising of 1830 Lelewel declared an agrarian revolution to be the only means of saving the country, but the Diet recognised this too late; during the insurrections of 1846 and 1848 the agrarian revolution was openly proclaimed.

From the day of their subjugation the Poles came out with revolutionary demands, thereby committing their oppressors more strongly to a counter-revolutionary course. They compelled their oppressors to maintain the patriarchal feudal structure, not only in Poland, but in all their other countries as well. The struggle for the independence of Poland, particularly since the Cracow uprising of 1846, is at the same time a struggle of *agrarian democracy* – the only form of democracy possible in Eastern Europe – against ***patriarchal feudal absolutism***.

So long, therefore, as we help to subjugate Poland, so long as we keep part of Poland fettered to Germany, we shall remain fettered to Russia and to the Russian policy, and shall be unable to eradicate patriarchal feudal absolutism in Germany ...

But the restoration of Poland and the settlement of her frontiers with Germany is not only necessary, it is the most easily solvable of all the political problems which have arisen in Eastern Europe since the revolution. The struggle for independence of the diverse nationalities jumbled together south of the Carpathians is much more

> complicated, and will lead to far more bloodshed, confusion and civil wars than the Polish struggle for independence and the establishment of the borderline between Germany and Poland.
>
> Needless to say, it is not a question of restoring a bogus Poland, but of restoring the state upon a viable foundation. Poland must have at least the dimensions of 1772. It must comprise not only the territories but also the estuaries of her big rivers, and at least a large seaboard on the Baltic.[23]

The criticism of the Polish aristocracy is here even sharper than in the Brussels speeches. Only a Poland of peasant democracy, carrying out an agrarian revolution simultaneously with the restoration of the country's national existence, only an independent Poland possessing a Baltic coast and the mouths of the Polish rivers, only such a Poland can constitute an insuperable barrier against Russian Tsardom. And the guarantee, the inevitability of the restoration of such a Poland lies, not in the development and strengthening of historical traditions, but in the fact that Poland forms a revolutionary portion of Russia, Austria and Prussia, that she has become a focus of European democracy, while Germany is still bogged down in the feeblest of empty constitutional ideology.

And how could Germany guarantee all this to Poland? Only 'if, after the revolution, they [the Germans] had had the courage, for their own sake, arms in hand, to demand that Russia relinquish Poland'.

This revolutionary war of Germany against Russia would not only have resulted in the liberation of Poland:

> A war with Russia would have meant a complete, open and effective break with the whole of our disgraceful past, the real liberation and unification of Germany, and the establishment of democracy on the ruins of feudalism, and on the wreckage of the short-lived bourgeois dream of power. War with Russia would have been the only possible way of vindicating our honour and our interests with regard to our Slav neighbours, and especially the Poles ... We shrank from it, and the inevitable happened – the reactionary soldiery, beaten in Berlin, raised their head again in Posen; under the pretext of saving Germany's honour and national integrity they raised the banner of counter-revolution and crushed our allies,

> the revolutionary Poles – and for a moment the hoodwinked Germans exultantly applauded their victorious enemies. The new partition of Poland was accomplished, and only the sanction of the German National Assembly was still missing.[24]

III

There can be no doubt that one must not assign the same importance, as expressions of political views, to private letters dictated by passing moods or special circumstances as to works intended from the outset for publication. Nevertheless, such private statements possess considerable interest, if only from the biographical standpoint. For this reason, I am giving here a summary of everything that is contained in the correspondence between Marx and Engels on the Polish question. After all, this correspondence is, for the period of 1851–64, often our only source for elucidating the views of Marx and Engels on certain matters.

Thus, Engels writes on 23 May 1851 a detailed letter to Marx about Poland:

> The more I think about it, the more obvious it becomes to me that the Poles are *une nation foutue* [a nation that is done for] who can only continue to serve a purpose until such time as Russia herself becomes caught up in an agrarian revolution. From that moment Poland will have absolutely no *raison d'être* any more. The Poles' sole contribution to history has been to indulge in foolish pranks, at once valiant and provocative. Nor can a single moment be cited when Poland, even if only by comparison with Russia, has successfully represented progress, or done anything of historical significance. Russia, on the other hand, is truly progressive in comparison with the East. Russian rule, for all its infamy, all its Slavic dirtiness, is civilising for the Black and Caspian Seas and Central Asia, for the Bashkirs and Tartars; and Russia has absorbed far more cultural elements, and especially industrial elements, than Poland, which by nature is chivalrously indolent. The very fact that the Russian aristocracy, from the Tsar and Prince Demidov[25] down to the most louse-ridden boyar, fourteenth class, who's merely *blagorodno*, well-born, manufactures, haggles, cheats, lays

itself open to corruption, engages in all manner of business, Christian and Jewish – that is in itself an advantage. Poland has never been able to naturalise foreign elements – the Germans in the cities are and will remain Germans. In Russia every second generation Russo-German is a living example of that country's ability to Russify Germans and Jews. There, even the Jews acquire Slav cheekbones.

Napoleon's wars of 1807 and 1812 provide striking examples of Poland's 'immortality'. The only immortal thing about the Poles is their aimless quarrelling. Moreover, the greater part of Poland, what is known as West Russia, that is, Byelostok,[26] Grodno, Smolensk, Minsk, Mogilev, Volhynia and Podolia, has, with minor exceptions, quietly allowed itself to be ruled by Russia since 1772: save for a few scattered members of the bourgeoisie and the nobility, *ils n'ont pas bougé* [they haven't stirred]. A quarter of all Poles speak Lithuanian, one quarter Ruthenian[27] and a small portion semi-Russian, while a good third of the Polish element proper is Germanised.

Fortunately, in the *Neue Rheinische Zeitung* we assumed no positive obligations towards the Poles, save the unavoidable one of restoration combined with a *suitable* frontier – and even that only on condition of there being an agrarian revolution. I'm convinced that such a revolution will sooner be fully effected in Russia than in Poland, because of the national character and because of Russia's more developed bourgeois elements. What are Warsaw and Cracow compared with St Petersburg, Moscow, Odessa, etc, etc?

Conclusion: To take as much as possible away from the Poles in the West, to man their fortresses, especially Posen, with Germans on the pretext of defence, to let them stew in their own juice, send them into battle, gobble bare their land, fob them off with promises of Riga and Odessa and, should it be possible to get the Russians moving, to ally oneself with the latter and compel the Poles to give way. Every inch of the frontier between Memel[28] and Cracow we cede to the Poles will, militarily speaking, be utterly ruinous to this already wretchedly weak frontier, and will leave exposed the whole of the Baltic coast as far as Stettin.

> Besides, I am convinced that, come the next fracas, the entire Polish insurrection will be confined to Poseners and Galician nobility, together with a few who have come over from the Kingdom, this having been bled so white that it's capable of nothing more, and that the pretensions of these knights, unless supported by French, Italians and Scandinavians, etc, and bolstered up by rumpuses on the part of the Czechs, will founder on the wretchedness of their performance. A nation which can muster 20,000 to 30,000 men at most is not entitled to a voice. And Poland certainly could not muster very much more.[29]

When we compare this onslaught with the articles in the *Neue Rheinische Zeitung*, the very great difference between them is immediately apparent. Such a sudden change of position by the highly impulsive Engels can be explained by the fact that in the conflict which was then in progress between the democrats and the Communists the Polish émigrés had sided with the former. True, he dwells only on the question of what concessions 'the Germans' can make to the Poles. In the *Neue Rheinische Zeitung*, Engels also sees the Poles as a predominantly agricultural people, and includes the Russians amongst those Slavonic peoples that possess a future.

Marx's reply is not known.[30] Probably, the two friends had the opportunity soon after this to exchange orally their views on this question, at the rendezvous about which they wrote at the time. In any case, the articles on the Polish question among those which they wrote in 1851 and 1852 for the *New York Tribune* are marked by less enthusiasm and categoricalness than the article in the *Neue Rheinische Zeitung* which Engels summarises for his new article:

> The revolution of 1848 calling forth at once the claim of all oppressed nations to an independent existence and to the right of all to settle their own affairs for themselves, it was quite natural that the Poles should at once demand the restoration of their country within the frontiers of the old Polish republic before 1772. It is true that this frontier, even at that time, had become obsolete, if taken as the delimitation of German and Polish nationality; it had become more so every year since, by the progress of Germanisation; but then, the Germans had proclaimed such an enthusiasm for the restoration of Poland that they must expect to be asked, as a first proof of the reality

of their sympathies, to give up their share of the plunder. On the other hand, should whole tracts of land, inhabited chiefly by Germans, should large towns, entirely German, be given up to a people that as yet had never given any proofs of its capability of progressing beyond a state of feudalism based upon agricultural serfdom? The question was intricate enough. The only possible solution was in a war with Russia. The question of delimitation between the different revolutionised nations would have been made a secondary one to that of first establishing a safe frontier against the common enemy: the Poles, by receiving extended territories in the East, would have become more tractable and reasonable in the West; and Riga and Mitau would have been deemed, after all, quite as important to them as Danzig and Elbing.[31] Thus, the advanced party in Germany, deeming a war with Russia necessary to keep up the continental movement, and considering that the national re-establishment of even a part of Poland would inevitably lead to such a war, supported the Poles; while the reigning middle class party clearly foresaw its downfall from any national war against Russia, which would have called more active and energetic men to the helm, and, therefore, with a feigned enthusiasm for the extension of German nationality, they declared Prussian Poland, the chief seat of Polish revolutionary agitation, to be part and parcel of the German Empire that was to be. The promises given to the Poles in the first days of excitement were shamefully broken. Polish armaments got up with the sanction of the government were dispersed and massacred by Prussian artillery; and as soon as the month of April 1848, within six weeks of the Berlin revolution, the Polish movement was crushed, and the old national hostility revived between Poles and Germans. This immense and incalculable service to the Russian autocrat was performed by the liberal merchant-ministers Camphausen and Hansemann.[32] It must be added that this Polish campaign was the first means of reorganising and reassuring that same Prussian army which afterwards turned out the liberal party and crushed the movement which Messrs. Camphausen and Hansemann had taken such pains to bring about. 'Whereby they sinned, thereby are they punished.' Such has been the fate of all the upstarts of 1848 and 1849,

> from Ledru-Rollin to Changarnier,[33] and from Camphausen down to Haynau.[34]

Marx also wrote about the Polish question in 1853 in his articles devoted to Palmerston's policy, which appeared almost simultaneously in the *New York Tribune* and the Chartist *People's Paper*.[35] But here we find only a merciless and sarcastic exposure of all the contradictions and all the hypocrisy that characterised Palmerston's attitude towards Poland.

Subsequently, Marx and Engels continued to raise doubts as to the correctness of their earlier views.[36] In order to settle these doubts, they went on studying the Polish question in depth. Evidence for this is provided by some letters of 1856. Thus, on 16 October of that year Marx writes to Engels:

> Herewith an extract from a book by Mieroslawski. As you know he's not without *esprit* [wit]. But there's also much *esprit de mauvais aloi* [wit of dubious quality] in his writing, in particular a great deal of the *style amphigourique* [stilted style] which the French have been at such pains to acquire since they became 'profound' and ceased being superficial Voltaireans.[37] Also much of that enthusiastic unguent used by 'unappreciated' nationalities to glorify their *passé* [past history]. Hatred of Russia, and even more of Germany; anti-Pan-Slavism,[38] but, on the other hand, free *confederation* of Slav *nations*, with the Poles as the *peuple-Archimède* [the nation that is to play the decisive role in bringing this change about]. Distinct emphasis on social revolution in Poland as the basic condition of the political one; but seeks to show by means of historical deduction, which proves exactly the *reverse*, that orthodoxy lies in restoring the old agrarian commune (*gmina* – the Russian commune *latinised*).[39]

Although Marx also criticises the tendency of the Polish émigrés, Mieroslawski included, to try and bring about 'a diplomatic revolution under the protection of Louis Bonaparte and Palmerston', he stays loyal to his previous opinion. On 2 December 1856, he writes to Engels:

> In my recent studies of Polish history what led me *décidément* [definitively] to plump for Poland, was the historical fact that the intensity and viability of all revolutions

> since 1789 can be gauged with fair accuracy by their attitude towards Poland. Poland is their 'external' thermometer. This is demonstrable *en détail* from French history. It is conspicuous in our German revolutionary period, likewise in the Hungarian.[40]

In his pamphlet *Herr Vogt*, Marx subjects the pro-Russian views of Karl Vogt to destructive criticism: 'Vogt demands not the emancipation of the Polish nationality from Russians, Austrians and Prussians, but the absorption by Russia and the annihilation of the entire former kingdom of Poland. *Finis Poloniae!*'[41]

Marx stresses especially the danger that would threaten Germany in that event:

> When Russia annexed by far the largest portion of Poland proper by virtue of the treaties of 1815, it gained a position which extended so far westward, and drove, as it were, a wedge not only between Austria and Prussia, but also between East Prussia and Silesia, that even at the time Prussian officers (such as Gneisenau)[42] pointed out that such frontiers could not be tolerated in relation to so powerful a neighbour. However, it was not until 1831, when the defeat of Poland put the whole territory at the mercy of Russia, that the true significance of the wedge became clear. The subjugation of Poland was no more than a pretext for constructing the grandiose chain of fortresses at Warsaw, Modlin and Ivangorod.[43] Its real purpose was complete strategic control of the basin of the Vistula, and the establishment of a base from which to launch attacks to the north, south and west. Even Haxthausen,[44] who enthused about the Orthodox Tsar and all things Russian, regards this as a very definite danger, and a threat to Germany. The Russian fortifications on the Vistula pose a greater threat to Germany than all the French fortresses put together, especially if and when Polish national resistance were to cease completely, and Russia were able to use Poland's war potential as its own force of aggression.[45]

The arguments used in the *Neue Rheinische Zeitung* had not included this, so to speak, strategic proof of the need to restore an independent Poland. Marx thought at this time that 'the emancipation of the serfs, as the Russian government sees it, would increase the aggressive power of Russia a hundredfold' – a view which he subsequently came to revise.[46]

IV

The Polish rising of 1863 aroused in Marx and Engels new hopes of revolution. A considerable role was played here by memories of the Cracow rising, which seemed to them to have been the forerunner of the revolution of 1848.

'What do you think of the Polish business?' Marx writes to Engels on 13 February 1863:

> This much is certain – the era of revolution has now fairly opened in Europe once more. And the general state of affairs is good. But the comfortable delusions and almost childish enthusiasm with which we welcomed the revolutionary era before February 1848, have gone by the board. Old comrades such as Weerth,[47] etc, are no more, others have fallen by the wayside or gone to the bad and, if there is new stock, it is, at least, not yet in evidence. Moreover, we now know what role stupidity plays in revolutions, and how they are exploited by blackguards. Incidentally, the 'Prussian' enthusiasts for the 'Italian' and 'Hungarian' nationalities are finding themselves in a fix. The 'Prussians' are not going to deny their Russian sympathies. This time, let us hope, the lava will flow from East to West and not in the opposite direction, so that we shall be spared the 'honour' of the French initiative.[48]

In his next letter, Marx proposes to Engels that they issue a manifesto in the name of the London Workingmen's Association: 'You must write the *military* bit, that is, on Germany's military and political interest in the restoration of Poland. I shall write the diplomatic bit.'[49]

Engels, who thought that if these 'splendid [Polish] fellows' could hold out until 15 March, rebellion would break out all over Russia, and that 'there would seem to be almost more chance of victory than of defeat',[50] at once approved Marx's project and suggested the following plan for the pamphlet:

> (1) Russia's military position vis-à-vis the West and South *before* (2) ditto *after* the 3 partitions of Poland (3) ditto after 1814: (4) the attitude of Russia and of Germany after the restoration of Poland. (Something will

> have to be said here about Prussian Poland, linguistic boundaries, and the statistical proportions of the mixed population). All in all, at most 3-4 sheets; title: 'Germany and Poland: Politico-Military Considerations on the Occasion of the Polish Uprising of 1863'.[51]

However, events moved faster than the friends had expected. Marx saw the appointment of Langiewicz[52] to be dictator as 'suspicious'. It was a fact which he could interpret as signifying the victory of the aristocratic section among the Polish émigrés. What also seemed to him suspicious was the attitude of the representatives abroad of the Polish national government towards the British and French governments. Finally, it became clear to him that Prussia's opposition to the revolt was very strong. He wrote to Engels on 24 March 1863:

> Politically, the view I have reached is this: that Bismarck and Vincke[53] do in fact *accurately* represent the principle of the Prussian state: that the 'state' of Prussia (a very different creature from Germany) cannot exist either *without* the present Russia as she is, or with an independent Poland. The whole history of Prussia leads one to the conclusion which was obvious long since to Messrs Hohenzollern (Frederick II included). This princely consciousness is infinitely superior to the limited mentality of the subject that marks your Prussian liberal. Since, therefore, the existence of Poland is necessary to Germany, and completely incompatible with the state of Prussia, the state of Prussia must be erased from the map. Or the Polish question simply provides further occasion for proving that it is impossible to prosecute German interests so long as the Hohenzollerns' own state continues to exist.[54]

Nothing came of the project for a pamphlet. In August 1863, Marx became acquainted with Colonel Lapinski,[55] who, along with Bakunin, undertook an expedition in aid of the Poles in revolt, which, however, ended in complete failure. As Marx writes to Engels on 12 September 1863, in London Lapinski set himself the task of raising 'a German Legion in London, even only 200 strong, so that he can confront the Russians in Poland with the black, red and gold flag, partly so to "exasperate" the Parisians, partly to see whether there is any possibility whatsoever of bringing the Germans in Germany back to their senses. What's lacking is money. Efforts are being made down here to exploit all the German societies, etc., to this end'.[56]

In London, the German Workers' Educational Association invited the German workers, in a special appeal, to contribute money to help the Poles. The principles set forth and the explanation given of the importance of the Polish question for Germany show clearly that the author of this appeal was Marx.

It differs from earlier declarations only in that it includes, in connection with the debates in the Prussian Chamber of Deputies about the convention between Prussia and Russia signed on 18 February 1863, a description of the position of the bourgeois parties on the Polish question:

> In this fateful moment, the German working class owes it to the Poles, to foreign countries and to its own honour, to raise a loud protest against the German betrayal of Poland, which is at the same time treason to Germany and to Europe. It must inscribe the ***Restoration of Poland*** in letters of flame on its banner, since bourgeois liberalism has erased this glorious motto from its own flag.[57]

And the appeal offers to the German workers as an example the conduct of the British working class, who by means of mass meetings prevented their ruling classes from intervening in favour of the American slaveowners.[58]

V

If any particular importance is to be attributed to the events which served, to a greater or lesser extent, as the *occasion* for the foundation of the International Workingmen's Association, then it must be acknowledged that the Polish rising played a central role here. Thus, British workers came together on 22 July 1863 at a meeting in St James's Hall in London in order to urge their government to intervene energetically on behalf of Poland. However, by the time the meeting was held, in St Martin's Hall on 28 September 1864, at which the International Workingmen's Association was formed, the Polish rising had already been finally crushed, and so the inaugural address composed by Marx and published by the Provisional Central Council in November 1864 confined itself to a protest against 'the shameless approval, mock sympathy or idiotic indifference'[59] with which the ruling classes looked upon the destruction by Russia of heroic Poland. No positive demand in relation to the Polish question was included in the address – which, however, was not a programme.

Naturally, Marx did all in his power to get the International Workingmen's Association to include the restoration of Poland in its programme. During the two years that preceded the first congress of the International, he made use of every opportunity to put forward and defend this demand. Thus, at the session of the Provisional Central Council on 29 November 1864, the following resolution regarding Poland was adopted: 'Resolved that the Polish war of independence was made in the general interests of the peoples of Europe; that in its defeat the cause of civilisation and human progress suffered a severe shock; second, that Poland has an unimpeachable claim upon the leading nations of Europe to contribute by every necessary means towards the restoration of her national sovereignty.'[60]

Moreover, in accordance with a resolution moved by Peter Fox,[61] it was also decided to publish an address to the Polish people in the name of the British members of the Provisional Central Council. In a letter to Engels of 10 December 1864, Marx writes the following in this connection:

> There was a subcommittee meeting last Tuesday, at which Mr Peter Fox (his real name is P Fox André) presented his address on Poland to us. (This kind of thing is always dealt with beforehand in the sub-committee before going to the General Committee.) The piece is not badly written and Fox has endeavoured to employ the concept of 'class', at least a semblance of it, although it is normally alien to him. His real forte is foreign policy, and it is only as a propagandist of atheism that he has had dealings with the working classes as such ...[62]
>
> Fox, like his friend Beesly (Professor of Political Economy at the University of London,[63] he took the chair at the founding meeting in St Martin's Hall) and other 'Democrats', have a fanatical 'love' of France,[64] which, as far as foreign policy is concerned, they extend not only to Napoleon I but even to Boustrapa,[65] as opposed to what they call, not without justice, the English aristocratic tradition, and as a continuation of what they call the English democratic tradition of 1791–92. Well! Not content in his address (which, incidentally, is not to appear as an address from the whole Association, but as an address from the ***English*** section concerning the Polish question, *endorsed* by the whole Committee) with telling the Poles, which is true, that the French people has been

> traditionally more sympathetic towards them than the English, Mr Fox winds up his address mainly by consoling the Poles with the passionate friendship that the English working classes have conceived for the French democrats. I opposed this and unfolded a historically irrefutable tableau of the constant French betrayal of Poland, from Louis XV[66] to Bonaparte III ... To cut matters short, Fox's address was accepted by the sub-committee on condition that he altered the 'tail' in accordance with my suggestions. Jung,[67] the Swiss Secretary (from French Switzerland) announced that, as a minority on the General Council, he would move that the address be rejected as altogether 'bourgeois'.[68]

After prolonged debates at the sessions of the Provisional Central Council on 13 December 1864 and 3 January 1865 it was resolved 'that, the views expressed in the address concerning the French foreign policy towards Poland not being borne out by historical facts, it be amended so as to accord with the truths of history'.[69] The subsequent fate of the address is unknown to me.

At its meeting of 10 January 1865, the Provisional Central Council received a deputation from the British 'League for the Independence of Poland' and representatives of the National Government of Poland, who proposed to the International Workingmen's Association that they hold a joint meeting. It was resolved 'that should the Polish Committee call the meeting, this Association pledges itself to assist by all means in its power the commemoration of the glorious, though unsuccessful, revolution of 1863'.[70]

But the organising of this meeting encountered difficulties. Marx writes about them in his letter to Engels of 25 February 1865:

> Incidentally, other parliamentarians, such as Taylor,[71] etc (fellows who have close links with Mazzini),[72] have taken it into their heads to tell us that the *time* was not *opportune* for a Polish meeting. I answered through our Council that the *working class* has *its own foreign policy*, which is most certainly not determined by what the *middle class* consider *opportune*. They have always considered it *opportune to goad on the Poles at the beginning of a new outbreak to betray them during its progress by their diplomacy, and to desert them when Russia had thrown them down*. In fact the chief purpose of the meeting is to raise money to support them.

> Are the poor émigrés (*this time mostly workingmen and peasants* and thus not in the least *protected by Prince Zamoyski & Co*) to starve because it appears to the *English middle class just not opportune to mention even the name of Poland?*[73]

Nevertheless, the meeting held on 1 March 1865 went very well. We know about this from a hitherto unpublished letter from Marx to Jung, which also throws much light on Marx's position on the Central Council.[74]

But interest in the Polish question was declining not only in bourgeois circles. It was on the decline also among a section of the British working class and, especially, among the French and Belgian workers. So far as France and Belgium were concerned, this was due to the increasing influence of Proudhonism at this time. Proudhon had already in 1861 opposed the restoration of Poland.[75] In December 1863, in his work *Si les traités de 1815 ont cessé d'exister. Actes du futur congrès*, he recommended acceptance of the power of Russia, and strongly opposed any support for the Polish cause by European democracy.[76] If we remember that Proudhon wrote this at the very time when Muravyov and Berg[77] were doing their frightful hangmen's work in Poland and Lithuania, we can understand the psychology of Marx's verdict on Proudhon – that in 'his last work, written against Poland ... for the greater glory of the Tsar, he expresses the cynicism of a cretin'.[78]

This idea of Proudhon's was advocated, though not so fervently, by his follower Hector Denis in a series of articles which appeared in the most advanced organ of the Belgian labour movement.[79] That these articles did not fail to influence the Belgian workers was brought home to Marx in September 1865 at the first conference of the International Workingmen's Association in London.

The Central Council put before the conference its proposed agenda for the coming congress. This included a point formulated by Marx: 'The Muscovite invasion of Europe and the restoration of an independent and integral Poland'. The Belgian delegate César Paepe[80] fervently opposed this item. The French delegates either remained neutral or also opposed. Among the British delegates, too, opponents were found. Nevertheless, in the end it was accepted. It is clear, however, that a strong resistance was to be expected at the coming congress. And, in fact, immediately after the conference, Vésinier[81] began a campaign against the Central Council which was focused on the question of Poland. Marx wrote to Engels about this on 5 January:

> The real crux of the controversy is *the Polish question*. The fellows have all attached themselves to the Muscovist line pursued by Proudhon and Herzen.[82] I shall therefore send you the earlier articles by the oracles in the *Tribune du Peuple* against Poland and you must do a refutation, either for our paper in Geneva (the 'German' one) or for the *Workman's Advocate*. The Russian gentlemen have acquired some brand-new allies in the Proudhonised section of *Jeune France*.[83]

Owing to a variety of circumstances, Engels' series of articles – which, moreover, remained unfinished – appeared not in the *Workman's Advocate*, but in its successor, *Commonwealth*.[84]

In his first article, Engels explains that the foreign policy of the working classes at the outset of the genuine labour movement can be summarised in a few words: restoration of Poland. Then he attacks Proudhon and his adherents, and shows in detail why it is *Russia* that, despite the roles played by Prussia and Austria, bears the main guilt for the partition of Poland. Engels concludes by setting out the conditions for Russia, as a nation, to be able to separate herself from Tsardom. If the Russian working class will adopt a political programme which includes the emancipation of Poland, then the Tsar's government alone will remain 'under accusation'.

In his second article, Engels argues against the assertion that the demand for the restoration of Poland amounts to a recognition of the Bonapartist 'principle of nationalities'.[85] Referring to historical facts, he shows that, on the contrary, this principle is a Russian invention, and establishes a distinction between the principle of nationalities and 'the old democratic and working-class tenet as to the right of the great European *nations* to separate and independent existence'.[86]

In his third article, Engels examines the principle of nationalities and its relevance to Poland. He does not deny that it was the aristocracy that brought Poland to ruin (this was the Proudhonists' favourite argument),[87] but at the same time he stresses the ruthlessness with which Russia exploited this weak point.

In the memorandum composed by Marx which the General Council submitted to the Geneva Congress in September 1866, he, for his part, tries to explain the importance of the Polish question and to answer the principal objections put forward by his opponents.

> (a) Why do the workmen of Europe take up this question? In the first instance, because the middle-class writers and agitators try to suppress it, although they

> patronise all sorts of nationalities, on the Continent, even Ireland. Whence this reticence? Because both aristocrats and bourgeois look upon the dark Asiatic power in the background as a last resource against the advancing tide of working-class ascendancy. That power can only be effectually put down by the restoration of Poland upon a democratic basis.
>
> (b) In the present changed state of Central Europe, and especially Germany, it is more than ever necessary to have a democratic Poland. Without it, Germany will become the outwork of the Holy Alliance; with it, the cooperator with republican France. The working-class movement will continuously be interrupted, checked and retarded until this great European question be set to rest.
>
> (c) It is especially the duty of the German working class to take the initiative in this matter, because Germany is one of the partitioners of Poland.[88]
>
> I pass over here the debates at the Geneva Congress. Despite all the efforts made by old Becker[89] and the delegates of the Central Council, they were unable to convince the majority. No resolution was adopted, and the congress merely expressed the wish that 'the growth and expansion of the International Working Men's Association will, of itself, call to life a social democratic Poland'.

A few months after the Geneva Congress, on 22 January 1867, the General Council organised, jointly with the Polish Workers Association, a public meeting to commemorate the anniversary of the rising of 1863. Jung took the chair. As usual at such meetings, the resolutions were moved and seconded by different speakers, so that each resolution advocated a particular point which was advanced in the speech made by its mover. The first resolution, on the significance and programme of the rising, was moved and seconded by the Poles Zabicki and Bobczynski.[90] It declared:

> The Poles here assembled to commemorate the anniversary of their insurrection declare that they faithfully adhere to the *Manifesto* of the Polish National Government, dated 22 January 1863, which *Manifesto* abolished all privileges, endowed the peasantry with land, and proclaimed all the inhabitants without distinction free and equal before the law, and they firmly believe

> that this is the only available means to resist the present nefarious attempts of the Muscovite Tsar to decompose Polish society into fragments of various classes, religions and races, and the only just principle whereon to consolidate the unity of the people, and to organise a national power sufficiently strong to recover their freedom and independence, and further, they appeal to this meeting to declare that in the prosecution of these aims they are entitled to the goodwill and cooperation of all free and civilised people, and, especially, the working classes throughout the world.

The second resolution, moved by Marx and seconded by Eccarius,[91] spoke of the importance of the Polish question for Europe and affirmed 'that liberty cannot be established in Europe without the independence of Poland'.[92]

I omit the third resolution, moved by the Frenchman Besson,[93] and the fourth, moved by the Englishman Fox.

The report of the meeting in the *Vorbote*[94] does not quote the individual speeches, but summarises them thus:

> All the speeches were brief and concise. What was chiefly stressed was that Poland had served for a century as the barrier between Western civilisation and Eastern barbarism, that Europe had been able to attain its present level of culture only because the Poles had stood on guard for it and prevented the advance of barbarism; that the partition of Poland had broken down that barrier, installed Russian barbarism in the very heart of Europe, as the ally of the ruling classes against the oppressed; and that the labour question in the West cannot be solved unless that dam protecting the cradle of bourgeois society is restored which an independent Poland would maintain against the Russian deluge; that nobody but the working class is capable of fighting for the restoration of Poland; and that this fight is a sacred duty for the workers.

Marx's speech in defence of his resolution was printed in the French journal *Le Socialisme*, in its issue for 15 March 1908, devoted to Marx, in a translation from the English original presented to the editors by Madame Lafargue.[95] Both the Lafargues and the editors of *Le Socialisme* thought that Marx delivered this speech in 1862, because he makes no mention in it of the Polish rising of 1863, but does mention the emancipation of the Russian peasants in 1861. They did not pay attention to the above-mentioned division of labour between the various speakers, or to the mention in the speech of other facts relating to a period later than 1862. Thus, for example, the speech opens with a reference to 'the last Russian ukases for the abolition of Poland', that is, the three ukases issued on 31 December 1866, by virtue of which Russian Poland was completely merged with Russia proper so far as administration was concerned. This is also the explanation for the adoption of the fourth resolution, which was moved at this meeting by P Fox and seconded by Dupont.[96] My supposition is likewise confirmed by Marx's sarcastic observation in which he attributes the advice given by the organ of the stock exchange (probably by the *Economist*) that these ukases be accepted calmly, to the fact that this would give further security to the six million pounds sterling which had recently been lent to the Tsar by British capitalists, a loan concluded on 4 November 1866.[97]

In support of the resolution he is moving, Marx begins with a survey of the history of the Polish revolution. This shows that it was only the rising in Poland that saved Europe from the conspiracy between Charles X[98] and Nicholas I and another anti-Jacobin war. Just as good service was rendered by the Poles in 1848–49, during the conflict between the revolution and Tsardom. Has the situation changed since then? Has the danger from Russia vanished? Has Poland become merely a sentimental memory? No, only the blindness of Europe's ruling classes is responsible for that. Russia's policy has remained the same: its methods and motives have changed, but not its ultimate aim, the empire of the world:

> As the greatest Russian diplomat of modern times, Pozzo di Borgo, wrote to Alexander I, at the epoch of the Vienna Congress, Poland is the great tool for the execution of the world-embracing dreams of Russia, but also her irresistible obstacle, until the Pole, fatigued by the accumulated treacheries of Europe, becomes her scourge in the hands of the Muscovite. Now, apart from the dispositions of the Polish people, has anything happened to thwart the plans of Russia or paralyse her action?[99]

Marx points to the successes of Russian policy in Asia. The sham war[100] waged by Britain and France resulted in Russian domination of the Caucasus and the Black Sea. New railways have concentrated Russia's strength. New fortifications in Warsaw, Modlin and

Ivangorod have increased her offensive capability. Panslavist propaganda has weakened Austria and Turkey. So far back as 1848 one saw what that meant. And Britain's persecution of the Irish has raised up new allies for Russia on the other side of the Atlantic.[101]

A continental European may answer that, with the emancipation of the serfs. Russia has become a civilised country: that the German power recently concentrated in Prussia's hands can serve as a barrier against Russia;[102] that a social revolution will put an end to all 'international conflicts'. An Englishman who reads nothing but the ***Times*** will think that, even if matters come to the worst, and Russia seizes Constantinople, Britain will then annex Egypt and thereby secure her route to India. However, the emancipation of the serfs has only removed those obstacles which the nobility opposed to centralisation: any attempt at raising the moral[103] level of the peasantry is subject to prosecution: and whatever expectations the emancipation has aroused regarding future developments, for the present it has merely increased the strength of Tsardom.

As to Prussia, in spite of everything, she remained bound to Russia, for without Russia's aid she could never have become a great power. Her ever-growing antagonism towards France and Austria makes the Russian alliance indispensable for Prussia. Besides, Russia is the prop of Hohenzollern absolutism. And the social revolution? It means nothing but the struggle between classes. Perhaps the struggle between workers and capitalists will be less bloody than was the struggle between feudalism and the bourgeoisie in France and England. But, in any case, it will oblige the ruling classes to desire strongly the receipt of aid from Russia. It is an illusion, too, to imagine that Russia will be satisfied with taking Constantinople; not to mention the fact that she can take it only against the opposition of France.

Thus, Europe is faced with only one choice – either Asiatic barbarism, under Muscovite leadership, will overwhelm Europe like an avalanche, or Europe must liberate Poland and thereby place a barrier of 20 million heroes between herself and Asia, until the hour strikes for Europe's social regeneration.

This is the last declaration in favour of Poland known to me which was made by the General Council in London under the influence and with the participation of Marx. As for the old International as a whole, after the Geneva Congress it had no further occasion to concern itself with the Polish Question. This matter played no role in the great dispute between Bakunin and Marx.

VI

The part played by Polish revolutionaries in the Paris Commune revived the old sympathy with oppressed Poland in the ranks of the labour movement, especially in France and Germany. At the same time, in Russia too there was the beginning of a divergence between 'government' and 'society' which pointed to a revolutionary movement in that hitherto immobile 'land of barbarians.' True, this movement, insofar as it was led by Bakunin, prepared a grave disappointment for Marx and Engels. Nevertheless, Marx, that fierce opponent of Tsardom, now became the General Council's secretary, not only for Germany, but also for Russia. And in 1872 there appeared in Russia the first translation of *Capital* to be published anywhere in Europe. In the face of these facts the two friends could not lump together any more, as Engels had still done in his English articles, the Russian government and the Russian people, putting them in the dock side by side.

All this explains why we hear a new note, already in 1874, in a fresh statement by Engels on the Polish question. The occasion for this statement was a proclamation issued by the Polish émigrés in London (who included Wróblewski, the well-known Communard and later secretary for Poland on the General Council)[104] in connection with the visit of Tsar Alexander II to the British capital.

The danger threatening Europe from Russia, writes Engels, is greater than ever before:

> Only because the Russian army prevented Austria from siding with France was Prussia able to defeat France and to complete the Prussian-German military monarchy. Behind all these grand performances of state we see the Russian army. And even if the victory of Germany over France will just as surely produce a war between Russia and Germany – *unless Russia's internal development soon enters a revolutionary flux*[105] – as the victory of Prussia over Austria at Sadowa entailed the Franco-German war, the Russian army will always be prepared to oppose any movement in the interior of Prussia. Even today official Russia is the stronghold and bulwark of all European reaction, her army the reserve of all other armies, ensuring the suppression of all the working-class in Europe.[106]

Then comes an explanation as to why the German labour movement has a particular interest in changing this intolerable situation.

> Yet it is the German workers who are first exposed to the onslaught of this large reserve army of oppression, both in the so-called German Empire and in Austria. As long as the Russians stand behind the Austrian and German bourgeoisie and governments, the sting is taken out of the entire German labour movement. So we, more than any others, have an interest in ridding ourselves of Russian reaction and the Russian army.[107]

Especially important is the conclusion of Engels' statement, which reads as follows:

> And for this task we have only one reliable ally, but one who is reliable regardless of the circumstances – *the Polish people*.
>
> Poland is faced, far more than France is, with the choice of either being revolutionary or perishing. And this scotches all the silly talk concerning the essentially aristocratic nature of the Polish movement. There are plenty of Polish refugees who have aristocratic cravings; but once Poland herself enters the movement it becomes revolutionary through and through, as we have seen in 1846 and in 1863. These movements were not simply national; they were also aimed directly at liberating the peasants and transferring landed property to them. In 1871 the great mass of the Polish refugees in France entered the service of the Commune; was this an act of aristocrats? Did that not prove that these Poles were at the very apex of the modern movement? Since Bismarck introduced the *Kulturkampf*[108] in Posen and, on the pretext of striking a blow against the Pope, searches out Polish textbooks, suppresses the Polish language and does his utmost to drive Poland into the arms of Russia, what happened? The Polish aristocracy is increasingly siding with Russia at least to reunify Poland under Russian rule; the revolutionary masses reply by offering to ally themselves with the German Workers' Party, and fighting in the ranks of the International.
>
> In 1863, Poland showed that she could not be done to death, and continues to show this every day. Her claim to an independent existence in the European family of nations is irrefutable. Her restoration, however, is a necessity for two nations in particular: for the Germans, and for the Russians themselves.

> A people that oppresses another cannot emancipate itself. The power it needs to oppress others is ultimately always turned against itself. As long as there are Russian soldiers in Poland, the Russian people cannot liberate itself politically or socially. At the present state of development in Russia, however, it is beyond dispute that the day Russia loses Poland, the movement will become strong enough in Russia to bring down the existing order. The independence of Poland and revolution in Russia – which is far closer than it would appear on the surface, given the complete social, political and financial breakdown and the corruption that pervades the whole of official Russia – mean for the German workers that the bourgeoisie, the governments, in short, reaction in Germany, will be reduced to their own forces – forces that we shall, in time, overcome.[109]

The difference between this article by Engels and his articles of 1866 and the motivation given by Marx in his Address to the Geneva Congress is obvious. The Polish question has now also become a Russian question, and is no longer merely a German one. The excommunication which in 1866 Marx and Engels pronounced upon the Russian people has been lifted. And Engels' argument not only became the common property of all the Russian revolutionaries of the 1870s, but also down to the most recent times part of the creed of the Russian Social-Democratic labour movement. There were still differences of view, but not on the question of the ***restoration of a democratic and independent Poland, only on the historical possibilities and conditions for this restoration***.

Marx and Engels went even further in their last joint statement on the Polish Question, at the end of 1880, in connection with the Jubilee commemoration of the rising of 1830, organised on 29 November 1880 in Geneva by the editors of the Polish Socialist journal *Równość* (Equality). This was a time when the revolutionary movement in Russia led by *Narodnaya Volya* was much stronger than the Polish movement, and 'by its self-sacrifice and heroism brought the autocracy to a position where it was already having to contemplate the possibility and conditions of capitulation'.

The declaration was signed by Marx, Engels, Lafargue and Lessner,[110] in their capacity as former members of the General Council of the old International.[111] It gave a concise historical outline of the role played by the Poles in all the wars of liberation and revolutions since the American War of Independence in the eighteenth century. 'Thus the cry "Long Live Poland!" really meant: Death to the Holy Alliance, death to the military despotism of Russia, Prussia and Austria, death to Mongol rule over modern society.'[112]

After the July revolution and the conquest of political power by the bourgeoisie in France and Britain, the working-class movement began to develop. In Britain, the ruling classes had to resort to armed force against the Chartists, the first militant organisation of the working class.

> Then in 1846 in the last corner of independent Poland, Cracow, the first political revolution to proclaim socialist demands broke out. From that time on Poland forfeited all the ostensible sympathies of the whole of property-owning Europe. In 1847 the first international congress of the proletariat met secretly in London. One outcome of this congress was the writing of the *Communist Manifesto*, which ended with the new revolutionary watchword: 'Working Men of all Countries, Unite!' Poland had its representatives at this congress, and at a public meeting in Brussels the famous Lelewel and his supporters declared their adhesion to the resolutions of the congress[113] – in 1848 and 1849 numerous Poles served in the revolutionary German, Italian, Hungarian and Romanian armies, distinguishing themselves as soldiers and commanders. Although the socialist aspirations of this age were drowned in the bloodbath of the June Days, the revolution of 1848 nevertheless – and this should not be forgotten – turned Europe for a moment into one community by seizing it almost entirely with its flame, and in this way prepared the ground for the International Workingmen's Association.
>
> The Polish insurrection of 1863, by giving rise to a joint protest of English and French workers at the international machinations of their governments, formed the starting point for the International, which was founded with the participation of Polish exiles. Finally, the Paris Commune found its true champions among the Polish refugees, and after its fall, it was sufficient to be a Pole to be shot by the war tribunals in Versailles.
>
> Thus outside the borders of their country the Poles have played a major part in the struggle for the emancipation of the proletariat; in this struggle they were its international combat force.

> May the struggle develop among the Polish people itself, may our propaganda and the refugee press support it, and may it unite with the ***unparalleled endeavours of our Russian brethren***; this will be yet another reason to echo the cry of old: 'Long live Poland!'[114]

The union between Polish and Russian revolutionaries was consummated soon afterward.[115] In 1884, the Polish revolutionary organisation *Proletariat* (whose prominent members were Warynski and Kunicki)[116] concluded with *Narodnaya Volya* a formal alliance for the overthrow of the Tsarist regime.

Marx died before the final defeat of *Narodnaya Volya*. Engels lived long enough, not only to follow the development of the young Russian Social Democratic movement, but also to give it vigorous support. To the first Russian Social Democratic journal, *Sotsial-Demokrat*, he contributed his work entitled 'The Foreign Policy of Russian Tsardom', which appeared later in *Die Neue Zeit* (Volume 8, pp145–154, 193–203).[117] In this Engels explained in detail to the Russian Social Democrats why the West European workers' parties were so much interested in the victory of the Russian revolutionary party. The restoration of Poland remains, as before, a point in the programme of the foreign policy of the European proletariat. In the internal struggle against Tsardom, the Polish proletariat functions now only as an ally of the Russian proletariat, which is waging this struggle, in the most vulnerable centres of Tsarist power, in St Petersburg and Moscow, inside Russia proper.

In 1892, Engels wrote a preface to the Polish edition of *The Communist Manifesto*. Deserving attention is his reference to the development of industry in Poland, which is creating in the numerous proletariat to which it gives rise a fresh guarantee of the coming resurrection. After this, since the Polish nobility has proved to be powerless, and the Polish bourgeoisie shows utter indifference to the question, the liberation of Poland can be achieved only by the Polish proletariat.[118]

Translator's note

The setting of Riazanov's work was this. In the later 1890s and early 1900s, three schools of thought existed in the Second International on the subject of Poland.

Firstly, there were those, particularly on the right wing of the Polish Socialist Party, who claimed that nothing had changed since the days of the First International, and the world's Socialist movement should fight for the reunification and independence of Poland.

Secondly, Lenin and his co-thinkers held that there had been important changes, notably the growth of the revolutionary movement in Russia and the rise of imperialism, with the consequent danger of inter-imperialist wars; and that, therefore, while recognising the Poles' right to self determination, the way Socialists should favour their use of this right must depend on circumstances.

Thirdly, according to Rosa Luxemburg, the changes had been so great – in particular, the integration of the economy of Russian Poland with that of Russia proper – that to talk of self-determination for the Poles was as absurd as to talk of self-determination for Ivanovo-Voznesensk, or any other province in the heart of Great Russia: history had simply eliminated the Polish question as a distinct question in politics. Lenin explains this controversy as he saw it in 'The Right of Nations to Self-Determination', published in April-June 1914 (*Collected Works*, Volume 20, Moscow, 1964, pp432–5) and 'The Discussion on Self-Determination Summed Up', published in October 1916 (*Collected Works*, Volume 22, Moscow, 1964, pp340–6).

Chronology of the Principal Events Mentioned in 'Marx and Engels and the Polish Question'

1794
Offensive by Prussia, Austria and Russia against Jacobin France prevented by revolt in Poland.

1814–15
Defeat of Napoleon; re-drawing of the map of Europe by the Congress of Vienna; formation of the 'Holy Alliance' of the reactionary powers – Russia, Prussia and Austria – to maintain this peace settlement and suppress revolutions.

1830–31
'July Revolution' in France overthrows King Charles X and establishes the constitutional monarchy of Louis-Philippe (1830–48); plans for intervention by the 'Holy Alliance' prevented by revolt in Poland.

1846
Revolt in Cracow, which the Congress of Vienna had made 'a free state under the protection of Russia, Austria and Prussia'.

1848–1849
Revolutions in France and Germany; revolt in Hungary, helped by

Polish émigrés, suppressed by Russian intervention in aid of the Austrian Emperor.

1851
Coup d'état in France establishes the 'Second Empire' under Napoleon III ('The Eighteenth Brumaire of Louis Bonaparte').

1863
Revolt in Poland.

1866
Austro-Prussian War; Battle of Sadowa.

1870–71
Franco-Prussian War; defeat and capitulation of French army at Sedan (2 September 1870); Paris Commune; establishment of German Empire dominated by Prussia.

Notes

1. Cf *Emigracju polska od 1831 do 1863. Krótki rys historyczny*, Leipzig, 1865; *Demokracja polska na emigracji, wyjatki z pism W Heltmana*, Leipzig, 1866; L Gadan, *Emigracja polska*, Cracow, 1901 (author's note).
2. L Sawaszkiewicz, *Notice sur la vie de Joachim Lelewel*, Brussels, 1862. A letter from Lelewel to Marx is printed in the latter's *Herr Vogt*, p188 (author's note) (Marx-Engels, *Collected Works*, Volume 17, Moscow, 1981, p322; New Park edition, London, 1982, p303. Translator's note).
3. Ludwik Oborski (1787–1873) was a member of the Society of Fraternal Democrats and of the General Council of the First International in 1865–67. He took part in the Polish uprising of 1831 and the 1848 revolution in Germany (translator's note).
4. Karl Schapper (1812–1870) took part in the 1848 revolution in Germany, and was a member of the Communist League and of the General Council of the First International in 1865 (translator's note).
5. Adam Jerzy Czartoryski (1770–1861) had been deputy Foreign Minister of Russia under Alexander I, when he put forward the idea of a union of all the Polish lands under the Russian crown; he headed the Polish National Government during the insurrection of 1830–31, where he obstructed reform (translator's note).
6. Cf B Limanowski, *Historja ruchu spolecznego w xix stuleciu*, Lwów, 1890; W Narkiewicz-Jodko and S Dickstein, *Polski socyalizm utopijny na emigracji*, Cracow, 1907; S Szpotanski, *Lud Polski*, Lwów, 1907 (author's note).
7. Ludwik Mieroslawski (1814–1878) fought in the 1830–31 rising, and had been sent to organise the revolt in Poznan in 1845. He subsequently tried to gain control of the movement for Polish independence in the emigration, and was proclaimed dictator at the start of the 1863–64 uprising (translator's note).
8. A Piller, *Historja narodu polskiego w 1861–64*, Paris, 1867–71, Volume 3; J Krajewski, *Jajne zwiazki polityczne w Galicyi, 1833–41*, Lwów, 1903; B Limanowski, *Historja demokracyi polskiej w epoce porozbiorowej*, part 9, Zurich, 1901 (author's note).
9. In the *eastern* part of Galicia (Austrian Poland), now the Western Ukraine, the peasants were mostly Ukrainian ('Ruthenian') and the landlords mostly Polish, and the national and religious antagonism between them played its part in these events. Actually, as Rosdolsky points out, Cracow being in *western* Galicia, the peasants who helped to put down the rising were *Polish* peasants (translator's note).

10. Ludwik Ozeasz Lubliner (1809–1868) was a Polish lawyer and revolutionary, who emigrated to Brussels after the failure of the Polish national uprising (translator's note).
11. Lucien Léopold Jottrand (1804–1877), a lawyer and journalist, was the President of the Brussels Democratic Association (translator's note).
12. Jacques Imbert (1793–1851), was a French journalist, democrat and Socialist, who was Vice-President of the Brussels Democratic Association (translator's note).
13. Cf L Bertrand, *Histoire de la démocratie et du socialisme en Belgique depuis 1830*, Volume 1, Brussels, 1906, pp250–70; L Jottrand, *Charles-Louis Spilthorn*, Brussels, 1872 (author's note).
14. This meeting was reported in the *Deutsche Brusseler Zeitung* of 9 and 12 December and the Paris *La Réforme* of 5 December 1847. The latter report was reprinted in C Andler's edition of *The Communist Manifesto* (*Bibliothèque socialiste*, no 8), Paris, 1901, pp76–9, and also, together with a second article in *La Réforme* attributed to Engels, in Bernstein's *Dokumente der Sozialismus*, Volume 1, pp218–24. Franz Mehring's *Einiges für Parteigeschichte*, in *Die Neue Zeit*, Volume 20, part 1 (1901–02), pp545–8 reproduced the speeches of Marx and Engels from the text given in the *Deutsche Brusseler Zeitung*. Cf also E. Dolléans, *Le Chartisme*, Volume 1, Paris, 1913, pp397–404 (author's note) (pp296–9 in the 1949 edition, translator's note).
15. Karl Marx, *Speech on Poland*, 29 November 1847, Marx and Engels, *Collected Works*, Volume 6, Moscow, 1976, pp388–9 (translator's note).
16. Frederick Engels, *Speech on Poland*, 29 November 1847, Marx and Engels, *Collected Works*, Volume 6, Moscow, 1976, pp389–90 (translator's note).
17. Jean Pellering (1817–1877), a shoemaker, was a working-class activist in Brussels and a member of the Democratic Association; Karl Wallau (1823–1877) had been chairman of a workers' union in Mainz, and was on the Central Authority of the Communist League (translator's note). The speeches by Marx and Engels were published in full in a pamphlet now very rare, being, as far as I know, available only in the Anton Menger Library in the Social Sciences Institute of Vienna University: *Célébration à Bruxelles du deuxième anniversaire de la révolution polonaise de 22 février 1846. Discours prononcés par Mm AS Senault, Karl Marx, Lelewel, F Engels et Louis Lubliner, avocat*, Brussels, CC Vogler, 1948 (author's note) (Marx-Engels, *Collected Works*, Volume 6, Moscow, 1976, pp544–52, translator's note).
18. 'Dniester' may be a slip of the pen for 'Dnieper' (translator's note).
19. Karl Marx, 'The Position of the Communists in Relation to the Various Existing Opposition Parties', in *The Communist Manifesto*, Marx and Engels, *Collected Works*, Volume 6, Moscow, 1976, p518 (translator's note).
20. *Aus dem literarischen Nachlass von Karl Marx, Friedrich Engels und Ferdinand Lassalle*, edited by Franz Mehring, Volume 3: *Gesammelte Schriften von Marx und Engels, 1841–1850*, pp134–82 (author's note).
21. W Jordan (1819–1904) was a writer and a member of the German National Assembly in 1848 (translator's note).
22. Here a distinction is made between the aristocracy, meaning the great feudal magnates, and the mass of the nobles, a class which was exceptionally numerous in Poland. The Constitution was adopted on 3 May 1791, and after Poland was re-established as an independent state in 1918, '3 May' was proclaimed the country's equivalent of '14 July' in France (translator's note).
23. Karl Marx, 'The Frankfurt Assembly Debates the Polish Question', *Neue Rheinische Zeitung*, no 82, 22 August 1848; Marx-Engels, *Collected Works*, Volume 7, London, 1977, pp350–2 (translator's note).
24. Op cit, pp352–3 (translator's note).
25. The Demidovs were a well-known family of mine owners in the Urals. Anatoli Demidov (1812–1870) married a niece of Napoleon and purchased the title of Prince San Donato (translator's note).

26. That is, present day Bialystok (translator's note).
27. Ukrainians under Austrian rule were officially called 'Ruthenes' (translator's note).
28. That is, present-day Klaipeda (translator's note).
29. *Briefwechsel zwischen F Engels und K Marx, herausgegeben von A Bebel und E Bernstein*, 1918, Volume 1, pp189–91 (author's note) (Marx and Engels, *Collected Works*, Volume 38, London, 1987, pp363–365. Translator's note).
30. Marx did write to Engels on 28 May 1851, but his letter does not mention Poland or Russia (translator's note).
31. That is, present-day Elblag (translator's note).
32. Ludolf Camphausen (1803–1890) was a leader of the Rhineland Liberals and premier of Prussia, 1848. David Justus Hansemann (1790–1864), another Rhineland Liberal, was Finance Minister in Prussia at the same time (translator's note).
33. Alexandre Auguste Ledru-Rollin (1807–1874) was a French politician, the editor of *La Réforme*, and Minister of the Interior in the Provisional Government of 1848; Nicolas Anne Théodule Changarnier (1793–1877) was the French monarchist general and politician responsible for dispersing the demonstration of June 1849 (translator's note).
34. Karl Marx, *Revolution and Counter-Revolution in Germany*, German translation by Karl Kautsky, Stuttgart, 1896, pp59–61. The English original was published by Marx's daughter Eleanor Marx-Aveling under the same title in London in 1896. From the correspondence of Marx and Engels it is clear that most of these articles were written by Engels (author's note). (Marx and Engels, *Collected Works*, Volume 11, London, 1979, pp44–46). Julius, Freiherr von Haynau (1786–1853) was known as 'Hangman Haynau' owing to the savagery with which he put down the Hungarian revolt of 1848–9 (translator's note).
35. 'Palmerston and Russia', *New York Tribune*, 4 November 1853, and also in the *People's Paper* of 5 November 1853 and the (Sheffield) *Free Press* of 17 November 1855, repeated in the London edition of the latter, 12 January 1856. This article was reprinted separately in Tucker's Political Flysheets under the title *Palmerston and Poland*, and in 1899 reappeared in the collection *The Story of the Life of Lord Palmerston* by Karl Marx, edited by his daughter Eleanor Marx-Aveling. (In this book pages 22 and 35 are edited in a particularly unsatisfactory way, author's note.) (Marx and Engels, *Collected Works*, Volume 12, Moscow, 1979, pp358, 368–9, translator's note)
36. Engels wrote to Weydemeyer on 12 April 1853: 'As for the former Polish provinces this side of the Dvina and the Dnieper, I have not wanted to hear anything about them ever since I learned that all the peasants there are Ukrainians, while only the nobles and some of the townsmen are Poles, and that for the peasant there the restoration of Poland would mean merely the restoration of the old rule of the nobility in full force, as was the case in Ukrainian Galicia in 1846. In all these areas, that is, outside the Kingdom of Poland proper, there are hardly 500 000 Poles!' (Marx and Engels, *Collected Works*, Volume 34, London, 1983, pp303–11; *Selected Correspondence of Marx and Engels*, Moscow, 1956, p91, translator's note)
37. François Marie Arouet de Voltaire (1694–1778), a French philosopher famous for his opposition to religious obscurantism, was noted for his ready wit (translator's note).
38. Panslavism was the movement in favour of a union of all the Slavs, including those in the Austrian and Turkish empires, under the Tsar of Russia (translator's note).
39. *Briefwechsel*, Volume 2, p129 (Marx-Engels, *Werke*, Volume 29, p79). The book referred to is L Mieroslawski, *De la Nationalité dans l'équilibre européen*, Paris, 1856. I have found very detailed excerpts from this book among Marx's papers, together with other excerpts from books on Polish history (author's note). Karl Marx, Letter to Engels, 16 October 1856, Marx and Engels, *Collected Works*, Volume 40, Moscow, 1983, p75 (translator's note).
40. *Briefwechsel*, Volume 2, p134 (author's note). (Karl Marx, Letter to Engels, 2 December 1856, Marx and Engels, *Collected Works*, Volume 40, Moscow, 1983, p85, translator's note)

41. According to legend, when Tadeusz Andrzej Bonawentura Kosciuszko (1746–1817), the leader of the 1794 rising in Poland, fell wounded in the last battle of the rising, he exclaimed: 'Finis Poloniae!' – 'This means the end of Poland!' (translator's note)
42. Field Marshal August Wilhelm Anton, Graf Neidhart von Gneisenau (1760–1831) was Blücher's Chief of Staff at Waterloo, and died campaigning against the Polish uprising (translator's note).
43. That is, present-day Dęblin (Demblin) (translator's note).
44. August Franz Ludwig Maria Haxthausen (1792–1866) was a Prussian official and economist, the author of several books (translator's note).
45. Karl Marx, *Herr Vogt*, London, 1860, pp78–9 (author's note). (Marx-Engels, *Collected Works*, Volume 17, Moscow, 1971, pp146–8; New Park edition, London, 1982, pp132–3, translator's note)
46. Marx and Engels, *Collected Works*, Volume 7, London, 1977, pp140–1; New Park edition, London, 1982, p127 (translator's note).
47. Georg Weerth (1822–56), one of the editors of the *Neue Rheinische Zeitung*, was a poet and a member of the Communist League (translator's note)
48. *Briefwechsel*, Volume 3, p116) (author's note). Karl Marx, Letter to Engels, 13 February 1863, Marx and Engels, *Collected Works*, Volume 41, London, 1985, p453 (translator's note).
49. *Briefwechsel*, Volume 3, p117 (author's note). Karl Marx, Letter to Engels, 17 February 1863, Marx and Engels, *Collected Works*, Volume 41, London, 1985, p455 (translator's note).
50. Letter of 17 February 1863, *Briefwechsel*, Volume 3, op cit, p118 (author's note). Frederick Engels, Letter to Marx, 17 February 1863, Marx and Engels, *Collected Works*, Volume 41, London, 1985, p455. The point of '15 March' is that this was the date when the emancipation of the peasantry from serfdom, decreed by the Tsar in 1861, was due to come fully into effect, and it was expected that the peasants, disappointed with the limited character of this reform, would rise in revolt (translator's note).
51. *Briefwechsel*, Volume 3, p120 (author's note). Frederick Engels, Letter to Marx, 21 February 1863, Marx and Engels, *Collected Works*, Volume 41, London, 1985, p459 (translator's note).
52. M Langiewicz (1827–87) emigrated to London after the failure of the 1863 uprising in Poland. He later went on to France, and then to Turkey (translator's note).
53. Georg, Baron von Vincke (1811–75) was the leader of the Prussian Liberals (translator's note).
54. *Briefwechsel*, Volume 3, p122 (author's note). Karl Marx, Letter to Engels, Marx and Engels, *Collected Works*, Volume 41, London, 1985, pp461–2 (translator's note).
55. T Lapinski (1826–1886) took part in the Hungarian uprising of 1848–49, fought for Turkey in the Crimean War and joined the Circassian resistance to the Russian advance in the Caucasus (translator's note).
56. *Briefwechsel*, Volume 3, pp145–6 (author's note). Karl Marx, Letter to Engels, 12 September 1863, Marx and Engels, *Collected Works*, Volume 41, London, 1985, p493. The 'Black-Red-Gold' flag was the flag of the German revolutionaries of 1848. It was adopted by the Weimar Republic of 1918–33, and post-war Germany (translator's note).
57. The appeal was printed on bluish paper, with no date or indication of where it was printed. The original, from Lessner's papers, is now in the Marx-Engels Institute (author's note). Karl Marx, 'Proclamation on Poland By the German Workers' Educational Society in London', November 1863, Marx and Engels, *Collected Works*, Volume 19, London, 1984, p297 (translator's note).
58. It is outside the scope of the present work to compare this document with the resolution on the Polish question introduced by Lassalle in the German Workers' Union. Marx's appeal lacks, of course, the moderation which Hermann Oncken finds praiseworthy in Lassalle's resolution (cf H Oncken, *Lassalle*, second edition, Stuttgart, 1912, pp403–4)

(author's note). Karl Gerhard Hermann Oncken (1869–1945) was a German historian (translator's note).

59. *Documents of the First International*, Volume 1, Lawrence and Wishart, London, 1963, p287 (translator's note).
60. From the manuscript minutes of the Central Council, which I intend to publish in the near future (author's note). *Documents of the First International*, Volume 1, op cit, pp54–5 (translator's note).
61. Peter Fox (Fox-André, d 1869) was the official press correspondent of the General Council of the First International from 1864, and one of the editors of *Commonwealth* (translator's note).
62. Fox was one of the most active members of the General Council, and after the Geneva Congress served as its principal secretary. He died in May 1869 in Vienna, where he was living as the correspondent of British newspapers (author's note).
63. Edward Spencer Beesly (1831–1915), professor of History and Political Economy at University College London, was a Positivist philosopher who presided at the inaugural meeting of the First International. He was associated with the beginnings of the Workingmen's College, St Pancras (translator's note).
64. The reference is to the support for revolutionary France given by Charles James Fox and his circle (translator's note).
65. 'Boustrapa' was a nickname given to the Emperor Napoleon III (Louis Napoleon) because he had made two unsuccessful attempts at *coups d'état*, in Boulogne and Strasbourg, before he finally succeeded in seizing power in Paris (translator's note).
66. Louis XV was King of France (1715–1774) (translator's note).
67. Hermann Jung (1830–1901) was a Swiss member of the General Council of the First International, 1864–72 (translator's note).
68. *Briefwechsel*, Volume 3, pp204–5 (author's note). Karl Marx, Letter to Engels, 10 December 1864, Marx and Engels, *Collected Works*, Volume 42, London, 1987, pp54–5. Marx's speech criticising Fox's address is included in Karl Marx, *Manuskripte über die polnische Frage*, edited by Conze and Hertz-Eichenrode, 1961, and in Karl Marx, *Beiträge zur Geschichte der polnischen Frage*, Książka i Wiedza, Warsaw, 1971 (translator's note).
69. *Documents of the First International*, Volume 1, op cit, p62; Marx and Engels, Collected Works, Volume 20, London, 1985, p356 (translator's note).
70. *Documents of the First International*, Volume 1, op cit, p64 (translator's note).
71. PA Taylor (1819–1891) was a radical MP (translator's note).
72. Giuseppe Mazzini (1805–1872), the Italian revolutionary and democrat, was at this time an exile in London, where he founded a 'Central Committee for European Democracy' which tried to infiltrate the International (translator's note).
73. *Briefwechsel*, Volume 3, p236 (author's note). Karl Marx, Letter to Engels, 25 February 1865, Marx and Engels, *Collected Works*, Volume 42, London, 1987, p110; *Documents of the First International*, Volume 1, op cit, pp386–7 (translator's note).
74. Marx-Engels, *Werke*, Volume 31, pp463–4 (translator's note). At this meeting, Fox moved the following resolution on behalf of the International: 'An independent and integral Poland is an indispensable condition of a democratic Europe', and Eccarius, after explaining the role played by Prussia, added that the restoration of Poland and the unification of Germany were impossible without the downfall of the Prussian monarchy (author's note).
75. 'But, as far as reviving a state condemned by its own kings and executed by virtue of the right of force and in accordance with the forms of war, I would rather hear of proposals to re-establish the Saxony of Witikind, the Kingdom of Austrasia, or that of the Visigoths.' (Proudhon, *La Guerre et la Paix*, Part 2, Brussels, 1861, pp448–9 (author's note). Witikind was the leader of the Saxons defeated by Charlemagne in 785. Austrasia was the Kingdom of the Eastern Franks, with its capital at Metz between 511 and 843. The Visigoths, or Western Goths, had a kingdom in the south-west of what is now France

centred on Toulouse in the fifth century (translator's note).

76. This pamphlet was printed as an appendix to a new publication: *On the Federal Principle*, etc, see pages 286–314, the chapter entitled 'The Polish Question': 'I say that the more progress Russia makes in civilisation and constitutional ways, the more she will lose her invading temper; that the more her recently emancipated peasants advance in education and prosperity, adapting themselves to the arts and customs of a settled way of life, the less need we shall have to fear them; that *that* is the true aspect of our security, the real buttress of Europe.' (Author's note) Proudhon, *Contradictions politiques*, 1932, p420. The point of the title of his pamphlet was that the map of Europe had been fixed by the treaties signed after the defeat of Napoleon in 1815, and if, as some were saying, these treaties were no longer effective, some future congress might consider how, or how not, to re-draw the map defined by the Congress of Vienna (translator's note).
77. General NN Muravyov (1794–1866) and Field-Marshal FF Berg (1793–1874) were the Russian commanders in charge of crushing the Polish rebellions of 1831 and 1863 (translator's note).
78. Karl Marx, 'On Proudhon', in the Berlin *Sozialdemokrat*, no 18, 5 February 1865 (author's note). Karl Marx, *The Poverty of Philosophy*, London, 1956, p227: Letter to Schweitzer, 24 January 1865 (translator's note).
79. 'Poland, The Polish People and Democracy', in *La Tribune du Peuple*, a fortnightly, in the issues of 5 and 26 March and 17 April, and 'A Note on Nationality', in the issue of 31 June 1864 (author's note). Hector Denis (1842–1913) was a Belgian supporter of Proudhon (translator's note).
80. César de Paepe (1842–90) was one of the founders of the Belgian section of the First International, and of the Belgian Workers Party (POB) in 1885 (translator's note).
81. Pierre Vésinier (1826–1902) was one of the organisers of the French branch of the First International in London, where he published the newspaper *Fédération*. Expelled from the International in 1869, he later participated in the Paris Commune (translator's note).
82. The Russian revolutionary exile Alexander Herzen (1812–1870) lost confidence in the movement in the West after the failures of 1848 and began to cultivate ideas of 'Russian Socialism' and 'democratic Panslavism' (translator's note).
83. *Briefwechsel*, Volume 3, p288 (author's note). Karl Marx, Letter to Engels, Marx and Engels, *Collected Works*, Volume 42, London 1987, p213 (translator's note).
84. From 10 February 1866, several members of the International, including Marx, served on the management committee of this journal (author's note). The three articles appeared in *Commonwealth* of 24 and 31 March and 5 April 1866. They are reproduced in Paul S Blackstock and Bert E Hoselitz, *Karl Marx and Friedrich Engels: The Russian Menace to Europe*, 1953, pp95–104, and in 'What Have the Working Classes to Do with Poland', Marx and Engels, *Collected Works*, Volume 20, London, 1985, pp152–4 (translator's note).
85. Napoleon III made 'the principle of nationalities', that every nationality was to be the arbiter of its own fate, the corner stone of his foreign policy (translator's note).
86. Marx and Engels, *Collected Works*, Volume 20, London, 1985, p155; Blackstock and Hoselitz, op cit, p99. In this article, Engels draws a distinction between 'nations' and 'nationalities': 'There is no country in Europe where there are not different nationalities under the same government. The Highland Gaels and the Welsh are undoubtedly of different nationalities to what the English are, although nobody will give to these remnants of peoples long gone the title of nations, any more than to the Celtic inhabitants of Brittany in France.' He ridicules those for whom 'the Roumans of Wallachia, who never had a history, nor the energy required to have one, are of equal importance to the Italians who have a history of 2000 years and an unimpaired national vitality'. He waxes ironic about the subversive activity of Russian agents among the Lapps: 'The "cry of anguish" of the oppressed Laplanders is raised very loud in the Russian papers... and indeed it is a frightful oppression to induce these poor Laplanders to learn the civilised Norwegian or Swedish language, instead of confining themselves to

their own barbaric half Esquimaux [*sic*] idiom.' (Friedrich Engels, 'What Have the Working Classes to do with Poland?', *Commonwealth*, 31 March 1866, in Karl Marx, *The First International and After*, [ed Fernbach], Harmondsworth, 1974, pp382–4. Engels's attitude towards the 'non-historic' peoples is discussed by Roman Rosdolsky, *Engels and the 'Nonhistoric' Peoples: The National Question in the Revolution of 1848*, Critique Books, Glasgow, 1986 (translator's note).

87. Marx and Engels, *Collected Works*, Volume 20, London, 1985, p159. Actually, Engels repeats here an idea which he had expounded in a letter to Marx on 21 April 1863: 'I must say that one would have to be an ass to enthuse over the Poles of 1772. Over most of Europe the nobility went down in those days with dignity, sometimes with esprit [wit], even though most of them believed that materialism consists in eating, drinking, fucking, winning at cards, or getting paid for knavery. No other nobility behaved so stupidly as the Poles in the way they sold themselves to the Russians.' (*Briefwechsel*, Volume 3, p129, author's note) Marx-Engels *Werke*, Volume 30, pp345–6 (translator's note).
88. Karl Marx, 'Memorandum for the Geneva Conference', Section 9, 'The Polish Question', Marx and Engels, *Collected Works*, Volume 20, London, 1985, p193; *Documents of the First International*, Volume 1, op cit, p350 (translator's note).
89. Johann Philippe Becker (1809–1886) was the organiser of the German-speaking sections of the First International in Switzerland, and editor of *Der Vorbote*, 1866–71 (translator's note).
90. Anton Zabicki (1810–1871) who had taken part in the Polish uprising of 1831 and the Hungarian uprising of 1848–49, was a member of the General Council of the First International, 1866–71; Konstantin Bobczynski participated in the 1863 Polish uprising, and was also a member of the General Council, 1865–69 (translator's note).
91. Johann Georg Eccarius (1818–1889), one of the founders of the London German Workers' Educational Association, was a member of the General Council of the First International, 1864–72 (translator's note).
92. *Documents of the First International*, Volume 2, London, 1964, pp277–8 (translator's note).
93. Alexandre Besson was one of the leaders of the French branch of the First International in London and a member of its General Council, 1866–68 (translator's note).
94. *Der Vorbote*, central organ of the German-language section of the International, edited by JP Becker, 1867, pp29–30 (author's note).
95. This was not among the papers of her father which Madame Lafargue handed over to me (author's note). Karl Marx, 'Speech at the Polish Meeting in London', 22 January 1867, Marx and Engels, *Collected Works*, Volume 20, London, 1985, pp197–8. A retranslation of Marx's speech from the French is given in Blackstock and Hoselitz, op cit, pp104–108. The original English text, which was in the possession of Bracke, one of the editors of *Le Socialisme*, is given in *Cahiers de l'Institut de Science Economique Appliquée*, no 109, January 1961, pp83–9 (translator's note).
96. 'That the recent abolition of the 'Congress Poland' by the Tsar is an insult to those great powers of Europe which promoted these arrangements by their connivance or mutual jealousies, but that we who represent the popular sentiment and interest cannot regret the sweeping away of the unrighteous and inevitably abortive compromise of 1815, but even are glad that henceforth the Polish question is necessarily reduced to this simple issue: either to acquiesce in the total disappearance of the name of Poland from the map of Europe, or to champion its re-establishment within the boundaries of 1772.' (*Documents of the First International*, Volume 2, op cit, illustration opposite p76) Eugène Dupont (1831–81) took part in the June 1848 workers' uprising in Paris, and was a member of the General Council of the First International, 1864–72 (translator's note).
97. The so-called 'second five-per-cent Anglo-Dutch loan'. Cf *Istoriya russkogo ministerstva finansov, 1802–1892 gg* (History of Russia's Ministry of Finance, 1802–1892), Volume 2, St Petersburg, 1902, pp446–7. This evidence suffices to establish the correct date when

Marx made the speech in question, and I therefore say no more for the moment. It is odd that even the Poles who published the speech did not notice the contradiction between its content and the date which they accepted (Cf *Marx, Engels, Liebknecht. Odbudowanie Polski*, Warsaw, 1910, pp147–52). The introduction and appendix were contributed by S Zawierucha. Another translation appeared in the journal *Mysl Socjalystyczna*, Cracow, May 1908, pp119–23. The anonymous translator was not categorical, saying merely that the speech was 'probably' made in 1862 (author's note).

98. King Charles X of France (reigned1824–1830) was a reactionary who sought to restore the royal power to what it had been before the French revolution (translator's note).
99. Karl Marx, Speech on the Polish Meeting in London, 22 January 1867, Marx and Engels, *Collected Works*, Volume 20, London, 1985, p199 (translator's note).
100. Marx and Engels saw the Crimean War of 1854–56 as a 'sham war' in which Britain and France did not want to beat Russia too severely because of its usefulness as a counter-revolutionary force (translator's note).
101. The Irish community in the United States, Marx implies, use their political influence to support Russia because they see it as Britain's adversary (translator's note).
102. Prussia had beaten Austria in the Battle of Sadowa (Königgrätz) in 1866 and formed a close alliance of all the German states (excluding Austria) under Prussian leadership – a step towards the creation of the 'Second Reich', established after the Franco-Prussian war of 1870–71 (translator's note).
103. Riazanov writes 'intellectual' (translator's note).
104. Walery Wróblewski (1836–1908) fought both for the Polish uprising of 1863 and the Paris Commune, and was on the General Council of the International in 1871–72 (translator's note).
105. My emphasis (author's note).
106. Frederick Engels, 'A Polish Proclamation', *Volksstaat*, 17 June 1874, Marx and Engels, *Collected Works*, Volume 24, London, 1989, p9; Blackstock and Hoselitz, op cit, pp113–5 (translator's note).
107. Frederick Engels, 'A Polish Proclamation', *Volksstaat*, 17 June 1874, Marx and Engels, *Collected Works*, Volume 24, London, 1989, p10 (translator's note).
108. The Kulturkampf was the name given to the series of measures taken by Bismarck in the 1870s against the Catholic Church in Germany, which he identified with Bavarian separatism and Polish nationalism. The struggle was waged in the name of 'modern civilisation' against 'medieval obscurantism' (translator's note).
109. Frederick Engels, 'A Polish Proclamation', *Volksstaat*, 17 June 1874, Marx and Engels, *Collected Works*, Volume 24, London, 1989, pp10–11; Blackstock and Hoselitz, op cit, pp113–5 (translator's note).
110. Friedrich Lessner (1825–1910) was a member of the Communist League, and took part in the 1848 revolution in Germany. After his imprisonment, he emigrated to London, joined the German Workers' Educational Association, and was on the General Council of the First International, 1864–72. He later played a part in the formation of the Independent Labour Party (translator's note).
111. Printed in *Sprawozdanie z międzynarodowego zebrania zwolanego w 50-letnia rocznice listopadowego powstania*, published in Geneva by *Równość*, 1881, pp30–2. Limanowski gives a different translation (author's note). This document is printed in Marx-Engels, *Werke*, Volume 19, pp239–40. There is a partial translation in Blackstock and Hoselitz, op cit, pp255–6 (translator's note).
112. Karl Marx and Frederick Engels, 'To the Meeting in Geneva Held to Commemorate the Fiftieth Anniversary of the Polish Revolution of 1830', Marx and Engels, *Collected Works*, Volume 24, London, 1989, pp343–4 (translator's note).
113. This is doubtless a lapse of memory: Marx and Engels have confused the meeting of the Fraternal Democrats with the congress of the Communist League (author's note).

114. Karl Marx and Frederick Engels, 'To the Meeting in Geneva Held to Commemorate the Fiftieth Anniversary of the Polish Revolution of 1830', 29 November 1880, Marx and Engels, *Collected Works*, Volume 24, London, 1989, pp344–5; it is partially quoted in Blackstock and Hoselitz, op cit, pp255–6 (translator's note).
115. In a letter to Kautsky of 7 February 1882, Engels wrote that, while continuing to fight for the independence of Poland, 'we do not take any position at this time on any future settlement between the Poles and the Lithuanians, Byelorussians and Ukrainians and the old Poland, nor on the frontier settlement with Germany' (Blackstock and Hoselitz, op cit, p120, translator's note).
116. Ludwyk Warynski (1856–1889) was a pioneer of the Socialist movement in Poland, a member of *Równość* and a founder of *Proletariat* in 1881; Stanislaw Kunicki (1761–1886) was also a founder of *Proletariat*, and editor of its theoretical organ, *Walka Klas*(translator's note).
117. Engels's article is reproduced in Blackstock and Hoselitz, op cit, pp25–55 and Marx and Engels, *Collected Works*, Volume 27, Moscow, 1990, pp11–48 (translator's note).
118. Engels wrote of 'the rapid development of Polish industry, outstripping that of Russia', and concluded: 'The nobility could neither maintain nor regain Polish independence; today, to the bourgeoisie, this independence is, to say the least, immaterial. It can be gained only by the young Polish proletariat ...' (Frederick Engels, 'Preface to the Polish Edition of *The Communist Manifesto*', 10 February 1892, Marx and Engels, *Collected Works*, Volume 27, Moscow, 1990, p274, translator's note)

Marx and Engels and the Balkan Question

D.B. Riazanov

I

Marx's views on the Eastern Question are usually identified with those expressed to Liebknecht in his well-known pamphlet *On the Eastern Question, or: Shall Europe Become Cossack?*[1] German, Russian and South-Slav Marxists have always supposed that Marx was just as much a Turcophil as the celebrated David Urquhart: that, like the latter and Liebknecht he was always a supporter of the *status quo* in the Balkan peninsula, and that he rejected any sort of 'right to self-determination' for the Slav peoples groaning beneath the Turkish yoke, and mocked at the 'stupid sentimentality' which saw 'in every brigand who comes into conflict with Turkey a representative of an oppressed nationality'. Marx's Balkan policy has thus been perceived as identical with that of the vulgar democrats, being, like theirs, determined exclusively by boundless hostility towards Russian hegemony in the Balkan peninsula.

'Behind the Balkan peoples' striving for independence is hidden the danger of Russian hegemony, and therefore it is necessary to oppose the national movement in the Balkan countries until the time comes when Europe's revolutionary liberty, in whatever national dress, shall unfurl its banner on the Bosphorus.' This is how Marx's views on the Eastern Question are formulated by Max Schippel.[2]

This former arch-radical, who has now almost completely severed his links with Marxism, believes that Marx drew all his evidence 'from a single source, from Urquhart's exposures, which today give the impression of morbid, pathological fantasies'. Marx is transformed into a parrot repeating uncritically all of Urquhart's revelations, and in this respect differing not at all from Lothar Bucher,[3] who in the 1850s denounced with equal fervour both the British parliamentary system and Palmerston, and who really did borrow all his arguments from the eccentric British publicist.

And yet one has only to glance through the Chartist journals of the 1850s to perceive that, even when Marx needed to seek out arguments for use against the domestic and external policies of Palmerston, he was not at all obliged to have recourse to the writings of that 'reactionary utopian', as he himself called Urquhart, for whom even the Chartist movement was the work of Russian intrigues and the Chartist leaders were puppets manipulated by Russian agents. In the brilliant articles and speeches of Harney[4] and Jones, those 'enemy brothers' of Chartism, Marx could find both merciless criticism of Palmerston's cheap 'liberalism' and independent attempts to lay the foundations of a Balkan policy inspired by the interests of the proletariat. Thus, Ernest Jones criticised very sharply the theory of maintaining the *status quo* in the Balkan peninsula, and saw young Greece as the most important factor in the political rebirth of the oppressed Balkan nationalities.[5] And if Marx was not altogether in agreement with Jones, the divergence of view did not relate to the question of maintaining the *status quo*, which Urquhart considered the keystone of his entire Balkan policy. Hatred of Russia's despotism made Marx, no more than Jones, a defender of Turkish 'civilisation', and he well understood that the maintenance of the status quo in the Balkan peninsula was the principal obstacle to the development of the Balkan peoples, the source of Russia's increasing influence among them, and, consequently, a cause of strength for this main enemy of the European revolution.

A closer study of Marx's articles on the Eastern Question written in the period of the Crimean War reveals as clearly as can be how ill-founded is the identification of his views with those of Urquhart. These articles were collected by the late Eleanor Marx in 1897, when the massacre of Armenians in Constantinople, the troubles in Crete and the Greco-Turkish War made the Eastern Question more topical. Unfortunately, this publication had shortcomings even more serious than those that marred her collection of Marx's articles on the history of diplomatic relations between Russia and Britain in the eighteenth century.

When I was preparing the German edition of the articles by Marx which had been collected by his daughter, I came to the conclusion that some of them could not have been written either by him or by

Engels, and also that there were gaps in the collection. I therefore considered it necessary to compare the articles in question with the originals in the *New York Tribune*. My suppositions were fully confirmed.

As is known, Marx began writing for the *New York Tribune* in 1851, with his articles under the title of 'Revolution and Counter-Revolution in Germany'.[6] In 1852, he became the permanent, though not the sole, correspondent of this newspaper in London. The first of his communications was printed on 21 August 1852, and this was followed by a series of others, in which Marx provided, once and sometimes twice a week, a review of current events, not only in Britain, but also throughout Europe. Although the Eastern Question had become a matter of general concern already by the end of 1852, Marx's first mention of it comes only in March 1853, when, following the extraordinary mission of Menshikov,[7] events in the Balkan Peninsula assumed a threatening character. It is in a message of this period that Marx promises to examine in detail the Eastern Question, that *pons asinorum*[8] of European diplomacy.

Marx fulfilled his promise in four articles which were published in the *New York Tribune* on 7, 12, 19 and 21 April 1853. Only three of these articles were reproduced in the collection published by Eleanor Marx: the fourth, which constitutes a necessary supplement and conclusion to the first three, was omitted owing to some blunder. Yet it is this article which radically refutes the old legend of Marx's 'Turcophilia'. True, it emphasises still further his hostility to uninvited 'civilisers' in the shape of various 'Tashkentsy',[9] but in this respect Marx is at one with all those who, already in the 1870s, exposed what really lay behind the campaign prepared with such pomp by 'the Turk within' against 'the Turk without'.[10]

Before reproducing the article by Marx which had remained lost in the columns of the *New York Tribune*, I must briefly set forth the content of the preceding articles, which were written jointly by him and Engels.

II

> Whenever the revolutionary hurricane has subsided for a moment, one ever-recurring question is sure to turn up: the eternal 'Eastern Question'. Thus, when the storms of the first French revolution had passed, and Napoleon and Alexander of Russia had divided, after the Peace of Tilsit, the whole of continental Europe between themselves, Alexander profited from the momentary calm to

march an army into Turkey and to 'give a lift' to the forces that were breaking up from within that decaying empire. Again, no sooner had the revolutionary movement of Western Europe been quelled by the congresses of Laibach and Verona, than Alexander's successor, Nicholas, made another dash at Turkey. When, a few years later, the revolution of July, with its concomitant insurrections in Poland, Italy and Belgium had had its turn, and Europe, as remodelled in 1831, seemed out of the reach of domestic squalls, the Eastern Question, in 1840, appeared on the point of embroiling the 'Great Powers' in a general war.[11] And now, when the short-sightedness of the ruling pigmies prides itself in having successfully freed Europe from the dangers of anarchy and revolution, up starts again the everlasting topic, the never-failing difficulty: what shall we do with Turkey?

Turkey is the living sore of European legitimacy. The impotence of legitimate, monarchical government, ever since the first French revolution, has resumed itself in one axiom: keep up the *status quo*. A *testimonium paupertatis*, an acknowledgement of the universal incompetence of the ruling powers, for any purpose of progress and civilisation, is seen in this universal agreement to stick to things as by chance or accident they happen to be ... Myrmidons of mediocrity, as Béranger calls them,[12] without historical knowledge or insight into facts, without ideas, without initiative, they adore the status quo they themselves have bungled together, knowing what a bungling and blundering piece of workmanship it is.

But Turkey, no more than the rest of the world, remains stationary; and just when the reactionary party has succeeded in restoring in civilised Europe what they consider to be the status quo ante, it is perceived that in the meantime the status quo in Turkey has been very much altered, that new questions, new relations, new interests have sprung up ...

Keep up the status quo in Turkey? Why, you might as well try to keep up the precise degree of putridity into which the carcass of a dead horse has passed at a given time, before dissolution is complete. Turkey goes on decaying, and will go on decaying as long as the present system of 'balance of power' and maintenance of the status quo goes on ...[13]

Marx proceeds to describe the situation in Turkey and among the various nationalities of the Balkan peninsula on the eve of the Crimean War. He comes to the conclusion that the Turks in Europe constitute a serious hindrance to the development of the 'Thraco-Illyrian' peninsula.[14] How far he is from seeing in the independence of the Balkan peoples a danger that Russia's hegemony will be strengthened can be seen from the following words, the truth of which has been confirmed by all subsequent history:

> There can be no doubt that, should the Greco-Slavonian population ever obtain the mastery in the land which it inhabits, and where it forms three-fourths of the whole population ... the same necessities would by and by give birth to an anti-Russian, progressive party, the existence of which has been hitherto the inevitable consequence of any portion of it having become semi-detached from Turkey.[15]

In the following article, Marx expounds the reasons why Britain must be the most earnest and uncompromising opponent of every attempt made by Russia to annex fresh territory in the Balkan peninsula. Britain cannot allow Russia to become mistress of the Bosphorus and Constantinople. If that were to happen, it would do enormous damage to Britain, both commercially and politically, and might, indeed, strike a mortal blow at her commercial and political power. To be convinced of this it is sufficient to take a look at Britain's trade relations with Turkey.

> The commercial battlefield between England and Russia has been removed from the Indus to Trebizond,[16] and the Russian trade, formerly venturing as far as the limits of England's eastern empire, is now reduced to the defensive on the very verge of its own line of custom-houses. The importance of this fact with regard to any future solution of the Eastern Question, and to the part which both England and Russia may take in it, is evident. They are, and always must be, antagonists in the East.[17]

The rapidly increasing commercial activity in the Black Sea depends, as Marx puts it, on the confidence that is felt in the country which controls the Dardanelles and the Bosphorus, which are the key to the Black Sea.

And who can expect that Russia, once she had got possession of

Constantinople, will keep open the door through which Britain has entered her trade space?

This commercial importance of the Dardanelles and the Bosphorus makes them also positions of first class naval importance – more so, even, than Gibraltar, or Helsingör on the Sound.[18] A few carefully built and well-armed fortifications, such as Russia would undoubtedly erect at once after taking over Constantinople, would defy the combined fleets of the entire world. And if Russia were to gain control of Turkey, her power would be increased to a colossal degree, and she would dominate all the rest of Europe. Such an event would do incomparable harm to the cause of the European revolution. To support Turkey's independence, or to prevent the realisation of Russia's plans if the Ottoman Empire should collapse, is a task of great importance. To this extent the interests of revolutionary democracy and those of Britain are the same.

In his third article, Marx returns to the theory of the *status quo*. To what, in practice, has the application of this theory led? Why, simply to this, that, thanks to the ignorance, inertia and cowardice of the West European governments, Russia has, slowly and steadily, implemented her policy in its essential points. And when this constant and successful advance by Russia at last evoked in the cabinets of the West European powers a vague premonition of impending danger, the diplomats opened up a new panacea: maintenance of the *status quo* in Turkey, they said, is a necessary condition for maintaining the peace of Europe. Either the Russians enter Constantinople, or the *status quo* has to be maintained – for European diplomacy and even for Europe's press there can be no other solution!

By way of illustration, Marx quotes the Conservative *Times* and the Liberal *Daily News*. The former was still at that time on Russia's side, and sought to show that the downfall of the Ottoman Empire would be far from having the frightful consequences that were feared by the opponents of Russia's Balkan policy. The Liberal *Daily News*, on the other hand, made every effort to show what danger threatened from Russia, and how needful it was to uphold the independence and integrity of Turkey. And Marx then venomously mocks the Turcophilia of the *Daily News* and its principal inspirer, David Urquhart:

> Is not the partition of Turkey a crime equal to the partition of Poland? Have not the Christians more religious liberty in Turkey than in Austria or Russia? ... Is not Turkey a paradise compared to Austria and Russia? Is not life and property safe there? And is not British trade with

> Turkey larger than with Austria and Russia put together, and does it not increase every year?

All these dithyrambs lead up, in the pages of the *Daily News*, to an outright apotheosis which is quite incomprehensible for the ordinary reader of the newspaper.

> The key to this strange enthusiasm for the Turks is to be found in the works of David Urquhart, Esq MP. This gentleman, of Scotch birth, with medieval and patriarchal recollections of home, and with a modern British civilised education, after having fought three years in Greece against the Turks, passed into their country and was the first thus to enamour himself of them. The romantic Highlander found himself at home again in the mountain ravines of the Pindus and the Balkan, and his works on Turkey, although full of valuable information, may be summed up in the following three paradoxes, which are laid down almost literally thus: If Mr Urquhart were not a British subject, he would decidedly prefer being a Turk; if he were not a Presbyterian Calvinist, he would not belong to any other religion than Islamism; and thirdly, Britain and Turkey are the only two countries in the world which enjoy self-government and civil and religious liberty.[19]

Even the Turcophils' argument that trade is developing under Turkish rule does not, in Marx's view, stand up to criticism: 'Remove all the Turks out of Europe, and trade will have no reason to suffer.' To whom is civilisation indebted for its progress in all parts of European Turkey? Not to the Turks, but to the Greek and Slav middle classes of the cities and the trading ports. 'Were it not for their monopoly of civil and military power, they [the Turks] would soon disappear ... The fact is, they must be got rid of. To say that they cannot be got rid of except by putting Russians and Austrians in their place, means as much to say that the present political constitution of Europe will last forever. Who will make such an assertion?'[20]

It is in the fourth article, which follows this one, and which has hitherto remained quite unknown, that Marx gives his answer to the question of how to remove these obstacles which hinder the development of the peoples inhabiting the Balkan peninsula.[21]

It would be strange, after all that has been quoted above, to assert, as do some Russian biographers of Marx, that in his views on the

Eastern Question he was a faithful 'pupil' of Urquhart. The article which I now give in full shows the role that he assigned to the South Slavs in the struggle against Russian hegemony in the Balkan peninsula.

III

We have seen how the obstinate ignorance, the time-hallowed routine, the hereditary mental drowsiness of European statesmen shrinks from the very attempt to answer this question. Aberdeen and Palmerston, Metternich and Guizot,[22] not to mention their republican and constitutional substitutes of 1848 to 1852 – who will ever be nameless – all despair of a solution.

And all the while Russia advances step by step, slowly, but irresistibly, towards Constantinople, in spite of all the diplomatic notes, plots and manoeuvres of France and England.

Now this steady advance of Russia, admitted by all parties, in all countries of Europe, has never been explained by official statesmen. They see the effect, they see even the ultimate consequence, and yet the cause is hidden from them, although nothing is more simple.

The great motive power which speeds Russia on towards Constantinople is nothing but the very device designed to keep her away from it; the hollow, the never-enforced theory of the *status quo*.

What is this *status quo*? For the Christian subjects of the Porte, it means simply the maintenance, for ever and a day, of Turkish oppression over them. As long as they are oppressed by Turkish rule, the head of the Greek Church,[23] the ruler of 60 millions of Greek Christians, be he in other respects what he may, is *their natural liberator and protector*. Thus it is that 10 millions of Greek Christians in European Turkey are forced to appeal to Russian aid by that very diplomatic scheme invented in order to prevent Russian encroachments.

Look at the facts as history records them. Even before the reign of Catherine II Russia never omitted an opportunity of obtaining favourable conditions for Moldavia and Wallachia. These stipulations at last were carried to such a length in the Treaty of Adrianople (1829) that the above-mentioned principalities are now more subject to

Russia than to Turkey. When, in 1804, the Servian[24] revolution broke out, Russia took the rebel Rayahs[25] at once under her protection, and in two treaties, after having supported them in two wars, guaranteed the internal independence of their country. When the Greeks revolted, who decided the contest? Not the plots and rebellions of Ali Pasha of Janina, not the Battle of Navarino, not the French army in the Morea, but the march of Diebitsch's Russians across the Balkan into the valley of the Maritza.[26] And while Russia thus fearlessly set about the dismemberment of Turkey, Western diplomatists continued to guarantee and hold up as sacred the *status quo* and the inviolability of the Ottoman territory!

So long as the tradition of the upholding, at any price, of the *status quo* and the independence of Turkey in her present state is the ruling maxim of Western diplomacy, so long will Russia be considered, by nine-tenths of the population of Turkey in Europe, as their only support, their liberator, their Messiah.

Now, suppose for a moment that Turkish rule in the Greco-Slavonian peninsula were got rid of; that a government more suitable to the wants of the people existed; what then would be the position of Russia? The fact is notorious, that in every one of the states which have sprung up upon Turkish soil and have acquired either total or partial independence, a powerful anti-Russian party has formed itself. If that be the case at a time when Russian support is their only safeguard against Turkish oppression, what, then, are we to expect, as soon as the fear of Turkish oppression shall have vanished?

But to remove Turkish authority beyond the Bosphorus; to emancipate the various creeds and nationalities which populate the peninsula; to open the door to the schemes and machinations, the conflicting desires and interests of all the great powers of Europe – why, is this not provoking universal war? Thus asks diplomatic cowardice and routine.

Of course, it is not expected that the Palmerstons, the Aberdeens, the Clarendons,[27] the Continental foreign secretaries, will do such a thing. They cannot look at it without shuddering. But whosoever has, in the study of history, learned to admire the eternal mutations of human affairs in which nothing is stable but instability, nothing constant but change; whosoever has followed up that stern march of history whose wheels pass relentlessly over the remains of empires, crushing entire generations, without holding them worthy even of a look of pity; whosoever, in short, has had his eyes open to the fact that there was never a demagogic appeal or insurgent proclamation as revolutionary as the plain and simple records of the history of mankind, whoever knows how to appreciate the eminently revolutionary character of the present age, when steam and wind, electricity and the printing press, artillery and gold discoveries cooperate to produce more changes and revolutions in a year than were ever before brought about in a century, will certainly not shrink from facing an historical question because of the consideration that its proper settlement may bring about a European war.

No, diplomacy, government according to the old fashion, will never solve the difficulty. The solution of the Turkish problem is reserved, with that of other great problems, to the European revolution. And there is no presumption in assigning this apparently remote question to the lawful domain of that great movement. The revolutionary landmarks have been steadily advancing ever since 1789. The last revolutionary outposts were Warsaw, Debreczin,[28] Bucharest; the advanced posts of the next revolution must be St Petersburg and Constantinople. They are the two vulnerable points where the Russian anti-revolutionary colossus must be attacked.

It would be a mere effort of fancy to give a detailed scheme as to how the Turkish territory in Europe might be partitioned out. Twenty such schemes could be invented, every one as plausible as the other. What we have to do is not to draw up fanciful programmes, but to seek general conclusions from indisputable facts. And from this point of view the question presents a double aspect.

Firstly, then, it is an undeniable reality that the peninsula commonly called 'Turkey in Europe' forms the natural inheritance of the South-Slavonian race.[29] That race furnishes seven millions out of twelve of its inhabitants. It has been in possession of the soil for twelve hundred years. Its competitors – if we except a sparse population which has adopted the Greek language, although in reality of Slavonic descent – are Turkish or Arnaut[30] barbarians, who have long since been convicted of the most inveterate opposition to all progress. The South-Slavonians, on the contrary, are, in the inland districts of the country, the exclusive representatives of civilisation. They do not yet form a nation, but they have a powerful and comparatively enlightened nucleus of nationality in Servia. The Servians have a history, a literature of their own. They owe their present internal independence to an 11 year struggle, carried on valiantly against superior numbers. They have, for the last 20 years, grown rapidly in culture and the means of civilisation. They are looked upon by the Christians in Bulgaria, Thrace, Macedonia and Bosnia as the centre, around which, in their future efforts for independence and nationality, all of them must rally. In fact, it may be said that, the more Servia and Servian nationality has consolidated itself, the more has the direct influence of Russia on the Turkish Slavonians been thrown into the background; for Servia, in order to maintain its distinct position as a Christian state, has been obliged to borrow from the West of Europe its political institutions, its schools, its scientific knowledge, its industrial appliances, and thus is explained the anomaly that, in spite of Russian protection, Servia, ever since her emancipation, has formed a constitutional monarchy.

Whatever may be the bonds which consanguity and common religious belief may draw between the Russian and the Turkish Slavonians, their interests will be decidedly opposite from the day the latter are emancipated. The commercial necessities arising from the geographical position of the two countries explain this. Russia, a compact inland country, is essentially a country of predominantly agricultural and perhaps, one day, manufacturing production. The Greco-Slavonic peninsula, small in extent, comparatively, with an enormous extent of shore on three seas, one of which it commands, is now essentially a country of commercial transit, though with the best capacities for independent production. Russia is monopolising, South Slavonia is expansive. They are, besides, competitors in Central Asia, but while Russia has every interest to exclude all but her own produce, South Slavonia has, even now, every interest to introduce into the Eastern markets the produce of Western Europe. How, then, is it possible for the two nations to agree? In fact, the Turkish South Slavonians and Greeks have, even now, far more interests in common with Western Europe than with Russia. And as soon as the line of railway, which now extends from Ostend, Le Havre and Hamburg to Pesth, shall have been continued to Belgrade and Constantinople (which is now under consideration), the influence of Western civilisation and Western trade will become permanent in the South-East of Europe.

Again: the Turkish Slavonians especially suffer by their subjection to a Mussulman class of military occupants whom they have to support. These military occupants unite in themselves all public functions, military, civil and judicial. Now, what is the Russian system of government, wherever it is not mixed up with feudal institutions, but a military occupation, in which the civil and judicial hierarchy are organised in a military manner, and where the people have to pay for the whole? Whoever thinks that such a system can have a charm for the South-Slavonians may study the history of Servia since 1804. Kara-George, the founder of Servian independence, was abandoned by the people, and Milosh Obrenovich, the restorer of that independence, was ignominiously turned out of the country, because they attempted to introduce the Russian autocratic system, accompanied with its concomitant corruption, half-military bureaucracy and pasha-like extortion.[31]

Here, then, is the simple and final solution of the question. History and the facts of the present day alike point to the erection of a free and independent Christian state on the ruins of the Moslem Empire in Europe. The next effort of the Revolution can hardly fail to render such an event necessary, for it can hardly fail to inaugurate the long-maturing conflict between Russian absolutism and European democracy. In that conflict England must bear a part, in whatever hands her government may for the moment happen to be placed. She can never allow Russia to obtain possession of Constantinople. She must, then, take sides with the enemies of the Tsar and favour the construction of an independent Slavonian government in the place of the effete and overthrown Sublime Porte.[32]

Not all of Marx's predictions became true. During the last 50 years, there have been great changes in the sphere of political and economic relations which could not be forecast on the eve of the Crimean War. Hardly had the antagonism between France and Britain, which determined the latter's policy in the Balkans in the eighteenth century and the first half of the nineteenth, been replaced by the antagonism between Britain and Russia, than, already in the mid-1880s, it became clear that Britain's chief rival in the Balkans was not Russia, but Germany, allied with Austria. The tremendous progress made by German industry and trade quickly reduced to a minimum the economic influence of Russia in both parts of Turkey, European and Asiatic alike. There is no need to speak of the South-Slav states. Furthermore, the foremost guardian of the independence and integrity of Turkey is now not Britain, but Germany. After Britain's seizure of Egypt, next on her agenda come the occupation of independent Arabia, the capitalist 'resuscitation' of Mesopotamia,[33] and the need to establish a 'firm foothold' on the shores of the Persian Gulf. But in all these undertakings Britain encounters resistance, not only from Turkey, but also, and mainly, from Germany. Romania has, like Austria, been converted long since into an advanced position of German capitalism against Russian pretensions in the Balkan peninsula. By means of alternate wheedling and threats, Germany is steadily eliminating Russia from the Near East, and urging her into the Far East – today against Japan, tomorrow against China.

And among the South-Slav states, alongside Servia, a new Bulgarian state has arisen, which has proved to be no less refractory towards its 'liberators' than were, in their time, the 'ungrateful' Serbs.

After 17 October 1905 came 24 July 1908 in Constantinople. In that matter, Marx's prediction was fulfilled to the letter. But the *status quo* collapsed not only in the Near East. This time, the wave of the European revolution rolled not merely as far as Constantinople: after a first approach (5 August 1906) which ended in failure, on 13 August 1909 it also overwhelmed Teheran. And now it has reached that eternal embodiment of the status quo, Peking.[34]

Nobody is working so industriously to clear its path as all these defenders of the status quo. Everything has changed during the last 50 years, but the old routine and traditional immobility of thought of Europe's 'statesmen' remains the same!

1913

Notes

1. There are several articles by Marx on the 'Eastern Question' written between 1853 and 1856. Cf Marx and Engels, *Collected Works*, Volume 12, Moscow, 1979 (especially 'The Turkish Question', pp112–4). The title of the pamphlet was inspired by a well-known remark made by Napoleon in 1816: 'The way things are now, within 10 years Europe will be either Cossack or everywhere republican'. By 'Cossack' he meant 'under Russian rule' (translator's note).
2. Max Schippel (1859–1928) was one of the leaders of the right wing of German Social Democracy (translator's note).
3. Lothar Bucher (1817–1892) had been a deputy to the Prussian National Assembly in 1848, but later became a National Liberal and a supporter of Bismarck (translator's note).
4. George Julian Harney (1817–1897) was a prominent supporter of the left of the Chartist movement (translator's note).
5. Greece became an independent kingdom in 1830, though within frontiers that excluded many Greek speakers (translator's note).
6. Karl Marx, 'Revolution and Counter-revolution in Germany', Marx and Engels, *Collected Works*, Volume 11, London, 1979, pp3–96 (translator's note).
7. In 1853, the Tsar sent Admiral AS Menshikov to Constantinople (Istanbul) to present an ultimatum to Turkey. The Sultan appealed for help to the Western powers, and the so-called Crimean War began (translator's note).
8. 'The bridge of asses' – originally Euclid's proposition that 'if two sides of a triangle are equal, then the angles opposite these sides are equal' (a stumbling-block to many schoolchildren). This expression has come to be used for anything that is found especially difficult by beginners (translator's note).
9. Riazanov here uses the title of a work by the Russian satirist Saltykov-Shchedrin (1826–1889) about the Russian colonisers of Turkestan, whose centre of operations was Tashkent (translator's note).
10. Russian revolutionaries answered official anti-Turkish propaganda by claiming that 'the Turk within', that is, the Tsar, was no better than 'the Turk without', that is, the Sultan (translator's note).
11. The Treaty of Tilsit was signed in 1807. The Russo-Turkish War had actually begun in 1806, and went on until 1812. The congresses of Laibach (Ljubljana) and Verona, in 1821 and 1822, were called to deal with revolts in Italy and Spain. The next Russo-Turkish war took place in 1828–29. In 1840, a revolt against the Sultan by Mehmet Ali, Viceroy of Egypt (1804–1849), was backed by France, but all the other great powers rallied to the aid of the Sultan (translator's note).
12. The French poet Pierre Jean de Béranger (1780–1857), a propagandist for Bonapartism, thus mocked the statesmen whom he saw as unworthy successors of the Emperor Napoleon I whom they had overthrown (translator's note).
13. Marx and Engels, Article in *New York Herald Tribune*, 22 March 1883, and *New York Daily Tribune*, 7 April 1883, Marx and Engels, *Collected Works*, Volume 12, Moscow, 1979, pp5–6 (translator's note).
14. In ancient times, the territory on the eastern shore of the Adriatic was called Illyria, and that on the north-eastern shore of the Aegean was called Thrace (translator's note).
15. Marx-Engels, *Collected Works*, Volume 12, Moscow, 1979, p11. The direct reference is to the appearance in Serbia, which had won a degree of autonomy, of the Constitutionalist Party headed by Ilija Garashanin (1812–1874), which opposed Russian domination (and kept Serbia neutral in the Crimean War) (translator's note).
16. Trebizond (Trabzon), at the south-eastern angle of the Black Sea, was where the principal trade route from Iran and Central Asia to Europe descended from the highlands of Armenia to the sea (translator's note).

17. Marx and Engels, 'The Real Issue in Turkey', *New York Daily Tribune*, 12 April 1853, Marx and Engels, *Collected Works*, Volume 12, Moscow, 1979, p15 (translator's note).
18. Helsingör (Elsinore) commands the entrance to the Baltic (translator's note).
19. Frederick Engels, 'The Turkish Question', March 1853, Marx and Engels, *Collected Works*, Volume 12, Moscow, 1979,pp25–6 (translator's note).
20. Marx and Engels, *Collected Works*, Volume 12, Moscow, 1979, p27 (translator's note).
21. Frederick Engels, 'What is to Become of Turkey in Europe?', *New York Daily Tribune,* 21 April 1853, and New York Weekly Tribune, 30 April 1853, Marx and Engels, *Collected Works*, Volume 12, Moscow, 1979, pp32–6. The article is here reproduced in full (translator's note).
22. George Hamilton Gordon, Earl of Aberdeen (1784–1860), the Tory leader, served as Foreign Secretary (1828–30, 1841–46) and then Prime Minister (1852–55) during the Crimean War. Clemens Wenzel Lothar, Prince of Metternich-Winneburg (1773–1859) was the Austrian Foreign Minister and Chancellor who tried to hold back the tide of nationalism in Europe. François Pierre Guillaume Guizot (1787–1874) was the historian and conservative statesman in charge of French foreign policy during 1840-48 (translator's note).
23. Since Peter the Great's time the Tsar had been the head of the Orthodox ('Greek') Church in Russia, and was looked to for protection by the mostly Orthodox peoples of Greece, Bulgaria, Serbia, Montenegro and Romania (Moldavia-Wallachia) (translator's note).
24. When Marx and Engels wrote, certain proper names were used in forms that have now become obsolete: 'Servia' for Serbia, 'Slavonian' for Slavonic, 'Mussulman' for Moslem (or Muslim) (translator's note).
25. *Rayah* (from the Arabic word for a herd of cattle) was the term used for a non-Muslim subject of the Sultan, who had to pay the poll-tax from which Muslims were exempt (translator's note).
26. The disloyalty of Ali Pasha Tepelenë (1744-1822) of Janina (Ioannina), in North-Western Greece (described by Byron in *Childe Harold's Pilgrimage*) helped to shake the Sultan's power in that country. At Navarino a joint Anglo-Franco-Russian expedition commanded by Admiral Codrington sank the Turkish and Egyptian fleet (1827). The advance of the army of Field Marshal Count Ivan Ivanovich Diebitsch (1785-1831) threatened the Sultan's capital itself (translator's note).
27. George William Frederick Villiers, Earl of Clarendon (1800-1870) served as Foreign Minister in several Liberal governments (1853-58, 1865-66, 1868-70) (translator's note).
28. Debreczin (Debrecen) was the headquarters of the revolutionary movement in Hungary in 1849 (translator's note).
29. 'South-Slavonian' embraces both Yugoslavs and Bulgars (translator's note).
30. 'Arnaut' means Albanian (translator's note).
31. George Petrovich, called Kara-George (1762-1817) had to leave Serbia in 1813, and Milosh Obrenovich (ruled 1815-39, 1858-60) in 1839 (translator's note).
32. The 'Sublime Porte' was a name for the centre of government in the Ottoman (Turkish) Empire. This article, entitled 'What is to Become of Turkey in Europe?', is in Marx-Engels, *Collected Works*, Volume 12, Moscow, 1979, pp32–6 (translator's note).
33. Mesopotamia is the present-day Iraq (translator's note).
34. 17 October 1905 is the date of the 'Manifesto' in which the Tsar made concessions to the revolution in Russia. 24 July 1908 saw the successful coup d'état by reform-minded officers (the 'Young Turks') in Constantinople. On 5 August 1906, the Shah of Iran yielded to popular pressure and promised to convene a national assembly. When this met, however, it was dissolved by the Russian-officered 'Persian Cossacks' in the Shah's service: on 13 July 1909 revolutionary forces entered Teheran, and the Shah had to take refuge in the Russian legation. In 1911–13, the 'First Chinese Revolution' overthrew the Emperor and established a republic (translator's note).

Appendix

Brian Pearce

Wilhelm Liebknecht's pamphlet mentioned by Riazanov (*Zur orientalischen Frage, oder: Soll Europa Kosackish werden?* 1878) did indeed go very far towards Urquhartism. The discontent of the Christians in Turkey he treated as '99 per cent a Russian lie' and the remaining 'one per cent a Russian manufacture', and went on: 'But the oppressed nationalities, the freedom-loving Southern Slavs! Bah! Bird-lime for bullfinches! ... The freedom-loving Southern Slavs are just as real as the South Russian villages which Potemkin[1] decked up for the Empress Catherine.'

But, whatever Marx or Engels wrote in 1853, Riazanov is quite wrong in claiming that this pamphlet was out of line with their thinking in 1878. Indeed, Liebknecht was able to use a letter which Marx had written to him on the subject, in the second edition of his pamphlet, though without indicating its provenance. On 4 February 1878, Marx wrote to Liebknecht in connection with the Russo-Turkish War then in progress:

> We are most decidedly espousing the Turkish cause and for two reasons: (1) because we have studied the *Turkish peasant* – that is, the mass of the Turkish people – and in this way have come to see him as indubitably one of *the ablest and most moral representatives of the peasantry in Europe*; (2) because the *defeat of the Russians* would have greatly *expedited social revolution in Russia*, of which all the elements are present in abundant measure, and *hence radical change throughout Europe*.[2]

He had already written to Sorge on 27 September 1877: 'Russia ... has long been on the verge of an upheaval; all the elements are to hand ... The gallant Turks have advanced the explosion by many years through the blows they have dealt.'[3] And he had supplied 'advice and material' to the journalist Maltman Barry[4] for three articles which the latter contributed to Conservative periodicals (see Marx to Engels, 5 and 7 March 1877).[5] The Liberal leader Gladstone[6] had been denouncing Turkish atrocities against the Bulgarians, calling for the Turks to be driven out of Europe 'bag and baggage', applauding the Russians for their initiative in that direction, and protesting against the pro-Turkish attitude of Disraeli's government. Barry's articles appeared in the *Whitehall Review* of 3 February 1877 ('Mr Gladstone and the Russian Intrigue') and in *Vanity Fair* of 3 and 10 March 1877 ('Mr Gladstone' and 'The Great Agitator Unmasked'). Their principal themes were: (1) What about Russian atrocities in Turkestan? and (2) Gladstone is under the influence of a Russian lady agent, Madame Novikova.[7]

It is true, however, that Marx does not directly refer to the question of the struggle of the Southern Slav peoples, as such. He simply ignores it. Engels, though, expressed himself on this subject with his usual freedom of language. Writing to Kautsky on 7 February 1882, he said: 'Now you may perhaps ask me whether I have no feeling of sympathy for the small Slav peoples and fragments thereof which have been split apart by these three wedges – the German, the Magyar and the Turkish – driven into the Slav domain? To tell the truth damn little ... Only when the collapse of Tsardom frees the national aspirations of these diminutive peoples from their entanglement in pan-Slav hegemonic tendencies, and only then can we let them do as they please.'[8] And in a letter to Bernstein dated 22–25 February of the same year, he reproaches his correspondent for misplaced sympathy with the 'oppressed' (Engels' quotation marks) Southern Slavs, and goes on to observe: 'Every one of us, in so far as he has first gone through a liberal or radical phase, has emerged from it with these feelings of sympathy for "oppressed" nationalities, and I for one know how much time and study it took me to shake them off – but then it was for good and all.'[9] Bulgarian rebels, he notes, are killing Turks, burning their houses and driving them out, and comments grimly: 'Had the Turks adopted the same course, instead of allowing them more autonomy and fewer taxes than they have at present, the world would no longer be troubled with a Bulgarian question.'[10] His thoughts, in the same letter, about the discontent with Turkish rule among the people of Herzegovina recall one of the phrases from Liebknecht's pamphlet to which Riazanov specifically objects:

> That independence consists in demonstrating their hatred of the oppressor by stealing cattle and other valuable chattels from their own 'oppressed' Serb compatriots as they have done for the past 1000 years, and any attack on their right of rapine is regarded as an attack on their independence. I am enough of an authoritarian to regard the existence of such aborigines in the heart of Europe as an anachronism. And even if these little folk had had a standing as high as Sir Walter Scott's vaunted Scottish Highlanders, who were also really shocking cattle thieves, the most we could do is condemn the *manner* in which they are treated by present-day society. If we were at the helm, *we too* should have to put an end to the Rinaldo Rinaldi Schinderhannes business, which, by long tradition, these laddies indulge.[11]

Notes

1. Prince Grigorii Alexandrovich Potemkin (1739–1791) was the chief minister and lover of Catherine the Great. He is famous for allegedly arranging a series of stage-set façades of ideal peasant villages to flank a royal progress through the countryside.
2. Karl Marx, Letter to Wilhelm Liebknecht, 4 February 1878, Marx and Engels, *Collected Works*, Volume 45, Moscow, 1991, p296.
3. Karl Marx, Letter to Friedrich Adolph Sorge, 27 September 1877, Marx and Engels, *Collected Works*, Volume 45, Moscow, 1991, p278.
4. Maltman Barry (1842–1909) was a British journalist who had supported Marx against Bakunin on the General Council of the First International.
5. Marx and Engels, *Collected Works*, Volume 45, Moscow, 1991, pp205–6, 209–10.
6. William Ewart Gladstone (1809–1898) was leader of the Liberal Party and Prime Minister on four separate occasions in the latter part of the nineteenth century.
7. Olga Alexeyevna Novikova (1840–1925) was a Russian journalist who lived for a long time in London, the wife of General Ivan Petrovich Novikov.
8. Frederick Engels, Letter to Kautsky, 7 February 1882, Marx and Engels, *Collected Works*, Volume 46, London, 1992, p194.
9. Frederick Engels, Letter to Bernstein, 22 and 25 February 1882, Marx and Engels, *Collected Works*, Volume 46, London, 1992, pp203–4.
10. Op cit, p208.
11. Op cit, p206. Rinaldo Rinaldi was a fictional character, the brigand hero of a novel by C.A. Vulpius, 1798. Schinderhannes was a real person, the leader of a band of brigands in the Rhineland, who was eventually caught and executed at Mainz in 1803.

Index